**W9-BSE-744**

Turning

Training

Into

Learning

Turning

Training

Into

Learning

How to Design and Deliver Programs That Get Results

Sheila W. Furjanic and
Laurie A. Trotman

AMACOM
American Management Association
New York • Atlanta • Boston • Chicago • Kansas City • San Francisco • Washington, D.C.
Brussels • Mexico City • Tokyo • Toronto

Special discounts on bulk quantities of AMACOM books are available to corporations, professional associations, and other organizations. For details, contact Special Sales Department, AMACOM, a division of American Management Association, 1601 Broadway, New York, NY 10019.
Tel.: 212-903-8316. Fax: 212-903-8083.
Web site: www.amanet.org

This publication is designed to provide accurate and authoritative information in regard to the subject matter covered. It is sold with the understanding that the publisher is not engaged in rendering legal, accounting, or other professional service. If legal advice or other expert assistance is required, the services of a competent professional person should be sought.

Library of Congress Cataloging-in-Publication Data

Furjanic, Sheila W.
    Turning training into learning : how to design and deliver programs that get results /
Sheila W. Furjanic and Laurie A. Trotman.
        p.   cm.
    Includes index.
    ISBN 0-8144-0519-3
    1. Employees—Training of.   I. Trotman, Laurie A.   II. Title.
HF5549.5.T7   F87   2000
658.3′12404—dc21   99–056994

Printing number

10   9   8   7   6   5   4   3   2   1

Contents

Acknowledgments

LEARN is the answer to a need we, as trainers, discovered. It is the missing link that enables training to live on long after a session has ended. We thank all of our past participants who entrusted us with their minds, experiences, and time. You were instrumental in the formation of LEARN.

We appreciate our friends, colleagues, and mentors who offered us their experience, wisdom, and support, especially Bola Akinola, Dr. Michael Bronner, Karen Carroll, Esther Chakes, Chester Delaney, Dr. Atul Dhir, Elizabeth Falter, Meryl Ginsberg, Doriane Gloria, Dr. E. Edward Harris, Avah Mealy, Susan Merrill, Joseph Miniace, John Murphy, Marilyn Norris, Dr. Bridget O'Connor, Dr. Theodore Repa, Dr. Joan Ritsch, Eileen Santos-Perez, and Mona Sonnenshein.

We also thank our families for their support and encouragement, and for putting up with the late nights, stressed moments, missed celebrations, and junk food—Bob, Cheryl, Mike, Ma, Dad, Mary, Delaina, and Jonathan. For our frequent unannounced work sessions, we thank Vanessa and Lindell for the use of their Staten Island retreat space.

We thank Kelly Anne Moore for reviewing our work when it was in its early development stage. Your keen feedback and comments motivated us as we continued to write each chapter.

We appreciate the swift kicks and creative input we received from our acquisitions editor, Jacquie Flynn; the careful editing work done by our associate editor, Mike Sivilli; the many hours of work of our copyeditor Sara Carrier of Maine Proofreading Services; and the meticulous proofreading of Judy Lopatin.

Turning
Training
Into
Learning

Introduction

Did you ever go to a training or education event and question why you were there? Did you ever find yourself tuning out the leader because there didn't seem to be anything in the presentation for you? When you discovered an interesting concept or potentially valuable skill at a training event, did you ever have it evaporate before you had a chance to try it on the job? In fact, how long did it take you to forget 80 percent of what you heard in the last training session you attended?

Three key questions in any training situation are: What's in it for me? Will it stick? Will I be rewarded for what I've learned in the training program? The only right answer to the first question involves a concept we call *learning,* which means being able to do something new or to do something differently or better than you've ever done it before. And if it doesn't stick, it *isn't* learning.

As a trainer, educator, consultant, or manager, you should be asking yourself, What's in this book for me? *Turning Training Into Learning* gives you the tools you need to identify, develop, and present the training your organization needs. More important, you will learn the techniques for "hard-wiring" your participants with skills and abilities that won't evaporate before they can use them on the job. The book is packed with guidelines, models, checklists, forms, templates, and other easy-to-use tools that will help you turn training into *learning.*

The heart of this book is the LEARN process. It is the natural process we all experience as learners before we can own and use what we've received in a training situation. LEARN is an acronym that represents the five-step process participants follow as they take in, practice, apply, and internalize skills and concepts. LEARN is the secret for turning training into learning. Each letter of this acronym stands for an important part of the learning process (see Figure I-1).

LEARN is the center and therefore the core piece of the puzzle that also includes the four parts of the traditional training cycle: assess, design, deliver, and evaluate (see Figure I-2). To present this concept, *Turning Training Into Learning* is divided into two major parts: Part One, The Training Process, and Part Two, The LEARN Process. Notice that all aspects of the training process touch and influence the LEARN process. The book includes a chapter for each of the four training process components as well as a chapter for each of the five steps in LEARN.

Figure I-1.   The LEARN process.

L   Listen and Understand—If you capture my attention and interest, I'll listen to what you have to offer and try to understand it.

E   Evaluate and Decide—When you help me see what's in it for me, I'll evaluate the competencies you've introduced and decide how I can use them on the Job or in my life outside the job.

A   Attempt and Build—If you help me build my skills step-by-step in a safe environment, I'll make a serious attempt to learn.

R   Return and Apply—When I feel comfortable with the skills and abilities I've learned, I'll return to the job and actually use what you've taught me. I'll be able to apply them to my own situation.

N   Natural Transition—Now these skills and abilities are mine. I own them. I may pass them on to other people or take them to the next level and learn more on my own.

Figure I-2.   The training process puzzle.

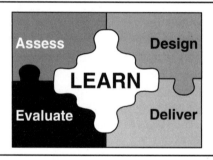

Part One—The Training Process: Creating the Foundation

Chapter 1, Assessing the Need for Training, sets the stage for learning by helping you to determine who needs training and why they need training. Assessment helps you to identify the driving forces behind training requests. It also helps you to evaluate what impact your training will have on bottom-line business results.

Chapter 2, Designing Learner-Based Training, helps you to identify training goals, recruit mentors, develop materials, select training methods, and determine schedules and resources.

Chapter 3, Delivering Training That Ensures Learning, introduces the needs of the adult learner and three different styles of learning. The chapter also features five secrets for transferring skills and abilities from your participants' short-term memories, where they will quickly disappear, and "hardwiring" them into participants' long-term memory.

Chapter 4, Evaluating the Training Process, focuses on evaluating the effectiveness of your training and determining how well it is received and applied by participants. The output of evaluation provides significant input for new and revised training efforts and links directly back to the assessment phase of the training cycle.

Part Two—The LEARN Process: Linking Training to Learning

Chapters 5 to 9 are each devoted to one letter in the LEARN acronym. The subtitle for each chapter is its secret to success because this is what the adult learner *really* wants. These chapters will lead you through the LEARN process and help you put yourself in the learner's shoes (see Figure I-3).

Chapter 5. If you capture my attention and interest—I'll *listen and understand.* This chapter gives you techniques for capturing your participants' attention and interest up front, because if you don't, you will be hard-pressed to capture it later.

Chapter 6. Help me see what's in it for me. This chapter presents a "road map" for the important process of getting your learners on board to learn. It shows you how to create an active learning situation that can involve your participants in the learning process, and shows you how to convince your learners that they should participate.

Chapter 7. Help me build my skills step-by-step. You will learn how to add activities to your presentation that will help participants remember what they have learned, realize the value on a personal level, and build the skills they need so they can apply them on the job.

Chapter 8. Send me back to use them on the job. To transition your learners from "Now I've tried it" to "I'll return and apply it" calls for planned follow-up activities as well as tools (the Return and Apply Model) to assist your learners in achieving training results that will stick on the job.

Chapter 9. Now they're mine—there's a natural transition. This chapter

Figure I-3. Outline of Chapters 5–9.

Chapter	Acronym Letter	Meaning	Chapter Subtitle (Secret to Success)
5	L	Listen and Understand	Capture my attention and interest
6	E	Evaluate and Decide	Help me see what's in it for me
7	A	Attempt and Build	Help me build my skills step-by-step
8	R	Return and Apply	Send me back to use them on the job
9	N	Natural Transition	Now they're mine

will help you understand both the natural transition process and the highest level of evaluation—transformation—from the learner's point of view.

Chapter 10, Putting It All Together, fits the pieces of the puzzle back together and reviews the entire process of *Turning Training Into Learning*. As we fit the pieces of the puzzle back together, we will discuss some of the pitfalls that may inadvertently occur in the training process and give you both some safety net solutions and tips to remember. We will also cover the training summary report.

PART ONE
The Training Process:
Creating the Foundation

This part introduces the process that creates the foundation for the main event—LEARN. The training process includes four stages that are performed by the trainer to successfully *deliver* training programs; they include assess, design, deliver, and evaluate. Each of these stages is presented in a separate chapter (see Figure P1-1).

Figure P1-1.   Stages of the training process.

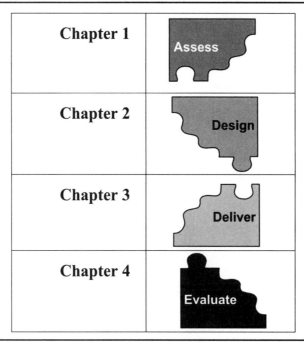

Chapter 1	Assess
Chapter 2	Design
Chapter 3	Deliver
Chapter 4	Evaluate

Each of the four stages in the training process plays an equally important part in shaping the success of the learning process. Without all four stages, there may not be learning (see Figure P1-2).

Figure P1-2.   The training process puzzle.

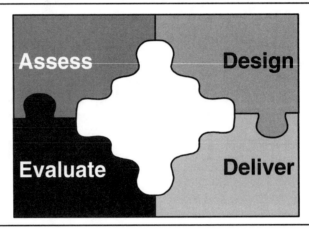

1

Assessing the Need for Training

While each of the four stages in the training process is important, assessment helps you aim the entire process in the right direction. The assessment stage helps you clarify the request, determine the driving force behind it, and decide whether or not training is the right response. It requires taking time to investigate each potential training situation before you start designing the training effort. Assessment can mean the difference between a training session that is nothing more than a recess from work and learning that gets results.

The ten basic questions shown in Figure 1-1 will help you assess the

Figure 1-1.   Guide to Chapter 1.

Training Stage	Questions to Ask
1. ASSESS	1. Who needs training?
	2. Why do they need training?
	3. Is a process the real problem?
	4. What are the driving forces behind the training request?
	5. Will the training be supported when the participant returns to the job?
	6. What are the barriers to success?
	7. Is the request realistic or a "magic wand" request?
	8. Is the problem worth fixing?
	9. Should design/delivery be outsourced?
	10. The big decision—Should training happen?

need for training. The first nine questions lead up to the big decision—Should training happen?

Question 1: Who Needs Training?

Your request for training can come from any one of a number of possible sources (or clients), including the top management of an organization, the management staff in a department or unit, and even front-line staff members. But proceeding with any training effort without first analyzing it can be a waste of your resources and your participants' time.

It is important to take a close look at the intended audience and ask some basic questions about the way your participants interact with each other on the job. Five different types of audiences are described in Figure 1-2, categorized by the way the participants interact with each other. This checklist will help you answer the question, Who needs training?

If your intended participants work together as team members or if they share the same function but are not considered a team, your job may be a little easier than if the participants are from various areas within the organization because:

- You can collect examples recognizable by the specific group.
- The participants will already know each other and can make your job easier by helping each other learn and retain what is learned.

Figure 1-2. Training checklist.

Who Needs Training?

1. Who is the intended audience?
   - ❐ *Intact work team members* who are dependent on each other to accomplish daily work and meet goals (e.g., a book publishing team made up of an acquisitions editor, marketing manager, production manager, art director, and team leader).
   - ❐ *Staff members who share the same function* and work toward the same goal but are not considered a team (e.g., cashiers from all shifts of a large supermarket).
   - ❐ *Members of special project teams* whose work flows directly from one department to another (e.g., hospital admitting representatives who capture insurance information, medical records representatives who code patient charts for billing, and billers who seek reimbursement from third-party payers).
   - ❐ *Any staff member at a specific level who chooses to attend* (e.g., any manager or supervisor who elects to attend).
   - ❐ *Any staff member who is given permission to attend* (e.g., any staff member who voluntarily elects to attend and obtains permission).

2. Will this training be required?   ❐ Yes (mandatory)   ❐ No (voluntary)

A copy of this form is provided as Figure B-1 in Appendix B.

- You will have support for the proposed training at the departmental level.
- You will have a smaller number of supervisors or managers to work with as you help participants return to the job and apply what they have learned.
- It will be easier to track your success.

On the other hand, if your participants come from a variety of locations throughout the organization, you may have an opportunity to develop more interesting class discussions because all participants have an opportunity to be exposed to other areas they may not be familiar with. The participants from diverse areas add a dimension to the learning due to their breadth of experiences and varied responsibilities within the organization.

Gathering Background Information

You will want to gain more information about groups of participants who work together, such as the way work flows from one person to another and the background of the participating group. Figure 1-3 lists some questions you might want to ask. Question 12, inviting the person who requested the training to open up and tell you more, often leads to information you wouldn't otherwise have learned.

You can sometimes uncover important information that will help you shape the training effort and defuse potentially difficult situations. One trainer was assessing a request to present customer service training to the staff in a large health and beauty aid store. By asking the right questions up front, he discovered that an assistant manager had been given the assignment of creating the same training program several months ago. She produced a training packet and ran one class, both of which were considered unsuccessful, so the project was taken away from her. Because the assistant manager was scheduled to be one of the training participants, the trainer had an opportunity to involve her in early planning sessions and build a positive working relationship from the start. By discovering background information and taking action up front, the trainer was able to avoid a potentially unpleasant situation during training.

Talking With Participants

Trainers often complete the assessment phase without taking advantage of a very valuable resource—the participants themselves. There are two basic reasons for making this type of contact during assessment:

1. To gather the information you need to develop effective training
2. To build rapport and trust with the participants

You can gather information from participants through brief written surveys, telephone interviews, or face-to-face conversations. Although written surveys are efficient because you can mass-produce them, they are often difficult to collect and provide very little opportunity for you to build rapport.

Figure 1-3.   Background questions.

Assessing the Training Request

1. Which employees are the intended training participants?

2. What part does each one play in the work that is done in the department?

3. Which participants are the most skilled at performing their jobs?

4. How well do the participants know each other?

5. Are there natural leaders among the participants? Who are they?

6. How familiar are the participants with the training subject?

7. Are there one or two participants who know the subject well?

8. Are any participants likely to resist training? Why?

9. Do any participants need special attention during the learning process?

10. What other types of training have these employees received?

11. How will employees perceive this particular training effort (positive, negative)?

12. Is there anything that hasn't been asked that will help assess this training request?

A copy of this form is provided as Figure B-2 in Appendix B.

While face-to-face contact can help you build rapport, the logistical problems can make it time-consuming and impractical. Telephone interviews, on the other hand, will provide you with an opportunity to build rapport with a relatively small time investment. Figure 1-4 lists questions you might ask intended participants for a middle-management leadership course.

Question 2: Why Do They Need Training?

It is very helpful to determine the situation that led to the training request. To answer this question, you will need to interview the client who initially requested the training. For example, a request to provide customer service training for the front-line staff throughout the organization could be motivated by a single incident in which one staff member who deals with the public was discourteous to one customer, who complained to a director. While customer service training is often a good thing, a training course prompted by a single discourteous incident may waste your training re-

Figure 1-4.   Sample telephone interview.

Telephone Interview With Intended Participants
for Middle-Management Leadership Course

Hi. My name is Marian Wong, and I've been asked to facilitate a course in leadership skills for all managers in the Advertising and Promition Department at Weston Corporation. Have you heard about this course? It is scheduled for _____. I'm trying to talk with all the people who are scheduled to participate in the course to gather some basic information that will help me develop a course that addresses your needs. Is this a good time to talk?

1.   How long have you been with Weston Corporation?

2.   How long have you been a manager?

3.   How many people report directly to you?

4.   What has been your biggest challenge as a manager?

5.   What has been your biggest success?

6.   To be of help to you as a manager, what topics/skills should this course focus on?

7.   Do you have any leadership hints, tips, or suggestions you can share with other managers?

8.   What else should I know before I begin planning this course?

A copy of this form is provided as Figure B-3 in Appendix B.

sources and be considered punitive by staff members. Unfortunately, some trainers are so eager to respond to requests from above that they leap into action without stopping to analyze the request. The questions in Figure 1-5 will help you analyze the training request to determine if it's an appropriate use of resources.

Question 3: Is a Process the Real Problem?

Sometimes a request for training can help you identify a process that isn't working. If you honor the request for training instead of taking the time to address the problem, you are, in effect, placing a Band-Aid on the problem. By fixing the problem, you can eliminate the need for any training at all. The steps in identifying and eliminating a process that isn't working are shown in Figure 1-6.

Let's look at an example that demonstrates how this process works. A manager requests training to help her billing staff. They are having difficulty reading a multipage, complex quarterly report of insurance claim informa-

Figure 1-5.   Analyzing the training request.

If you ask these questions, you will save your time and conserve the organization's resources:

1. What prompted you to request this training?

2. How long has this been a problem?

3. How often does it occur?

4. What is the process that leads up to the problem?

5. Have you already tried training as a solution? What happened?

A copy of this form is provided as Figure B-4 in Appendix B.

Figure 1-6.   Steps to fix the process problem.

1. **Request**—What is the nature of the problem? How will the requested training solve the problem?

2. **Root Cause**—Why is it a problem? What is the root cause?

3. **Options**—What are the options? Is there another way to do it? What are the alternatives?

4. **Solution**—What is the best solution for the organization and the participant?

5. **Action**—Develop the action plan for the best option.

A form based on this figure is provided as Figure B-5 in Appendix B.

tion. They need to extract the dates on which their denied claims are appealed. Instead of proceeding automatically with the training, the trainer sets up a meeting with the manager who requested the training and the person who issues the quarterly report. Together they examine the current process. Why does the report come on a quarterly basis instead of monthly or even weekly? Why does it contain so many pages? How is the appeal information coded? As a result of this examination, they decide that the multipage report can be streamlined. With a minimum of effort, they create a user-friendly, single-page report to substitute for the complex report. They also decide to report information on a weekly basis instead of a quarterly basis in order to keep the billing staff better informed. The training is no longer necessary, and there is a solution to the problem. This example demonstrates that training isn't always the solution.

Question 4: What Are the Driving Forces Behind the Training Request?

The answer to this question will provide you with the broad background information you need to develop effective training for training requests. The

Figure 1-7. The driving forces model for training.

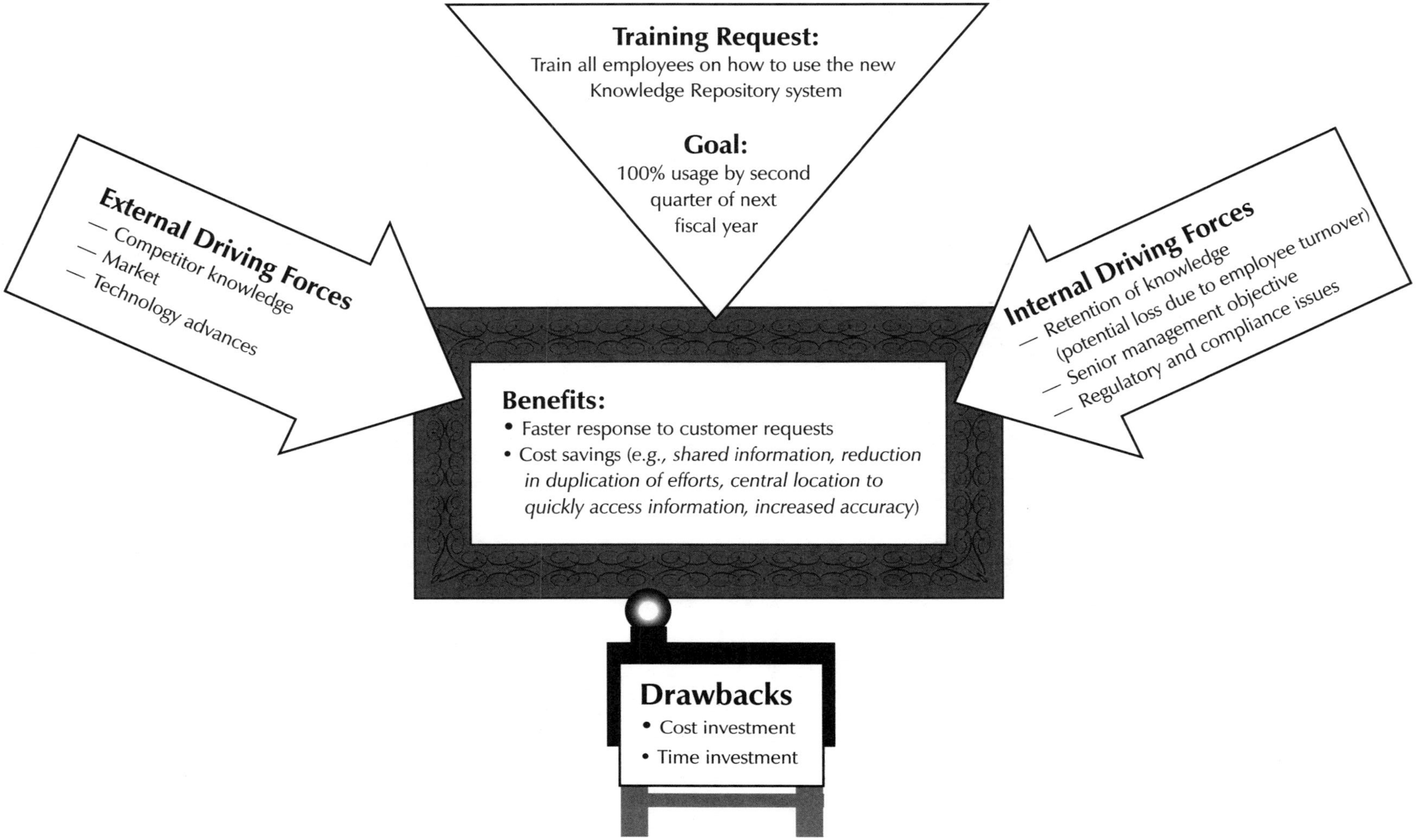

Training Request:
Train all employees on how to use the new Knowledge Repository system

Goal:
100% usage by second quarter of next fiscal year

Internal Driving Forces
— Retention of knowledge due to employee turnover)
— (potential management objective
— Senior and compliance issues
— Regulatory

External Driving Forces
— Competitor knowledge
— Market
— Technology advances

Benefits:
• Faster response to customer requests
• Cost savings (e.g., shared information, reduction in duplication of efforts, central location to quickly access information, increased accuracy)

Drawbacks
• Cost investment
• Time investment

driving forces model in Figure 1-7 will help you figure out what internal and external forces are driving the training request. It will also help you clarify the training goal, examine the internal and external forces behind that goal, and identify both the advantages and drawbacks of proceeding toward that goal by fulfilling the training request. For example, what is the training request and the goal of that request? Too often trainers get requests that training alone will not be able to address. That is why it's important to understand the driving forces behind the request. As a trainer, you should ask some key questions. Why is training needed? What factors are driving the need for training? Are these factors internal or external? What is within the control of the training department? You will also need to assess the benefits and drawbacks of the request so you can determine the real training need.

The driving forces model will also help you determine who is supporting the training request and why they are supporting it. Is the training request in response to organizational needs? Is it market-driven? Does it represent individual needs or responses to the external environment? What barriers (if any) are preventing the training? Sometimes the forces are a combination of all these drivers. To fill in the blanks to questions posed in the driving forces model, you will need to work with the client who is requesting the training.

For example, you receive a training request from one of the directors in your organization, who asks you to train all employees on how to operate the new knowledge management software system that will soon be put online. To understand the training request, you will need to make an appointment with the director requesting the training. The purpose of this meeting will be to examine the big picture before you dive into the process of creating the requested training solution.

At the meeting, you review market trend information and learn that your organization has decided to invest in a new knowledge repository database to better manage information that can be shared across the organization. Your CEO supports this new system and is very eager to roll it out. In fact, the implementation of the knowledge repository database is one of her goals for the second quarter of the year.

Information in the driving forces model will be useful not only in clearly defining training requirements but in setting the stage for successful communication and buy-in for the training. It also enables you to justify the time, effort, and resources needed to roll out training solutions. The driving forces model can also help you develop any advertising you need to promote this training effort to various audiences within your organization.

Participants are not always told why something new is being implemented (i.e., why the change is taking place). So, outlining these reasons or justifications up front enables you to become more successful in answering the learner's question, What's in it for me?

Question 5: Will the Training Be Supported When the Participant Returns to the Job?

This is a key question that can spell the difference between successful learning and forgotten training sessions that are little more than short vacations

Figure 1-8.   Questions to ask when clarifying support for participants.

- How important is this training to your department's operations?
- How long do you feel this training effort should take?
- What do you want participants to accomplish in that length of time?
- If more sessions are required, will your staff be encouraged to participate?
- How are you prepared to support the training on the job?
- How will you measure the success of the training?
- Are you or members of your staff willing to serve as mentors to the participants when they return to the job?
- Have you tried training for this before? If yes, why are you doing it again?
- If follow-up activities or sessions are necessary, will your staff members be encouraged to attend?

A form based on this figure is provided as Figure B-6 in Appendix B.

from work for the participants. In Chapter 2, you will learn how to develop a training contract with each participant's supervisor. By doing this, you are putting the supervisor in the roll of mentor.

If it is clear during the assessment phase that the requested training will not be supported on the job, you will want to weigh this request against others that may have higher priority and that may yield better returns on the time and resources invested. The supervisor should be ready and willing to help the participant apply what has been learned. Questions from a supportive supervisor might include: How was the class? What did you learn? How will you use it on the job? How can I help you put it into practice?

The questions in Figure 1-8 will help you assess the level of support that participants will receive when they return to the job to apply what they have learned.

Question 6: What Are the Barriers to Success?

What can go wrong to affect the success of the training effort? Not understanding the driving forces behind a request, as described in Question 4, can become a major barrier to success. Other common factors include time constraints, equipment and system issues, and organizational culture issues.

- *Time constraints.* The most well-meaning supervisor can inadvertently cause training efforts to fail by waiting too long to let participants apply what they have learned, simply because there is too much work to do and too little time to do it in. After a period of several weeks, the participant is no longer able to remember the skills acquired in class well enough to apply them. This is especially true for computer-related training programs.

- *Equipment and system issues.* The shortage of equipment and system implementation problems can also create the type of time lag that jeopardizes learning. If participants learn how to use a new document-imaging system in January and are not able to put their learning to use until the terminals are installed in April, they will probably have to be retained. Much of the training that involves the application of computer- or system-related skills is much more effective as just-in-time training—timed to be presented immediately before implementation.

■ *Organizational culture issues.* Failure to understand the culture of the organization and the particular group of participants you will be working with can result in training that is largely ignored by the participants, the supervisors, and the organization itself.

To lead a learning effort, you need to have an understanding of the organization's beliefs and values and how they are evidenced in the way the organization operates. Where these beliefs and values are present in organizational life, they affect everything in the organization, including the norms that guide the behavior or managers, supervisors, and employees. The information you gather in order to answer Questions 1 through 4 will help you gain an understanding of *some* of these cultural norms. In addition, you need to be alert to the subtle behaviors that give you clues so you can determine how well your intended training efforts will be received.

One area you should explore is the history of both successful and unsuccessful past training initiatives. If an initiative was considered successful, what made it successful? Was it the process, the outcomes, the instructor, the refreshments, the location, or the handouts? All of these answers give you information that will affect the way you go about responding to the training request. Unless you ask the right questions, you might miss an opportunity to capitalize on this information.

You should also be particularly alert to any unsuccessful training attempt. Why was it perceived as unsuccessful? You might learn, for example, that a past training program was considered unsuccessful because the learning techniques focused on games that were considered too "fluffy."

You need to understand how or if the management responsible for the training values it. If the manager clearly doesn't value the training and considers it a vacation day for his or her staff, this presents a barrier you must overcome before proceeding. To overcome these barriers, follow the process outlined in this book.

Question 7: Is the Request Realistic or a "Magic Wand" Request?

"Magic wand" requests are unrealistic requests for single-event training sessions to solve major problems, such as poor attitude, absenteeism, lateness, poor use of grammar, and lack of communication between staff and management, within the organization. The person requesting the training doesn't have a lot of time to devote to fixing this type of problem and wants you to take care of it quickly by waving your "magic wand" at a room full of staff members who will immediately change their behavior (see Figure 1-9). An example of this type of training might be a request for a one-hour grammar course for customer service representatives who are using improper grammar

Figure 1-9. "Magic wand training."

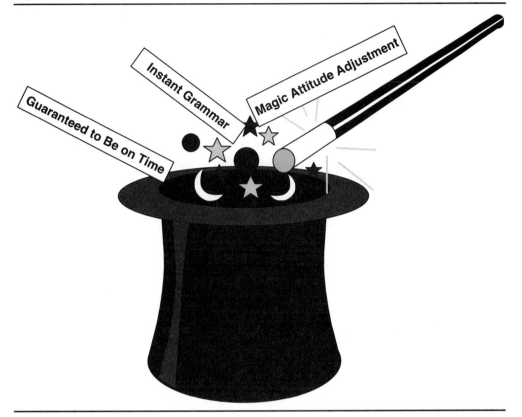

in their phone contact with customers. This request is the result of a high-level manager who received a complaint from an important customer. While the grammar used by customer service representatives is definitely an important issue, a one-hour session will have virtually no impact in correcting grammar mistakes. While the supervisor realizes that this is an issue worth fixing, he is not willing or able to monitor the grammar used by representatives after the one-hour session.

Unfortunately "magic wand" requests are doomed to failure because the vast majority of identified problems can't be addressed with quick fixes. If this type of request can't be restructured into a request that allows enough time and resources to accomplish the goals of the client, it is the type of request that should *not* be granted. "Magic wand" problems will continue whether or not participants are exposed to a short training session. By talking with the person requesting the training and managing his or her expectations, you can decide together that the training should not take place. By having this discussion, you can save yourself the effort required to create and implement the training and avoid the problems caused when it fails.

Another type of "magic wand" request is the request for instant training. While the scope of the training is appropriate, the person requesting the training wants it to start immediately. Because of the urgency of the situation, there will be no time to develop the training in an appropriate way. Although this type of request can create an atmosphere of excitement, the request can lead to problems for the requester, the participants, and the trainer. The person requesting the training will not get what he or she needs because it is impossible to create; the participants will not receive appropriate training; and the failed training effort may be blamed for any difficulties that occur in the urgent implementation of this new program.

Question 8: Is the Problem Worth Fixing?

Problems not worth fixing are ones that either will correct themselves or will have very little detrimental effect on the goals of the organization. If employees in a department that has just switched from a touch-screen method of entering data to a keyboard method request a keyboarding refresher, the training is appropriate for a short period of time. After that time, the problem will correct itself. If there is time to offer the refresher the week before implementation or the week of implementation, it is worth the time and effort involved. But each day or week that goes by renders the training effort less necessary. Soon employees who had rusty typing skills are able to build up speed and recapture accuracy. After the first week of implementation, any keyboarding issues that remain are probably not worth fixing.

Requests for training to solve problems that are not worth fixing include the creation of training programs and/or manuals that will add little or no value to the current process. A manager whose staff is effectively and efficiently scanning documents for use by the department requests that a training manual be created to formalize the scanning process. All staff members in the scanning department are working at peak efficiency, and no new employees are being hired. The training manual and course are for a supposed problem—lack of documentation and formal training—that is not worth fixing if resources can be devoted to higher-priority projects. The decision matrix in Figure 1-10 lists some of the questions you will want to answer when you are deciding whether the problem is worth fixing.

Question 9: Should Design/Delivery Be Outsourced?

Before beginning the development process for a new training program, it's important to see if that program is available from another resource. Courses in software programs, management skills, leadership, time management, project management, business English, listening, sexual harassment prevention, union negotiations, and a wide variety of other topics are available from outside training firms. If the number of participants who need a specific type of training is relatively small and the course is available on the outside, you may want to invest in the registration fee for the few participants who want to attend instead of taking time to develop your own course. Some outside firms are willing to negotiate a price for bringing their training programs into an organization. Before beginning the development process, it is always a good idea to investigate the feasibility of going outside for the training. If you

(text continues on page 22)

Figure 1-10.   Decision matrix.

CONFIDENTIAL IS THE PROBLEM WORTH FIXING?			
Question	Yes	Maybe	No
1. Does the client (person requesting training) have realistic expectations?			
2. If we do nothing, will the problem go away?			
3. If we do nothing, will the problem get worse?			
4. Will correction of this problem have a positive effect on the goals of the organization?			
5. Will failure to correct the problem have a negative effect on the goals of the organization?			
6. Are higher-priority programs competing for training resources earmarked for this effort?			
7. Is this training effort strongly supported by management?			
8. Is the value of this training effort being questioned by management?			
9. Will this training effort be supported when the participants return to the job?			
10. Can this training be handled effectively in the department without the help of the training department?			

A copy of this form is provided as Figure B-7 in Appendix B.

Figure 1-11. Proposal training matrix.

THE BIG DECISION:
SHOULD THIS TRAINING TAKE PLACE?

This matrix will help you determine whether the requested training should take place. Possible scores range from 7 to 35. The higher the score, the more certain you can be that training is the appropriate response to the request.

Consideration	5	4	3	2	1
1. Is the problem really a process problem?	☐ The process is sound. Training will help staff members learn to use the process.	☐	☐ The process might be able to be improved, but the improvement is impractical at this time.	☐	☐ An improvement in the process could increase productivity and make the requested training to be unnecessary.
2. What are the driving forces behind the training?	☐ Strong driving forces both internally and externally. Solidly backed by senior management.	☐	☐ Some degree of both internal and external driving forces, but not a priority training effort.	☐	☐ No strong driving forces, either internally or externally.
3. Will the learning be supported when the participant returns to the job?	☐ There is a support plan in place. A mentor has been appointed. The participant will be encouraged to apply the learning and return for help if needed.	☐	☐ The participant's supervisor seems mildly enthusiastic about the training, but no support plan is in place.	☐	☐ The supervisor is reluctant to let the participant attend class, and considers this training a waste of valuable time.

	☐	☐	☐
4. Will there be barriers to success in implementation?	The training requested is "do-able," and the time allotted, both for preparation and implementation, are appropriate.	There may be some delay in implementing the training due to equipment or systems problems, but they are being corrected.	There will be no implementation for at least 3 months while system and equipment problems are resolved.
5. Is this a "magic wand" request?	The requester's expectations are right on target.	The requester may be expecting too much.	This is clearly a "magic wand" request. Even Houdini couldn't make this happen.
6. Is the problem worth fixing?	Yes. If it is not fixed, there will be serious consequences. This problem will not go away on its own.	The problem is worth fixing, but there are other higher-priority problems that should be addressed first. There will be no serious consequences if it is not addressed now.	The problem will either go away or cause no serious consequences if it is not addressed.
7. Is the training available from another resource?	No. This has to be a custom-made training effort.	Outside resources are available, but they will have to be customized or supplemented to fit this effort.	Yes. Outside resources are readily available, and will address the needs of the requester.

A copy of this form is provided as Figure B-8 in Appendix B.

elect an external vendor, make sure you preview and research the material thorougly before formally contracting out training.

Question 10: The Big Decision—Should Training Happen?

The matrix in Figure 1-11 will help you make the big decision—Should training happen? The higher your proposed training effort scores on the scale of 7 to 35, the easier it will be for you to proceed to development. If the proposed effort receives a low score, you will probably want to work with the person requesting the training to determine whether there is a more appropriate solution.

Resources

Nelson, Bob. *1001 Ways to Energize Employees* (paperback). New York: Workman Publishing Co., 1997.

O'Connor, Bridget N., Michael Bronner, and Chester Delaney. *Training for Organizations.* Cincinnati: South & Western Educational Publishing, 1996, 358 pages. (This comprehensive training text provides strong and theoretical foundations for the training process. It places particular emphasis on needs assessment and on planning for the evaluation of training.)

Schein, Edgar H. *Organizational Culture and Leadership*, 2nd edition. San Francisco: Jossey-Bass, a division of Simon & Schuster, 1997, 448 pages.

Schein, Edgar H., and Warren Bennis. *The Corporate Culture Survival Guide: Sense and Nonsense About Culture Change.* San Francisco: Jossey-Bass, a division of Simon & Schuster, 1999, 224 pages.

2

Designing Learner-Based
Training

You have assessed the training request and decided that training is the right response. Now it's time to design training that meets the needs of both the learners and the organization. The time and effort you take in designing the training can spell the difference between a program that gets results and one that doesn't.

There are seven steps to the design process: (1) gather background information; (2) develop and sign the training contract; (3) identify desired skills and skill gaps; (4) develop learning objectives; (5) recruit mentoring support; (6) develop presentations, materials, and activities; and (7) determine schedules and needed resources. These steps and the questions that will help you answer them are shown in Figure 2-1.

Step 1: Gather Background Information

Before designing any portion of your course, you need to answer two critical questions:

1. What skills and behaviors do you want participants to exhibit?
2. What skills and behaviors do they exhibit now?

The answers to these simple questions can make an enormous difference in the success of your training effort. It's hard to tell whether or not training is successful if you don't know what it's supposed to be accomplishing.

Surprisingly, many training efforts proceed when neither the trainer nor the client has answers to these questions. When this type of disconnect occurs, the trainer can devote time and effort to developing a good training effort that doesn't produce the results the client was expecting. How can this happen? The training scenario might go something like this:

SITUATION

Dave Martin, the refreshment stand manager from a large theater, is having a bad week. His forty employees staff three separate refreshment stands from noon to midnight each day.

Figure 2-1.   Guide to Chapter 2.

Training Stage	*Process Steps/Questions to Ask*
2. DESIGN 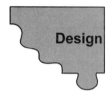	**1. Gather background information**
	2. Develop and sign training contract
	3. Identify desired skills and skill gaps ■ What should participants be able to do? ■ What can participants do now?
	4. Develop learning objectives ■ Cognitive learning ■ Affective learning ■ Psychomotor learning ■ Combining all three types of learning ■ Writing simple learning objectives ■ Designing pretests and posttests
	5. Recruit mentoring support ■ Who will support this training when the participant returns to the job? ■ How can mentors be included in the training development? ■ How can you enable proactive learning on the job?
	6. Develop presentations, materials, and activities
	7. Determine schedules and needed resources ■ How many sessions are required? ■ Who should present the material? ■ Where will the sessions be held? ■ What equipment and resources are needed? ■ The final check ■ Making your final plans

This week he has received complaints about ten of his employees. According to the complaints, some of these staff members are taking too long to fill orders, making incorrect change, and being discourteous to customers. The theater manager, Gianna Grecco, calls and says that your staff needs training! *Now!*

REQUEST FOR TRAINING

The refreshment stand manager calls the manager of training and development for the mall and asks for assistance.

Manager: My staff needs some training. They seem to be slacking off, and their customer service skills have gone downhill.

REQUEST FOR CLARIFICATION

The trainer has an all-purpose customer service course that can be customized to meet the needs of various audiences.

Trainer: What's the problem? When do you need help?

Manager: My staff is a good bunch of people, but some of them seem to be moving in slow motion, and some of them have forgotten everything they know about how to treat customers. Can you give them a refresher course? I heard that the one you did for the staff over at the stationery store was pretty good.

Trainer: How soon do you need it? I'm booked next Monday, Tuesday, and Wednesday, but I might be able to do something for you toward the end of the week.

Without further clarification, neither the refreshment stand manager nor the trainer will be able to fill the needs of this group of employees. Let's listen to more of their conversation:

Trainer: What should participants be able to do when they complete the training?

Manager: I want every one of our counter people to be efficient and more courteous to customers.

Trainer: How will you be able to tell that the training is successful?

Manager: I'll stop getting complaints, or at least they'll decrease.

If you were designing this training, you would not yet know specifically what employees need to do to improve their performance, but you would be able to write the training contract.

Step 2: Develop and Sign Training Contract

Once you have agreed to meet the training request, you should formalize the request by preparing a formal training contract. This document clearly states the goal, learning objectives, key performance measures, target audience(s), requirements, budget/cost, and manager follow-up activities. Figure 2-2 is a sample training contract and Figure 2-3 is an example of a completed training contract.

The purpose of the contract is threefold: (1) It formalizes the request, (2) it specifies the expected outcomes in terms that both the training department

(text continues on page 28)

Figure 2-2.   Training contract.

Training Contract	
Requesting Department: _____ **Sponsoring Manager:** _____ **Date:** _____	**Telephone Number:** _____ **FAX Number:** _____ **E-Mail Address:** _____

Background Information ■ Identify why training is needed ■ Identify relevant events that prompted the training request
Training Goal ■ Identify the overall goal for the training program
Training Learning Objectives ■ Identify the learning objectives to be achieved during the training
Key Performance Measures ■ Answer the question, How will you know training has been successful? What changes are required?
Target Audience(s) ■ Identify the participants/audiences you are targeting for the training
Requirements ■ List any requirements the requester would be responsible for performing prior to and during training
Budget/Cost *(only applicable for internal chargebacks)* ■ Identify any cost/budget requirements
Manager Follow-Up Activities ■ Identify follow-up activities the requesting sponsor (management) needs to perform

Approval	
I agree with the terms of this contract. _____ Requester Approval	I agree with the terms of this contract. _____ Training Department Approval
Dates of Actual Training: **Participants:** **Comments:**	

A copy of this form is provided as Figure B-9 in Appendix B.

Figure 2-3. Sample completed training contract.

Training Contract	
Requesting Department: Refreshment Stand **Sponsoring Manager:** Dave Martin (requester) **Date:** March 1, 2000	**Telephone Number:** *555-555-3070* **Fax Number:** *555-555-5050* **E-Mail Address:** David.Martin@lcmall.com

Background Information
- Identify *why* training is needed (to improve customer service/reduce complaints)
- Identify relevant events that prompted the training request (demand from theater manager)

Training Goal
- Identify the *overall goal* for the training program (improved customer satisfaction; reduced complaints because currently receive complaints about 25% of employees)

Training Learning Objectives
- Identify the *learning objectives* to be achieved during the training (see Figure 2-8)

Key Performance Measures
- *How will you know training has been successful?*
  (customer service complaints will decrease gradually over the next two months; by that time, there will be complaints on no more than 5% of employees)
- What changes are required?
  (increased skill in register handling, customer service, and pricing)
- Complete the Measuring Business Results form.

Target Audience(s)
- Identify the *participants/audiences* you are targeting for the training (100% of refreshment stand staff)

Requirements
- List any requirements the requester would be responsible for performing prior to and during training
  (provide a list of staff members, their positions, and their hours)

Budget/Cost *(only applicable for internal chargebacks)*
- Identify any cost/budget requirements (N/A)

Manager Follow-Up Activities
- Identify follow-up activities the requesting sponsor (management) needs to perform
  (weekly meetings/rewards for improved performance)

Approval	
I agree with the terms of this contract. *David Martin* Requester Approval	I agree with the terms of this contract. *Patricia Dunn* Training Department Approval

Dates of Actual Training:
Participants:
Comments:

and the person requesting the training understand and agree to, and (3) it clearly states what is required of the person requesting the training before the entire process can begin. The real value of the training contract is the fact that it identifies the goals, objectives, and key performance measures for the training initiative in such a way that both progress and success can be measured.

Step 3: Identify Desired Skills and Skill Gaps

Next you will need to determine what participants should be able to do and what they can do now.

What Should Participants Be Able to Do?

The key to figuring out what participants should be able to do is to ask the manager to be specific, and to identify *observable* behaviors that the participants should be performing. The three important questions the trainer should ask are:

1. What should employees be able to do?
2. How well should they do it?
3. How can you tell that the desired behaviors are being performed?

Remember that you are looking for observable behaviors, which are also referred to as *competencies.* You can't observe a participant appreciating something or understanding something, but you can observe a participant explaining why something is important or describing how something works. See Figure 2-4 for an example of how these three questions could be answered for refreshment stand employees.

What Can Participants Do Now?

When you know which skills participants should possess to perform a job effectively, you compare the list of skills required with the skills they possess now. The skill gap assessment guide in Figure 2-5 will help you pinpoint the needed training. If you plan to train in a group setting, you can complete this guide for the entire group; if you are planning individual training, you can complete this guide for individual employees who are new or who need refresher training.

In some cases, you will be responsible for determining organizational or departmental learning needs at a macro level (e.g., if you were asked to design customer service training for all employees who come in contact with customers at the theater or at the entire mall). In this case, you would need to conduct a more formal needs assessment. Figure 2-6 describes six of the more popular methods for collecting these data and shows the advantages and disadvantages of each method.

(text continues on page 32)

Figure 2-4. Questions to identify skills.

What Should Employees Be Able to Do?	How Well Should They Do It?	How Can You Tell It's Being Done This Way?
Operate the cash register correctly.	Key in all information correctly for each of the 48 items sold at the refreshment stand.	Register balances at end of day.
Charge the correct amount for each of the 48 items.	Be 100% accurate—no customers are overcharged or undercharged.	No complaints from customers who have been charged incorrectly.
Operate the popcorn machine correctly.	Have a batch of popcorn ready in 5 minutes without wasting oil or popcorn.	No spoiled batches of popcorn.
Operate and refill the soft drink machine.	Make soft drinks that pass taste test.	Drinks taste as expected, with no wasted syrup.
Smile and use approved greetings with customers. (Hello/May I help you?/ May I take your order?/ Who is next, please?)	Greet 100% of customers appropriately. Never use greetings such as "Yeah," "Yup," "Next," and "Uh-huh."	Observations by manager and no complaints by customers.
Say "Thank you" after customers are served.	Thank 100% of the customers.	Observations by manager.
Serve customers quickly and efficiently.	Serve approximately 20 customers in 15 minutes.	Observations by manager.
Demonstrate commitment to serving all customers with an equal level of courtesy.	Serve all customers efficiently, with a pleasant attitude.	Observations by manager and no customer complaints about lack of courtesy.
Handle difficult customers without alienating them.	Provide appropriate solutions to difficult customers or refer them to management.	No customer complaints or referrals to management.
Demonstrate commitment to maintaining a pleasant attitude during busy times.	Serve customers efficiently with a pleasant attitude during peak operating times.	Observations by manager and no complaints by customers upset by employees with bad attitude.

A form based on this figure is provided as Figure B-10 in Appendix B.

Figure 2-5.   Sample skill gap assessment guide.

Training Skill Required	Assessment of Trainee Skill	Skill Gap
Skill: Operate the cash register correctly. **How well?** All information keyed in correctly for each of the 48 items sold at the refreshment stand.	Operates the register quickly and successfully.	Has no skill gap.
Skill: Charge the correct amount for each of the 48 items. **How well?** No overcharged or undercharged customers.	Frequently confuses popcorn and soft drink prices. Has difficulty making correct change.	Needs training on correct prices and sizes. Needs training and practice on counting change.
Skill: Operate the popcorn machine correctly. **How well?** Batch of popcorn in 5 minutes, no wasted popcorn or oil, no spoiled popcorn.	Has never learned to make popcorn.	Needs training on the popcorn machine.
Skill: Demonstrate commitment to maintaining a pleasant attitude during busy times. **How well?** No complaints.	Has demonstrated unpleasant attitude that resulted in customer complaints 4 times during the past 3 weeks.	Needs customer service training.

A form based on this figure is provided as Figure B-11 in Appendix B.

Figure 2-6. Data collection methods.

Method	Advantages	Disadvantages
Observations	■ Are based on firsthand experience ■ Are accessible when appointment is made ■ Gauge atmosphere and working conditions	■ Can be an isolated example; may not be there at right time ■ Need follow-up visits to validate findings ■ Can be highly subjective
Interviews	■ Can ask follow-up questions and probe according to the information obtained ■ Increase the opportunity for open and honest feedback (if not recorded)	■ Can be timely ■ Can be costly ■ Require note transcription/tape recording, which can make people nervous
Focus Groups	■ Are fairly quick ■ Are information-rich	■ Require time commitment ■ May encourage groupthink—participants swayed by domineering participant
Surveys	■ Are anonymous—increase honesty ■ Are information-rich ■ Can obtain a statistically sound representative sample	■ Require tabulation ■ Can have a poor response rate ■ May have no follow-up opportunity ■ May be limited to simple responses like yes or no
Market Trend Research	■ Is valid source *(if reputable journal is used)* ■ Is inexpensive	■ Data not necessarily tailored to organization culture
Skills Assessments	■ Provide baseline to develop key performance measurements ■ Provide quantitative analysis to determine training effectiveness	■ May increase participant anxiety

Figure 2-7 is a training request form to complete during the data collection process that will help you capture information from both managers and individual staff members who request training. This form combines demographic information with learning needs, related competencies, and key performance measures. It is a convenient tool for clarifying and tracking training requests because key items of information are located on one simple form.

Step 4: Develop Learning Objectives

Learning objectives are the cornerstone of your training; they specify what your participants will be able to do when they have completed the training. Objectives are based on *competencies,* which are the behaviors and skills that predict success in a particular job or activity. If you have identified desired skills and subsequent skill gaps, you can develop your learning objectives by selecting skill gaps that need to be filled.

Examples of learning objectives for the refreshment stand are shown in Figure 2-8. Notice that these objectives are for desired sets of behavior that

Figure 2-7. Training request form.

Name _____	Date Requested _____
Department _____	Date to Be Conducted _____
Department Head _____ *Department Head Approval Required?* Yes ☐ No ☐	**Telephone** _____ **E-Mail** _____ **Fax** _____
Project Description:	
Training Requested:	

Learning Needs	Related Competencies	Key Performance Measures
(What are the learning needs?)	(What skills are related to the learning needs?)	(How will effectiveness of the training be measured?)

A copy of this form is provided as Figure B-12 in Appendix B.

Figure 2-8. Learning objectives for the refreshment stand.

Overall Training Goal

1. Customer satisfaction at the Theater Refreshment Stand will improve and customer complaints will decrease.
2. Within 2 months, no more than 5% of the employees (2 employees per month) will receive complaints from customers.

Handling Difficult Customers

1. At the completion of this training, you will be able to demonstrate your ability to handle a transaction with a difficult customer. You will listen without interrupting the customer, use eye contact, restate the customer problem, answer without raising your voice, and attempt to handle the problem without passing it off to your supervisor.
2. Management will receive no complaints from difficult customers you handle.

Handling the Cash Register

1. At the completion of this training session, you will be able to ring up 5 items correctly on the cash register without help.
2. In the next 2 weeks, you will be able to ring orders correctly for a 2-hour period without assistance.
3. At the completion of this session, you will be able to ring sales without voiding them.
4. In the next month, you will have no more than 2 voided sales.

Charging the Correct Amount

1. At the completion of this session, you will be able to identify and price the 3 sizes of soft drinks and the 4 sizes of popcorn.
2. In the next month, the number of inventoried popcorn and soft drink containers will correspond with the sales indicated on the cash register.

participants will demonstrate in the training session as well as back on the job. *Turning Training Into Learning* focuses on getting results. It's crucial that the skills developed during training be applied and expanded by the learner when they are applied to actual work situations.

Traditionally learning objectives call for three different types of learning:

- Cognitive learning
- Affective learning
- Psychomotor learning

A single training situation can call for one, two, or all three types of learning (see Figure 2-9).

Figure 2-9. Three types of learning.

Type of Learning	Cognitive	Affective	Psychomotor
Description	Calls for remembering and applying specific information. Includes making decisions based on information.	Calls for demonstrating attitudes, feelings, and preferences.	Involves the development of skills that require the learner to use his or her muscles. Calls for following procedures, learning techniques, and operating equipment, which become automatic after practice.
Example	At the refreshment stand, workers need to learn the correct price of each of the 48 items sold at the stand and how to identify each of the items.	Refreshment stand workers need to be committed to maintaining a pleasant attitude during busy times.	Workers need to learn how to operate the cash register and the popcorn machine.

Cognitive Learning

Cognitive learning calls for remembering specific information, applying that information to the job at hand, and making decisions based on that information. Most training situations will call for cognitive learning. At the refreshment stand, some of the employees need to learn the prices of products, the recipe for how to make specific products, and the proper words to use when servicing customers. In a union workshop, managers need to learn the clauses in the union contract. In the purchasing department, the staff needs to learn the names of the venders and products.

There are five different levels of cognitive learning; it is important to be sure that your training includes the higher levels of learning as well as the lower levels. Figure 2-10 shows all five levels, gives a description of each one, and lists the action verbs you can use to describe learning at each level.

Using the refreshment stand example, workers need to be able to identify the price of each of the forty-eight items (knowledge). They have to be able to distinguish one popcorn size from another and select the right box for each order (comprehension). When it's time to refill the soft drink machine, they need to use the right combination of water and syrup to make the soda taste like it should (application). When the soft drink machine or the popcorn machine breaks down, at least one person on each shift should be able to take the machine apart, analyze the situation, and detect the problem (analysis and synthesis). If the machine still isn't working right, the person who is trying to fix it needs to decide whether to keep working on it or call a repair technician (evaluate).

Affective Learning

Affective learning involves attitudes the learner has about what is being learned and the work being done. Affective learning is tricky because you can't see someone's attitude; you can only pinpoint the specific behavior that results from that attitude. Yet the staff members who are slacking off and treating customers inappropriately are demonstrating their attitudes toward work and the customers.

Figure 2-11 shows the levels of affective learning and highlights the behaviors you can and cannot see during customer service training. It's important to note that *saying* the customer is important doesn't necessarily mean *believing* the customer is important and being able to demonstrate that belief.

Psychomotor Learning

When you drive the car, type an e-mail into your computer, make copies at the copy machine, or work a cash register, you are using psychomotor learning. The first time you drove a car, you had to think about every part of the process. You adjusted the mirror, fastened the seat belt, and turned the key. Then you put the car into drive and inched forward. When you came to a corner, you were very conscious of using the hand-over-hand technique to turn the wheel just enough to make your right or left turn. Whether you were

(text continues on page 38)

Figure 2-10.   Levels of cognitive learning.[1]

Evaluation

Description: Judges which data or actions are appropriate for a given situation.
Action Verbs: Assess, conclude, decide, defend, determine, judge, predict.

Analysis & Synthesis

Description: Gathers facts from a variety of sources and determines possible courses of action.
Action Verbs: Analyze, arrange, construct, create, design, detect, develop, estimate, explain, formulate, infer, sequence, weigh.

Application

Description: Uses previously learned facts and information in new situations.
Action Verbs: Apply, classify, connect, demonstrate, interpret, relate, translate, use.

Comprehension

Description: Demonstrates an understanding of facts and information by restating, explaining, discussing, or describing it.
Action Verbs: Compute, describe, differentiate, distinguish, match, arrange in order, organize, and select (facts and information) appropriate for a particular situation.

Knowledge

Description: Recalls facts and terms, and distinguishes among items.
Action Verbs: Define, identify, list, name, recognize, and state (facts and information).

Figure 2-11.   Levels of affective learning during customer service training.

Internalizing

Description: Uses good customer service skills as an automatic part of his or her general behavior pattern.
Observable: It may take a little while for the participation to be able to develop consistent, automatic responses, but you will be able to tell that he or she has the proper attitude and is trying.

Organizing

Description: Recognizes the value of good customer service, and figures out how to exhibit the desired behavior.
NOT Observable: You can't tune in to this process. The participant who is quiet could be figuring out how to use customer service skills or planning the menu for tonight.

Valuing

Description: Sees the value in good customer service skills, and recognizes why this is important to the refreshment stand and the theater.
NOT Observable: You can't observe the thinking process. The participant *could* be thinking that everything you are saying is ridiculous instead of important.

Responding

Description: Reacts by answering questions, participating in a discussion about why good customer service is important, and participating in role-playing.
Observable: You can observe and hear the answers. But giving the right answer doesn't necessarily mean believing.

Receiving

Description: Starts to think about the customer service behavior you're describing during a training session.
NOT Observable: You can't observe the thinking process. The staff member may appear to be paying attention, but you can't tune in to his or her thoughts.

on a country road or a highway, your attention was focused on staying in your lane, giving the gas pedal just the right amount of pressure, and applying the brake just firmly enough for a smooth stop.

Now you use the car as a form of transportation without thinking about the details of how it operates or how you operate it. Every part of the process you learned when you began to drive has become automatic. The process of acquiring a motor skill well enough for it to become automatic is *psychomotor learning*. The same process occurs whenever you learn a skill that requires the performance of procedures, operations, methods, or techniques.

Usually psychomotor learning is teamed with cognitive and affective learning. When you're teaching staff members to use the cash register, you are teaching the techniques for ringing orders (cognitive), using customer service skills (affective), and manipulating the machine (psychomotor). When you are teaching someone to drive, you are teaching rules of the road (cognitive), the importance of driving safely (affective), and the skills needed to operate the car (psychomotor). The psychomotor learning process shown in Figure 2-12 helps us see how a skill is learned step-by-step.

Figure 2-12.   Levels of psychomotor learning while mastering the cash register.

Communication

Uses the cash register as an automatic tool to record sales, with no effort or special attention required to operate the register.

Application

Level 4: Rings orders automatically and correctly while concentrating on customer service problem.
Level 3: Rings order automatically and correctly during busy period (before the movies).
Level 2: Rings automatically and correctly during slow period (while the movie is showing).
Level 1: Rings orders quickly and correctly during practice.

Acquisition

Level 4: Rings items correctly during practice without conscious attention to each step in the process.
Level 3: Experiments by ringing more items to build up speed.
Level 2: Imitates the instructor and tries ringing up items as described.
Level 1: Follows directions given by the instructor and presses keys.

Combining All Three Types of Learning

Most learning objectives are a combination of two or three types of learning. Take a minute to look back at the learning objectives in Figure 2-8. You will see that the cash register training objectives are a combination of cognitive learning (knowing the prices of items and being able to use those prices to ring up correct sales) and psychomotor learning (operating the cash register automatically and correctly).

The handling difficult customers objective calls for both cognitive learning and affective learning. There are three levels of cognitive learning involved—knowledge of the proper responses to use with upset customers, application of those responses, and evaluation of the situation to determine whether a manager should be called. It also calls for valuing customer service (affective learning) and developing consistent, automatic responses to demonstrate that value.

Writing Simple Learning Objectives

When you are writing learning objectives for use in your training sessions, less is more. The less complicated you make the objectives, the more effective they will be in communicating the desired outcome—learning to be accomplished. Each learning objective is really made up of three parts: (1) the condition of performance, (2) the actual performance expected of the learner, and (3) the criteria for success.[2]

Although the objectives in Figure 2-8 do not use the term "the learner," it is a commonly used term when writing objectives. But an objective such as "Given five sample items (conditions), the learner will demonstrate the ability to record the sale of these items on a computerized cash register model 4358A (performance) within 3 minutes to 100% accuracy (criteria)" is a definite turnoff. Although it is important for you to understand all the details of each objective, the learner only needs the important facts: "By Friday, you will be able to ring a five-item cash register sale without making any mistakes."

To simplify learning objectives, try using actual dates and common expressions.

Instead of:	*Use:*
At the completion of the course	By Friday
The learner	You
With 100 percent accuracy	Correctly

Designing Pretests and Posttests

When you've completed the development of your learning objectives, you know the content of both your pretest and posttest. If you plan and develop both the pretest and posttest at this time, you will be able to coordinate your presentations, materials, and activities with these evaluations. Both pretests and posttests are described in more detail in Chapter 4.

Step 5: Recruit Mentoring Support

The process of turning training into learning is a team effort. It calls for a well-planned and skillfully delivered training effort with mentors involved, a learner who will be proactive in finding learning opportunities . . . a carefully designed, mentor-supported follow-up program when the learner returns to the job.

Who Will Support This Training When the Participant Returns to the Job?

If the training effort has been developed to the specifications of supervisors or managers at their request, you will have less difficulty recruiting support than if the training is offered to a larger audience.

A supervisor who does not believe in or support the training a learner has received can undo that learning before you know it. The time to recruit committed mentors and plan the mentoring effort begins *now*, while you are designing the learning.

The most effective way to ensure that learners will have an opportunity to apply what they have learned and adapt it to their specific needs is to recruit a committed mentor for each learner. If the training involves several sessions, your committed mentor will help you ensure that your participant is able to attend each session. Your mentor will partner with you to make sure the learning is used to improve job performance—since ultimately that's what all training initiatives hope to accomplish. The supervisor commitment grid in Figure 2-13 (to be completed by the trainer with the sponsor) will help you assess your ability to get buy-in from sponsors. This grid suggests that you review training requests with the trainee's supervisor/manager if the level of commitment is too low.

The training partner matrix in Figure 2-14 will help you summarize and track your findings after using the supervisor commitment grid in Figure 2-13.

How Can Mentors Be Included in the Training Development Process?

An effective way to involve mentors in the development process is to give them formal responsibility for customizing the training their employees receive. One example of a successful training program that involved mentors in the development process is a program created for new sponsoring editors at a large book company. Because these editors came from eight divisions that varied widely, the course was designed as a combination of large-group instruction and individualized learning. Each participant's individualized learning goals were customized and directed by his or her supervisor. To facilitate this process, each participant was provided with a deck of EDIT (editor-directed instructional technique) cards representing 167 possible competencies that could be needed to perform well as a sponsoring editor. Figure 2-15 shows the information given to the supervisors whose employees participated in the training program.

Figure 2-13.   Supervisor commitment grid.

Training Planned _____

Participant _____

Supervisor/Manager _____

Department Head _____

Level of Commitment

Use the grid below to gauge the level of commitment that the supervisor, who will support your participant on the job, has with regard to the training.

	Level	Commitment Description
❑	1	**Not Committed:** Is not in favor of training. Reluctantly has agreed to let staff members attend. Has not had time to discuss needs or implementation plans.
❑	2	**Passive Participant:** Seldom has time to discuss training needs. Supports training but believes that the responsibility for implementation belongs to the staff member and the trainer. Has not had time to discuss implementation.
❑	3	**May Be Moldable:** Has consulted with you about training needs and supports training but indicates that he or she has no time to devote to implementation.
❑	4	**Active Supporter:** Has actively participated in discussing and contributing to learning needs, supports training, and is willing to serve as mentor to staff members when they return to the job.
❑	5	**Cheerleader:** Enthusiastically supports training. Has helped you create relevant content. May even participate in the pilot session. Is a model mentor, allowing staff members to become comfortable using their new skills on the job.

Note: If commitment level is not above 3, review training requirements with your trainee's supervisor/manager and discuss the importance of his or her level of commitment to achieve buy-in. Reiterate the message that most training efforts fail to be transferred to the job because there are no follow-up support mechanisms in place once participants return to work.

A copy of this form is provided as Figure B-13 in Appendix B.

Figure 2-14. Training partner matrix.

Use the matrix below to:

▪ List participants.

▪ Identify supervisor/manager who supports each participant.

▪ Identify training needs.

▪ Indicate whether or not supervisor has been actively involved in communicating the training needs to participants. List date of last discussion.

▪ Determine the commitment level (see Figure 2-13).

Participant	Supervisor/ Manager	Training Need	Actively Involved (yes or no and date)	Commitment Level (1 not committed– 5 very committed)

This form is primarily useful in supporting the training contract.

A copy of this form is provided as Figure B-14 in Appendix B.

How Can We Enable Proactive Learning on the Job?

If you design training efforts that encourage learners to take charge of their own learning, you will automatically gain the assistance of the most valuable members of your team—the learners. One way to encourage your participants to take charge of their own learning is to use a learner-controlled approach such as the one described in Figures 2-15 and 2-16. Parts A and B of Figure 2-16 show the program description that was given to the participants who used the deck of EDIT cards.

Step 6: Develop Presentations, Materials, and Activities

The development of actual presentations, materials, and activities is essential to any learning effort. Chapter 3 and the entire second part of this book (Chapters 5–9—LEARN) will provide valuable information on the development of presentations, materials, and activities that will help you turn training into learning.

Figure 2-15.   Supervisors' training information.

___

The Supervisor's Role
in the Editorial Training Program

As the supervisor of a participant in the editorial training program, your role is an important one. Your support and cooperation will help to ensure that the program is an effective one that will, in turn, help your employee become more valuable.

The editorial training program involves two types of training: group and individual. The group sessions will be general enough to meet the needs of editors from every division in the Book Company. These sessions will give participants an opportunity to discuss the role of the sponsoring editor with a number of key Book Company resources. They will also have several opportunities to exhibit the behavior expected of successful sponsoring editors in realistic case problems and simulations.

The group sessions are only half of the editorial training experience. The individual instruction portion of the program will enable participants to apply what they have learned in the group sessions to their own situations and needs. ***Your role as the supervisor of a participant is to be that person's primary training resource.*** Your involvement will call for work with two key components of the program—the sponsor competencies and the EDIT cards. The use of these two components is fully explained in the attached description (see Figure 2-16). Specifically, your responsibilities will involve the following activities:

1. Working with your employee to tailor the sponsor competencies to his or her own particular position.
2. Working with your employee to sort the 167 EDIT cards that are provided to facilitate individualized instruction.
3. Helping your employee to select resources who can answer the questions on the EDIT cards and answering as many of the questions as you can yourself.
4. Releasing your employee for approximately three hours each week so that he or she can participate in the individualized instruction portion of the program. (This is essential to the success of the program.)
5. Monitoring your employee's progress and making yourself available for consultation whenever it is needed.
6. Providing an opportunity and a safe environment in which your employee can become comfortable in using his or her newly developed skills.
7. Providing constructive feedback and additional training when needed.

YOUR SUPPORT AND COOPERATION ARE VITAL TO THE SUCCESS OF THIS PROGRAM, and a successful program will help to produce a more valuable employee.

___

Supervisor/Date	Employee/Date

Figure 2-16.   Sponsor competencies and EDIT cards.

To develop proactive learners, one company gave the responsibility for learning to the learners themselves by presenting each of them with:

- A set of competencies that each learner could tailor to his or her own needs (with the help of a supervisor).
- A box full of question cards to shuffle and deal. Each learner worked with his or her supervisor to pick the most appropriate cards. Then the learners took responsibility for finding the right resources, and seeking out the answers.

Two key components of this program are the sponsor competencies and the EDIT cards. You will find the sponsor competencies in your notebook behind each of the seven tab dividers. Your deck of EDIT cards is in the black file box.

What Are Sponsor Competencies?

The sponsor competencies represent a combination of procedures and ideas taken from each of the eight divisions of the Book Company. These competencies will provide you with a list of job responsibilities in seven different areas:

1. Market need and marketing
2. Finances and publishing (with special emphasis on ROI)
3. Project authorization
4. Contract negotiations
5. Editing, design, and production
6. Author relations
7. Manufacturing and inventory

These competencies are generally representative of the sponsor's job throughout the Book Company. You should discuss the competencies with your supervisor and use them to develop a comprehensive set of competencies for **your** job. (Delete inappropriate competencies, change others, and add new ones where needed.)

What Are EDIT Cards?

Your pack of color-coded EDIT cards is the key to the learner-controlled instruction portion of the editorial training program. This instruction is directed by you, the learner, instead of the instructor. The degree of success of this program is up to you.

The group sessions will be general enough to suit the needs of editors from every division of the Book Company. You are responsible for applying the general information from the group session to your **own** needs. The tool you will use in this application is your deck of EDIT (editor-directed instructional technique) cards.

How Should You Use the EDIT Cards?

1. With the help of your supervisor, sort the cards:
   a. Eliminate any questions that are not appropriate for your position.

    b. Add other questions using the 16 blank cards at the back of your EDIT card pack.

    c. Put the cards in priority order.

2. With the help of your supervisor, select resources who can answer the top-priority questions. Each week you should work on the cards that have the highest priority for your own position.

3. Call the people you have selected as resources to set up appointments. Use the resource appointment form to confirm the time of each appointment and to explain the use of the EDIT cards.

4. As you talk with each resource, control the discussion so that you receive answers that are meaningful for you. The back of each card is blank so that you can take notes if they will be of help to you.

5. When your resource has answered the question on the card, ask him or her to initial the Completed Box ❐ in the lower right-hand corner of the card.

6. If you are able to answer the question on the card without the help of a resource, feel free to initial the Completed Box ❐ on that card yourself.

7. Use your EDIT card time sheet to keep a record of the cards you have answered, the resources you have used, and the time you have spent with the cards.

8. If you have any problems obtaining answers to the questions on your EDIT cards, share those problems with the other participants at the next group session. They may have overcome similar problems.

By participating in the learner-controlled instruction portion of the editorial training program, you will have an opportunity to ask the questions you want answered and talk with the people within your division who are most qualified to answer them.

Figure 2-17 shows a course plan that will help you design each course. By taking the time to develop a first draft of the complete plan before you begin developing your presentations, materials, and activities, you will be able to manage the entire process more easily. This plan can then serve as a working document as you finalize your course.

Step 7: Determine Schedules and Needed Resources

Your course planning template and course-at-a-glance grid can become a reality only if you have taken the time and effort to attend to all the logistics required to make any course a reality. You need to consider four key questions:

    1. How many sessions are required?

    2. Who should present the material?

    3. Where will sessions be held?

    4. What equipment and resources are needed?

Figure 2-17. Sample course plan.

Course/Session Title: Customer Service/"Top-Flight Customer Service"

Date:

Objective	Content (topics)	Time Frame	Presenter	Teaching Method
Explain why customer service is important to Thompson's.	Start with introduction/customer service discussion.	10 min.		Discussion
Describe why everyone makes a difference. Explain and demonstrate the concept of perception.	A customer's perception is the truth as far as that customer is concerned. Everyone contributes to the perception.	10 min.		Discussion
Describe how you would have felt if you were one of the customers on the customer service video.	Use the customer service video from Thompson's headquarters.	30 min.		Video Small-group discussion
Use the customer service bull's-eye and the moment-of-truth circle to illustrate the opportunities we all have to give external and internal customers a favorable impression.	The customer is the focus of our efforts (bull's eye). Positive moments of truth build satisfaction; negative ones have the opposite effect. Everyone contributes to moments of truth.	30 min.		Team activity Demonstration
Develop a plan of action that identifies 3 things you can do to improve customer service in your own department.	We are all responsible for customer service. Every department will have an action plan.	10 min.		Individual activity Discussion Posting of actions

A copy of this form is provided as Figure B-15 in Appendix B.

How Many Sessions Are Required?

As you develop a plan for the number of sessions required to complete training, you may be influenced by managers and supervisors who want learning to happen in as little time as possible. They want their staff members to return as quickly as possible to their jobs with better skills, a better attitude, and more willingness to work. At the same time, you are trying to accomplish a series of learning objectives that have been identified for a specific group of participants. Be careful not to shortcut the training time allotted; don't pack too much content into the session. When you do either, learners become overloaded.

As a general rule, it is better to present material in two half-day sessions than in one full-day session because learners are generally "filled up" and unable to absorb any more by the middle of the afternoon. If participants are expected to practice a technical skill on the job, several one-hour or ninety-minute sessions spaced a week apart, instead of one three-hour session, will yield much better results.

If the training is a large-scale effort, you need to consider the number of participants to be trained and factor that into the room size to know how many sessions you need to schedule. You also need to know the makeup of the audience. This will allow you to decide whether you should divide your participants by functional area or department. Assume, for example, that you have scheduled 200 staff members to participate in a new training program that requires hands-on practice on the new online system. You are limited to twenty people per course because your computer lab has only twenty terminals. You can either market the course as an open-enrollment course and register participants on a first-come, first-serve basis or hold the same number of sessions but select the participants by department or unit. All of your finance personnel may go through the course in a single session, and your HR personnel may go through the training in another session. Although this approach allows you to tailor the course to meet the specific needs of each department, it is sometimes difficult to schedule this type of training, as department heads may not want all their people attending training at the same time. Whatever method you choose to adopt, make sure it is feasible for the departments involved.

Who Should Present the Material?

One of the most valuable roles a trainer can serve is that of a resource broker who both helps clients identify needs and skill gaps and finds resources who can help fill those gaps. Your subject-matter experts can come from either outside or inside a department.

Outside Subject-Matter Experts. In some cases, you may want to involve a subject-matter expert (SME) to deliver a training program or portions of the program. To guide this process, refer to Figure 2-18, the subject-matter expert invitation. This letter is a mini-contract agreement for which you confirm the SME's involvement and communicate what is expected of him or her. The invitation should also include a copy of the course plan and any additional information needed. You might want to include a list of participants (if avail-

Figure 2-18.   Subject matter expert invitation.

To: <insert subject-matter expert name>

From: Training Coordinator

Date: <insert date>

Re: Invitation to <insert training course name>

Thank you for agreeing to be the subject-matter expert for the <insert training course name> to be held on <insert date and time>, in room <insert location>.

To assist with the <insert company name> ongoing training and education efforts, the <insert training course name> course will be offered to <insert audience>. The objective of this course is to <insert training objective>.

As a subject-matter expert, we would like you to complete the attached training plan. This plan enables the training department to identify, at a glance, your expectations for participants in this course. Also attached is a biography for you to complete so we can advertise the course, identifying your background.

If you are unable to attend the course, it is critical that you find a replacement with a relevant background to teach the course or notify us at least two weeks in advance so we can reschedule the course.

Please complete the training plan and the bio and return them to our office no later than <insert return due date>. Feel free to either e-mail them to <insert e-mail address> or fax them to <insert fax number>.

We look forward to working with you on the <insert course name>.

A copy of this form is provided as Figure B-16 in Appendix B.

able) as well as their level and position within the organization. If this list is not available, you will want to specify who the target audience is so your SME has an idea of how to tailor material to target varied audiences. Another important element of the SME packet is the biography (see Figure 2-19). The bio gives you more background information on the SME. This information is useful for two reasons: (1) You can include information in future course marketing communications, and (2) you can integrate the bio information as you introduce your SME.

Department-Based Subject-Matter Experts. Often there is someone within the department requesting the training who has the expertise to run the course but does not have the expertise to develop training plans, presentations, and materials. If you can identify this person, you can work as a team to create a custom-made training course. You should first help this person organize or structure his or her thinking regarding the course material. You might ask questions such as:

- What are the three most important things I should know about <insert training course topic> as a new staff member?
- Pretend I am a staff member in the department. Describe the process to me step-by-step.

Figure 2-19.   Subject matter expert biography.

Name:	**Telephone Number:**
Fax Number:	**E-Mail Address:**
Mailing Address:	**Secretary/Administrative Assistant (name and number):**

Please describe your last three positions (and length of time in each position), as well as the organization and your job responsibilities below.

1. **<Insert position, organization, length of time in position, and description>**

_____

_____

_____

2. **<Insert position, organization, length of time in position, and description>**

_____

_____

_____

3. **<Insert position, organization, length of time in position, and description>**

_____

_____

_____

Use the space below to describe additional relevant experiences

_____

_____

_____

_____

Education

Degree   *School*   *Major/Minor*

_____   _____   _____

_____   _____   _____

_____   _____   _____

Certifications/Licenses

_____

A copy of this form is provided as Figure B-17 in Appendix B.

▪ What are the three most common things that can go wrong with the process? How do you overcome these problems?

Often the person who has the expertise to be an internal trainer has never had the coaching necessary to clarify his or her thinking well enough to share it with someone else. If you can train or coach an internal expert through this clarification process, you may be able to groom a valuable training resource.

Senior management speaker. It may be appropriate to have a member of senior management kick off the training, especially if the course is critical to the organization. This type of course introduction demonstrates buy-in and helps you promote the course.

Where Will Sessions Be Held?

After you've thought through when the training will take place and identified the faculty involved in helping you deliver the program, you need to determine where the program will be held. You can begin by reviewing your course plan and determining what type of setup you need for delivery. If you are planning to involve participants in small-group work, you don't want a room with permanent theater-style seats. If you are planning to serve lunch, you want the room to have tables, not just chairs. If you are showing a video, you want to make sure the room can be darkened.

You will also want to consider the number of participants. You don't want to select a room size that is too large or too small. If it's too large, your participants will feel lost, and at times you might too! Large rooms also create acoustics problems and may require advanced projection equipment so your learners will be able to hear you and be able to effectively view overhead and video presentations. If the room is too small, your participants may become uncomfortable and restless. So when selecting the location, consider appropriateness for your particular needs and comfort level of the room.

What Equipment and Resources Are Needed?

Your next consideration is the logistics for the implementation of the course. Figure 2-20 shows a logistics requirements checksheet that outlines all your logistics considerations. There are four major sections to the form: equipment, room schematic (layout), training materials, and refreshments.

Equipment. You will want to consider all types of equipment. Determine if you need an overhead, microphone, PC, flip charts, TV/VCR, podium, electronic LCD panel, slide projector, facilitator tables, etc. Be sure to think through the entire course and identify all your needs.

Room Schematic (Layout). Figures 2-21 to 2-25 show five different room layout choices. The small-group and large-group layouts will enable you to move into and out of discussion activities without having to rearrange the room. If the course is primarily a video forum with little discussion or group

(text continues on page 57)

Figure 2-20.   Logistics requirement checklist.

Course Name _____

Instructor _____ **Date** _____

Use the following checklist to determine logistics requirements for training. This may be used with or without your client.

Equipment

❏ Overhead   ❏ Flip charts *(quantity)*   ❏ Electronic LCD panel projection

❏ Microphone   ❏ TV/VCR   ❏ Slide projector

❏ PC   ❏ Podium   ❏ Facilitator tables *(quantity)*

❏ Other _____

⊗ Contact the Audiovisual Department with request.

Room Schematic (Layout) *(see diagrams in Figures 2-20 to 2-24)*

Location (room number and floor) _____
❏ Individual   ❏ Large group   ❏ Classroom style
❏ Small group   ❏ Boardroom style   ❏ Other

Breakout session space/rooms required?
❏ Yes   ❏ No

⊗ Contact the Building Services Department with request.

Training Materials
❏ Overhead transparencies of course materials
❏ Prepared flip charts
❏ Icebreaker props/exercises
❏ Group exercise materials
❏ Name tents/cards
❏ Masking tape/pushpins
❏ Handouts (list)   _____
                    _____
                    _____
                    _____

Refreshments
❏ Breakfast   ❏ Lunch   ❏ Dinner   ❏ A.M. Break   ❏ P.M. Break

⊗ Contact the Catering Department with request.

A copy of this form is provided as Figure B-18 in Appendix B.

Figure 2-21. Individual setup.

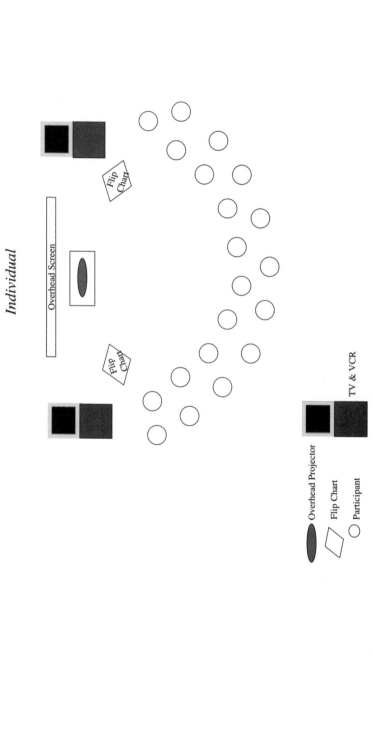

Room Setup A

Individual

Overhead Screen

Flip Chart

Flip Chart

TV & VCR

Overhead Projector

Flip Chart

Participant

Figure 2-22.   Small-group setup.

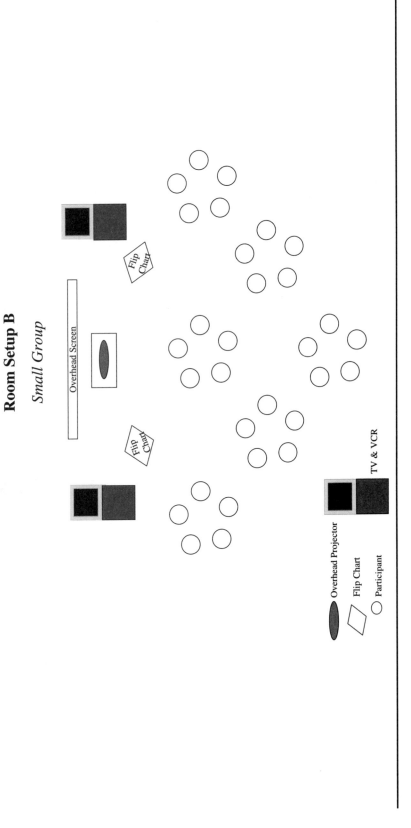

Room Setup B

Small Group

Overhead Screen

Flip Chart

Flip Chart

TV & VCR

Overhead Projector

Flip Chart

Participant

Figure 2-23.   Large-group setup.

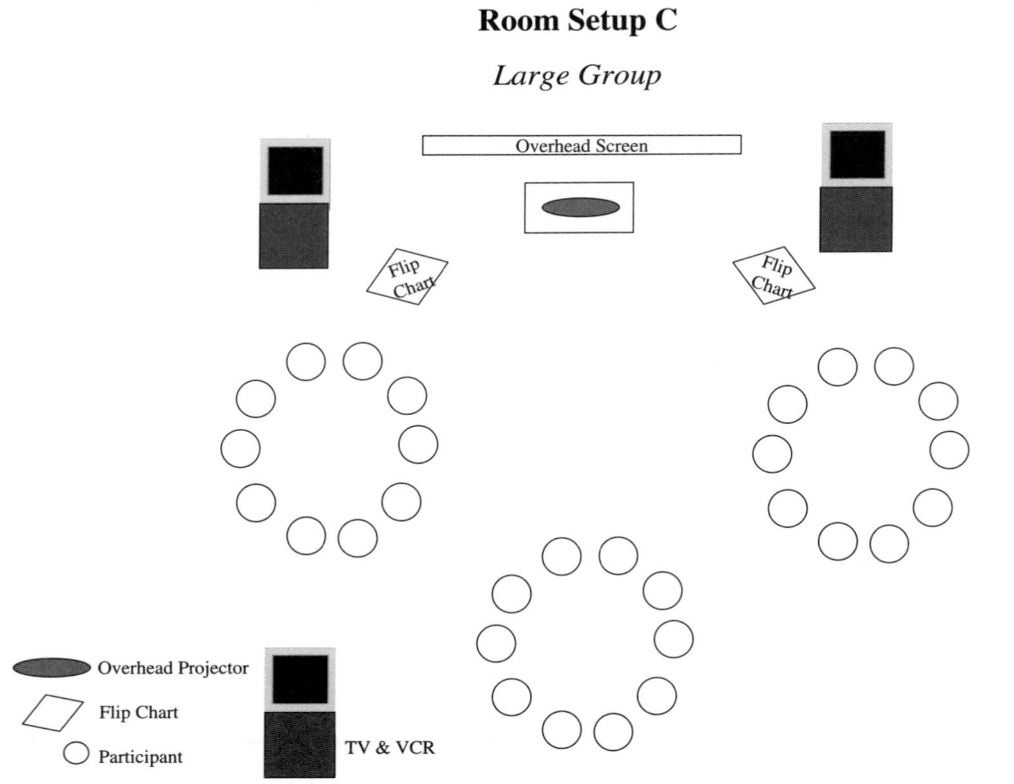

Room Setup C

Large Group

Overhead Screen

Flip Chart

Flip Chart

TV & VCR

Overhead Projector
Flip Chart
Participant

Figure 2-24. Boardroom setup.

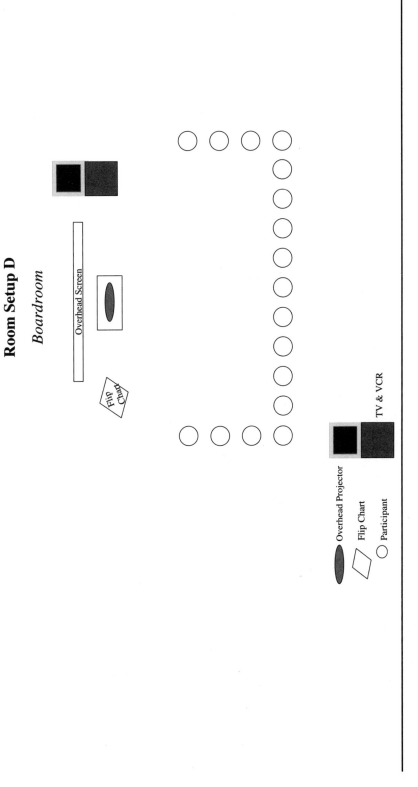

Room Setup D

Boardroom

Overhead Screen

Flip Chart

TV & VCR

Overhead Projector

Flip Chart

○ Participant

Figure 2-25. Classroom setup.

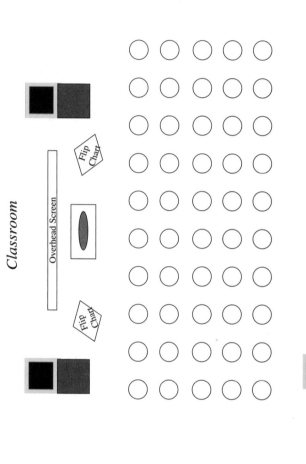

Room Setup E

Classroom

interaction, you may want to use the classroom style because all participants are facing the TVs. If the course will involve the whole class in one large discussion, you will want to select an individual or boardroom layout because participants can see each other and, at the same time, have a clear view of the front of the room.

Training Materials. Listing the materials you need to prepare ahead of time and bring to a session can be an invaluable technique that can save you last-minute rushing or the embarrassment of forgotten materials.

Refreshments. If you decide during the planning stage what refreshments will be served, be sure to select items that will allow you to accommodate the dietary needs of your participants. You can also ensure that you have budgeted sufficient funds and ordered in enough time to ensure delivery when needed.

The Final Check

Figure 2-26 is a precourse last-minute checklist that can help you make sure that all logistics have been taken care of and that all enabling departments—those departments you rely on for supplies and services—are committed to the time, place, and specific needs of your training session. Audiovisual equipment that fails to arrive or a training room that is locked can throw an unexpected monkey wrench in your well-developed plans. Taking the time to complete this checklist can alert you to details you may have forgotten and save you last-minute anxiety on the day of the course.

Making Your Final Plans

Figure 2-27, the course-at-a-glance grid, divides the course into time segments (as guided by the learning objectives) and indicates which materials are needed for each segment. If you take the time to complete this grid, you will be better able to keep your course on target during the actual delivery.

(text continues on page 60)

Figure 2-26.   Precourse checklist.

---

1. Visit room and check:

❒ Lighting
❒ Electrical outlets (actually working)
❒ Room setup (select schematic)
❒ Window shades (appropriate for effective illumination of AV equipment)

2. Contact all enabling departments to ensure delivery of their services.
   Catering:

❒ Menu
❒ Beverages
❒ Timing
❒ Cleanup
❒ Contact name and number (in case of problem)

Audiovisual:

❒ Equipment
❒ Delivery time
❒ Pickup time
❒ Contact name and number (in case of problem)

Environmental Services:

❒ Room setup
❒ Moving of equipment/furniture
❒ Delivery time
❒ Pickup time
❒ Contact name and number (in case of problem)

Security:

❒ Confirm room unlocked/locked at appropriate times
❒ Number and contact name (in case of an emergency)

A copy of this form is provided as Figure B-19 in Appendix B.

Figure 2-27.   Sample course-at-a-glance grid.

Course at a Glance: Top-Flight Customer Service		
Time	*Objective*	*Materials*
2 min.	**Introduce Course** Introduce participants, leader, and purpose of the course.	Slide 1, flip chart, markers, laptop and LCD projector*, table tents
8 min.	**Warm-Up Activity** Lead participants in short activity to launch discussion of customer service/customer satisfaction.	Perception activity
10 min.	**Discuss Customer Service and Link to Perception** Discuss meaning of customer service, concept of perception, connection between customer service and perception, everyone's contribution to customer service, and link to perception.	Slides 2, 3, 4, 5, 6, perception activity
2 min.	**Introduce Video** Introduce purpose of video and participant assignments during video.	Slides 7 and 8, video reaction form
18 min.	**Show Video** Show customer service video in its entirety, without stopping. Remember to watch video (again) with participants.	Customer service video (in its entirety, without stopping), VCR, TV
10 min.	**Ask for Video Reactions** Solicit (but don't comment on) reactions to video and record them for group to see.	Slide 9
15 min.	**Discuss Customer Service Bull's-Eye** 1. Discuss why everyone makes a difference. 2. Show that customer is the center of all our efforts.	Slides 10 and 11
10 min.	**Introduce Moment-of-Truth Opportunities** 1. Introduce moments of truth. 2. Define moments of truth. 3. Annotate moments of truth.	Slides 12, 13, and 14, what-if activity

(continues)

Figure 2-27. (Continued)

5 min.	**Introduce Customer Service Report Card and Review Everyone Makes a Difference** 1. Introduce concept of report card. 2. Discuss what participants expect as customers. 3. Ask participants to explain why everyone makes a difference.	Slides 15 and 16
10 min.	**Complete Action Plans, Verify Supervisor Buy-In, Set Date for Progress Checkup** 1. Encourage each participant to complete action plan. 2. Facilitate discussion of supervisor buy-in. 3. Set date for progress checkup.	Discussion, slides 17 and 18

*Have a set of overheads and an overhead projector available as backup.

Notes

1. The three types of learning have been a part of education and training for many years. The original sources of these theories are shown in the Resources.

2. The person who set the standard for learning objectives was Robert Mager. His books about goals, objectives, and instructional design are classic guides for anyone who is preparing instructional materials.

Resources

Bloom, Benjamin, et al. *Taxonomy of Educational Objectives: The Classification of Educational Goals, Handbook I: Cognitive Domain.* New York: David McKay Company, Inc., 1956.

Harrow, Anita, *A Taxonomy of the Psychomotor Domain.* New York: David McKay Company, Inc., 1972.

Krathwohl, David R., et al. *Taxonomy of Educational Objectives: The Classification of Educational Goals, Handbook II: Affective Domain.* New York: David McKay Company, Inc., 1964.

Mager, Robert. *Preparing Instructional Objectives,* 3rd edition. Atlanta: Center for Effective Performance, Inc., 1997, 202 pages.

3

Delivering Training That
Ensures Learning

Training is only successful when your participants have learned; learning happens only when participants can recall the skills and abilities that were taught and put them to work on the job. How can you be sure learning will happen in your training events? This chapter introduces the needs of the adult learner and three different styles of learning. The chapter also features five secrets for transferring skills and abilities from your participants' short-term memories, where they will quickly disappear, and "hardwiring" them into long-term memory, as well as approaches for reaching both the right brain and left brain of your participants (see Figure 3-1).

In Chapter 6, Help Me See What's in It for Me, and Chapter 7, Help Me Build My Skills Step-by-Step, you will learn how to use additional tools that will help you apply the information in this chapter to your own training/ learning situation.

How Adults Learn

If you want to deliver messages that will capture your learners' attention and interest, it is helpful to understand adult learning and try to mold your training experiences to the orientation of the adults in your sessions.

The Science of Andragogy (Adult Learning Theory)

The art and science of adult learning is called *andragogy,* and was introduced by Malcolm S. Knowles in the early 1960s. He compared andragogy with pedagogy, the art and science of how children learn, and focused on the fact that adults prefer learning that is life-centered, task-centered, and problem-centered. While individual learning styles differ, the study of adult learning by Knowles and others helps us make some general assumptions about how we need to offer learning to adults so we can avoid treating them like children.

Figure 3-1.   Guide to Chapter 3.

Training Stage	Process Steps
3. DELIVER 	**1. How adults learn** • The science of andragogy (adult learning theory) • Five guidelines for adult learning **2. Learning style links** • Visual learners • Auditory learners • Kinesthetic learners • The art of reaching all learning styles **3. Memory basics** • Short-term memory and long-term memory • How the memory system works • Secrets for transferring/"hardwiring" skills **4. The whole-brain approach to learning** • Right-brain/left-brain thinking • Stimulating the whole brain

Five Guidelines for Adult Learning

There are five general guidelines for adult learning.

1. *Allow for some self-direction.* Adults need to feel they have some control over their learning. Because they need to be self-directing, they will resist situations in which they feel as if they are being placed in dependent, childlike roles. One form of learning that satisfies the need to be self-directed is *goal-based scenario learning,* which is a form of learning that targets self-directed work teams and adults. It uses a case scenario as the basis for the course. A team of adult learners is responsible for getting through the materials by themselves. They may have a coach to guide them through the process, but essentially they are making their own decisions.

When goal-based scenario learning is not an option, it is important to find some portion of the learning over which participants can exercise control. You might give them a choice of activities or invite them to use their own job situations as the basis for in-class projects.

2. *Value their experience and build on it.* Adults come to training with a wealth of experience. They can, and will, relate new learning to their experience. You have an opportunity to capitalize on the accumulated experience of your participants by asking them to help you relate new learning to what they already know.

3. *Recognize their readiness to learn.* The adults in your sessions will come ready to learn what they need for practical use. They want practical, hands-on sessions as opposed to theory-based sessions. If you teach them a new communications system, show them how to use it today with someone on the job or at home. If you teach them a new database system, show them how they can use it right away to make their work and their home record keeping easier.

4. *Help them solve problems.* Children who learn are usually trying to master a subject area so they can pass a test and be promoted to the next level. Adults are learning because they are interested in acquiring the actual skills and abilities they need to solve their own real-life problems.

5. *Recognize internal motivation.* Most adults are motivated more by internal factors, such as increased self-esteem and pride, than they are by external factors, such as pay increases, bonuses, and promotions.

You can use the checklist in Figure 3-2 to help you prepare learning experiences that are appropriate for your adult learners.

Learning Style Links

Variety is the spice of life when it comes to the learning styles of your participants and the types of learning materials that are best suited to their learning. According to Rita Dunn (learning style authority from St. John's University in Jamaica, New York), a person's *learning style* is the way that person concentrates on, processes, internalizes, and remembers new and difficult academic information or skills.[1] Although we are all capable of receiving and processing information in a variety of ways, each person has a preference and is most comfortable in a learning environment that supports this preference.

There are three distinct learning styles: visual, auditory, and kinesthetic. At any time in one of your training sessions, you will probably have participants who are comfortable using all three styles.

Visual Learners

Your participants who are most comfortable with visual learning are the ones who are busy taking notes—on everything you say. They may be writing these notes by hand or keying them into a laptop. They may even ask you to slow down your presentation to make sure they have captured everything you say. It's almost as if the concepts you are presenting orally don't actually exist until the visual learner can write them down.

Visual learners often think in images or pictures, instead of words, and may report very clear visual images when they are thinking about something. They are adept at seeing connections and patterns in what you present. You can reach visual learners effectively if you supplement your oral presentation with charts, graphs, slides, pictures, videos, etc. You might also encourage your visual learners to create their own examples of these aids.

Figure 3-2.   Checklist on adult learning experiences.

**Are Your Sessions Geared to the
Needs of Adult Learners?**

Your answers to these questions will help you determine if your sessions are suited to adult learners.	*Seldom*	*Sometimes*	*Usually*
1. I build options into my lessons for the participants to choose from.	❑	❑	❑
2. I value the experience my adult participants have had and try to base learning on their real-life examples.	❑	❑	❑
3. I build practical, hands-on experiences into each session.	❑	❑	❑
4. I try to avoid teaching theory that participants won't find practical and useful.	❑	❑	❑
5. I relate learning to real life and help participants see how it can help them become better problem solvers.	❑	❑	❑

A copy of this form is provided as Figure B-20 in Appendix B.

Authorities in neurolinguistics believe that when a person is engaged in visual learning, he or she may use words that refer to pictures or characteristics of pictures:[2]

- I *see.*
- It's *clear* to me now.
- I get the *picture.*
- My proposal *focuses* on the customer *viewpoint.*
- Your ideas are a little *fuzzy* to me.

In addition to using charts, graphs, and tables, your visual learners will respond well to flash cards, color coding, highlighting, flyers, and any type of job aid you can invent.

Visual learners are also well suited to both developing and learning from *mind maps,* which are drawings that show the relationships among thoughts. You might refer to a mind map as a way to plot an individual brainstorm. Figure 3-3 shows some basic rules for mind mapping. Figure 3-4 shows an

Figure 3-3.   Basic rules for mind mapping.

1. Start in the center of the page and work outward. Use the center to name your topic, for example, "Analysis of Participants Before Training." You can circle it if you want.

2. Draw one line from the center for each main thought or question you have relating to that topic:

    - Why this class?
    - Wants
    - Fears
    - Already Knows
    - Learning Distractions

3. Keep the thoughts flowing. For each main thought, record your next thoughts. For Fears, it might be "looking stupid," "wasting time," and "other participants."

4. Don't think and write in sentences.

5. Use key words and colors.

6. If you want, use icons, pictures, etc.

7. Let one idea lead to another.

8. If you run out of space, tape more paper to the sides of your mind map and keep going.

Figure 3-4.   Template for mind mapping.

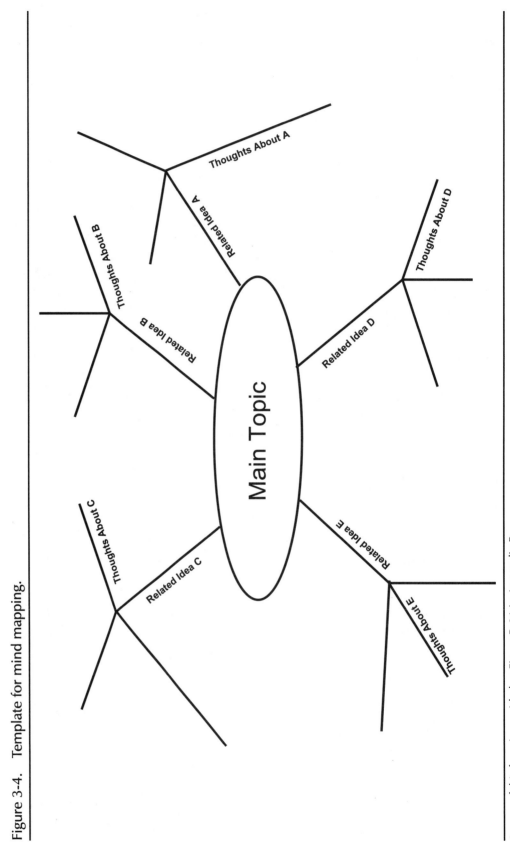

A copy of this form is provided as Figure B-21 in Appendix B.

outline of a mind map. The mind map in Figure 3-5 is a visual representation of the way in which you might analyze the probable needs of participants in an upcoming training class. See Figure 3-6 for a checklist that summarizes some of the activities that will appeal to your visual learners.

Auditory Learners

Your participants who are comfortable with auditory learning are the ones who are listening to your lecture and referring to the printed handouts you distributed. They probably haven't written anything all session, but they may be holding a tape recorder so they can capture every word you say. Auditory learners learn best by hearing, seeing, and saying words. According to neurolinguistic authorities, a person who is engaged in using auditory learning might use words that refer to sounds or characteristics of sounds:

- I *hear* what you're saying.
- That *sounds* good to me.
- That name *rings* a bell.
- I can't *say* which way the vote will go.

The information written in the handouts will have more significance for auditory learners after they hear it spoken out loud. It is natural for auditory learners to remember with little effort what they have heard. They also tend to be good readers because reading relies on auditory processing instead of visual processing.

Your auditory learners will probably be good speakers and may specialize in subjects such as law or public relations. If you have to supervise auditory learners, you will find that you only have to tell them once to do something and you can be sure it will be done. But because they strongly prefer face-to-face communication, auditory learners may pay less attention to the information you distribute to them in memos, e-mails, and other written forms. You may also find that they are easily distracted when there is a lot of noise or other conversations going on in the room.

Your auditory learners can absorb material they hear on audiotapes. If they don't have a handheld recorder in class, they may record the main points of your presentation after class and play it every day for a week—usually while they are walking or commuting to work. They find this to be an easy way to remember information with very little effort.

Another device that is well suited to auditory learners is the use of *mnemonics,* which means an aid to memory; mnemonic devices are words or even sentences that serve as automatic links to other information.

- HOMES is a common mnemonic for the five Great Lakes—Huron, Ontario, Michigan, Erie, and Superior.
- FACE and Every Good Boy Deserves Fudge are memory devices that have helped music students remember the music notes for many years.
- "A rat in the house might eat the ice cream" is a memory device for correctly spelling the word "arithmetic."

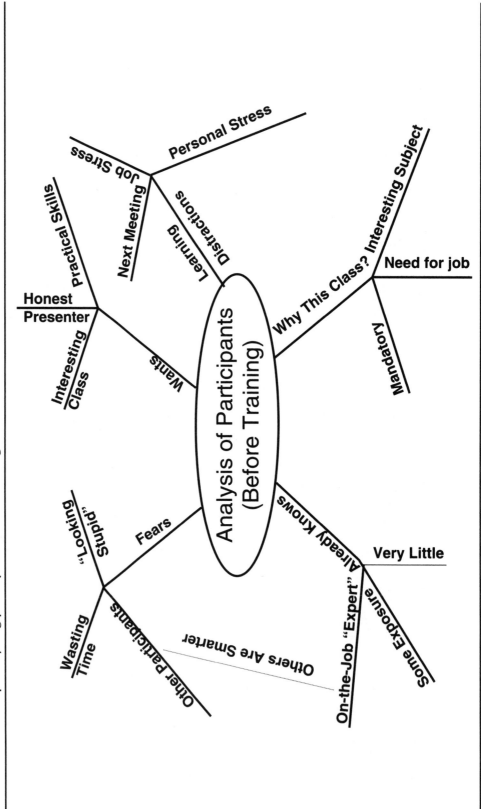

Figure 3-5. Mind map analyzing participants before training.

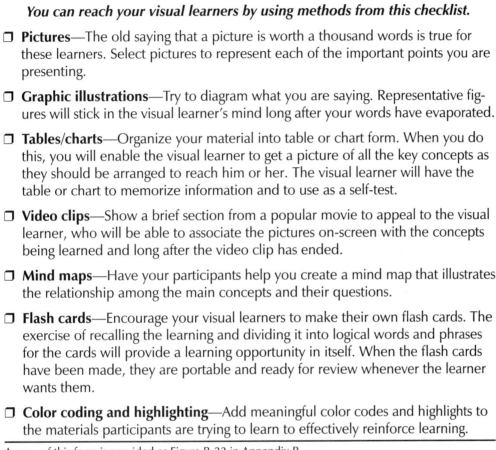

Figure 3-6. Reaching your visual learners.

You can reach your visual learners by using methods from this checklist.

❒ **Pictures**—The old saying that a picture is worth a thousand words is true for these learners. Select pictures to represent each of the important points you are presenting.

❒ **Graphic illustrations**—Try to diagram what you are saying. Representative figures will stick in the visual learner's mind long after your words have evaporated.

❒ **Tables/charts**—Organize your material into table or chart form. When you do this, you will enable the visual learner to get a picture of all the key concepts as they should be arranged to reach him or her. The visual learner will have the table or chart to memorize information and to use as a self-test.

❒ **Video clips**—Show a brief section from a popular movie to appeal to the visual learner, who will be able to associate the pictures on-screen with the concepts being learned and long after the video clip has ended.

❒ **Mind maps**—Have your participants help you create a mind map that illustrates the relationship among the main concepts and their questions.

❒ **Flash cards**—Encourage your visual learners to make their own flash cards. The exercise of recalling the learning and dividing it into logical words and phrases for the cards will provide a learning opportunity in itself. When the flash cards have been made, they are portable and ready for review whenever the learner wants them.

❒ **Color coding and highlighting**—Add meaningful color codes and highlights to the materials participants are trying to learn to effectively reinforce learning.

A copy of this form is provided as Figure B-22 in Appendix B.

- The core of this book—LEARN—is a mnemonic device for the steps in learning: listen and understand, evaluate and decide, attempt and build, return and apply, and natural transition.

See Figure 3-7 for a checklist that summarizes some of the activities that will appeal to your auditory learners.

Kinesthetic Learners

Participants who are most comfortable with kinesthetic learning will not enjoy sitting through a period of lecture; in fact, they are often the people tapping the table and squirming in their seats. They need to get up and walk around the room. Kinesthetic learners may have difficulty remembering a phone number until you hand them a telephone. As soon as they come in contact with the Touch-Tone phone and can move their fingers over the numbers, they quickly remember the phone number. A person who is engaged in kinesthetic learning may use words referring to touch, taste, smell, or emotions:

Figure 3-7.   Reaching your auditory learners.

You can reach your auditory learners by using methods from this checklist.

❐ **Storytelling**—Almost all learners, not just children, enjoy learning through story-telling, and auditory learners lead the group of people who will respond to case situations, examples, and personal stories that illustrate the points you are trying to make.

❐ **Small-group discussions**—Auditory learners will benefit from listening to other members of a small group as much as from contributing to it. However, auditory learners are often good speakers, so they will make substantial contributions to discussion groups.

❐ **Debates**—As keen listeners and good speakers, auditory learners are natural de-baters. They can remember key points without notes and expend little effort hearing, understanding, and preparing rebuttal for opposing arguments.

❐ **Audiotapes**—If you encourage your auditory learners to prepare their own au-diotapes, they will benefit from organizing the information to record it and from having the tapes available to listen to repeatedly.

❐ **Mnemonics**—If you can, create mnemonics that will help auditory learners bet-ter remember what is being taught; it will be a great help to them. If you are unable to do this, you can encourage your participants to come up with their own mnemonics based on examples you might provide.

A copy of this form is provided as Figure B-23 in Appendix B.

- I can't *grasp* the meaning of this section.
- Jim *threw* me a curve when he told me this was due next week.
- Something *smells* funny about this whole thing.
- I have a *feeling* this is going to be a success.

Kinesthetic learners are hands-on learners who need to be actively in-volved in the learning process. They like games, role plays, and practice sessions. Although it may take longer to prepare for sessions in which you are trying to accommodate the needs of kinesthetic learners, the result is worth the effort. Once they learn how to do something through hands-on learning, they can do it consistently without reminders or memory aids. They can work in busy, noisy surroundings without being distracted because it doesn't interfere with their thought processes. See Figure 3-8 for a checklist that summarizes some of the activities that will appeal to your kinesthetic learners.

The Art of Reaching All Learners

Although a variety of tests are available to help you determine the learning styles of participants, many facilitators have neither the budget nor the time to administer them. According to Rita Dunn, the distribution of learning styles in the average class is:[3]

- Visual learners   30–40 percent
- Auditory learners   20–30 percent
- Kinesthetic learners 30–50 percent

Figure 3-8.   Reaching your kinesthetic learners.

You can reach your kinesthetic learners by using methods from this checklist.

❑ **Role playing**—Your kinesthetic learners will be eager for you to stop talking so they can get into the role-playing exercise. They need to be up moving around and will be your most animated role players.

❑ **Practice**—Any opportunity for hands-on practice will appeal to these learners. Let's say you are learning about print advertising. Your kinesthetic learners won't be comfortable with the learning process until they have pens, scissors, and glue in hand and can create an ad that exemplifies the concept you are presenting.

❑ **Site visits**—Kinesthetic learners will be eager participants in any learning that allows them to leave the traditional classroom setting. They will learn rapidly if they have a chance to participate in hands-on demonstrations during site visits.

❑ **Lab work**—Kinesthetic learners will gravitate to the computer lab to try the technical concepts you have been teaching them. While participants from all three learning styles need time in the lab to make sure learning sticks, these learners can't wait to get their hands on the keyboard.

❑ **Games**—Any learning game that makes sense and reinforces the content presented in class will be a welcome activity for your kinesthetic learners, who may be your most eager participants.

A copy of this form is provided as Figure B-24 in Appendix B.

If each of your sessions has a mix of participants with different learning styles, you will be more effective if you:

- Become aware of your own learning style and learn to become comfortable using styles other than your own when you facilitate.
- Are sure that you can be heard and that your visuals can be seen in the back (especially if the room is large).
- Learn to switch styles several times in each session so you can accommodate the styles of all your participants. For each concept, you will cover all the bases if you remember to have ESP in your sessions:
  E—Explain it in words.
  S—Show it on overheads, pictures, graphs, tables, charts, etc.
  P—Practice it with games, role plays, and other activities.
- Place brightly colored, scented markers and highlighters on the table during your session for visual learners who need to annotate their notes.
- Track your main points on a flip chart or whiteboard so they are available for all to view as you progress.

- Are sure there is enough light in the room for note takers when showing videos.
- Switch to another method of conveying the information if you see your participants losing attention.

Memory Basics

How many times have you heard something in a training session that you want to remember and use, only to have it disappear from your mind before you have a chance to recall it and put it to use? Regardless of the type of learning styles you and your participants have, you will be better able to deliver training that sticks if you learn some basic information about the way memory works. All of us have two different kinds of memory—temporary short-term memory and more permanent long-term memory.

Short-Term Memory and Long-Term Memory[4]

Short-term memory is the temporary storage system we have for retaining the information we are dealing with at the moment. It is active all the time and has a very limited capacity, holding only about seven pieces of information (give or take two) at a time. This means if we pack too much information into short-term memory, all except seven items will disappear. How short is short-term memory? Most psychologists estimate that information only lasts twenty seconds in short-term memory before it either is transferred to long-term memory or disappears.

Long-term memory is a relatively permanent storage system that we have for retaining a great deal of information for a long period of time. It's like a file cabinet with much information stored in logical sequence and available for our use when we need it. But unlike short-term memory, long-term memory is not in use at all times; we access it when we need to find something in the "file." See Figure 3-9 for an illustration of these two memory systems.

How the Memory System Works

Because our short-term memory only holds around seven pieces of information for twenty seconds, it needs to be as efficient as possible to enable us to retain as much information as possible and transfer that information into long-term memory. If we peek into our brains, we can see what's going on in short-term memory (see Figure 3-10). There are three distinctly different types of processes going on—often simultaneously: learning effort, message decoding, and distractions.

1. *Learning effort.* This is an effort directly related to the process of transferring the information being received into long-term memory. It includes creating pictures in your participants' minds, mentally arranging the information they are receiving so they can find it later, relating what they've just heard to information they have already stored in long-term memory, and

Figure 3-9. Short-term and long-term memory.

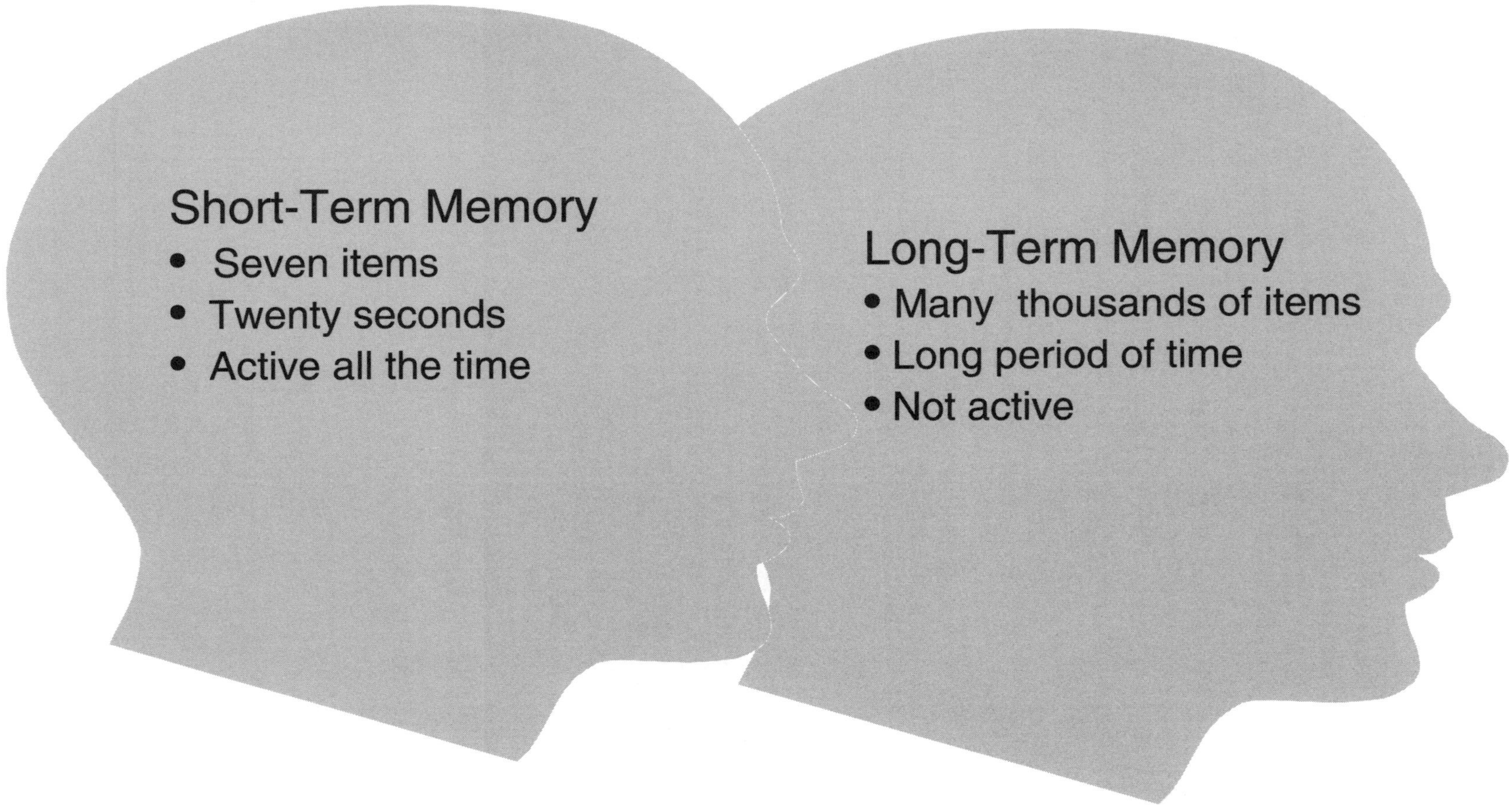

Short-Term Memory
- Seven items
- Twenty seconds
- Active all the time

Long-Term Memory
- Many thousands of items
- Long period of time
- Not active

Figure 3-10.   Short-term memory processes.

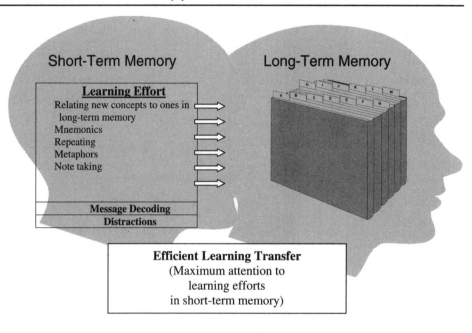

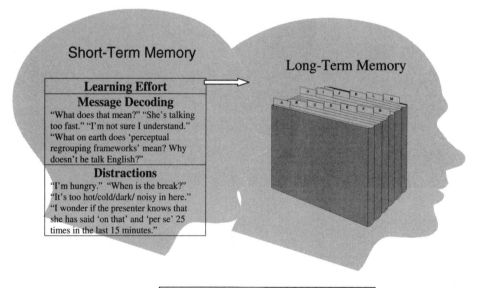

having them repeat information to themselves so they can transfer it into their long-term memory.

2. *Message decoding.* This is a short-term effort expended as participants try to understand the material that is being presented. The more complex the message, the more effort it takes to understand the information being presented. It doesn't matter whether this is material presented in a book, in handouts, or in presentation form in a training session. Message decoding effort interferes with learning effort. The more time and energy your participants expend on trying to figure out what you are trying to tell them, the less effort they can expend on actually learning the concepts and skills.

3. *Distractions.* Valuable short-term memory is used up when participants have difficulty concentrating on the learning at hand. They might be hungry, hot, tired, stressed, angry, etc. Maybe the room is too hot or too cold; the seats might be uncomfortable. Maybe your presentation is not as smooth or professional as it should be. Distractions are in direct competition with learning effort. They can leave little room for the learning effort your participants must exercise to move concepts from short-term memory to long-term memory.

Secrets for Transferring/"Hardwiring" Learning

For training to become learning, the concepts you are teaching need to move from short-term memory into long-term memory, and the skills you are teaching need to be learned to such a point that the learner is comfortable using them. Impossible? Not at all. But it will take careful planning on your part.

Did you ever feel confident at the end of a computer class because you mastered a software program such as Excel? What happened to your skill level if you didn't practice? Even though the skill was in long-term memory, it almost certainly faded. Without any form of practice, your learned skill is gone in a few weeks.

Because you can't follow each learner back to the job and make sure he or she practices, you take the opportunity to "hardwire" as many skills as you can while the participant is in the training classroom. Experts say that it takes six repetitions of a skill or ability before you own it.[5]

Unfortunately, most training courses are designed to allow for one brief practice session, at best, before the participant returns to the job. Often a slightly confused participant is walking out of a session and returning to the job (and a desk full of unfinished work) with every intention of practicing a newly developed skill, but the demands of the job make it impossible to devote time and energy to the effort. Then, when the skill is needed, it's no longer accessible in long-term memory.

Figure 3-11 shows the seven basic steps to "hardwiring" skills. As the participant progresses through six separate practice sessions, the skill becomes automatic. To allow for "hardwiring" to occur during training, you may have to think about the scheduling of training in a different way. If a participant were able to practice the entire skill two times on Monday, two times on Wednesday, and again two times on Friday, for example, the skill

Figure 3-11.   Steps for "hardwiring" skills into memory.

1. Describe to the learners the skill you are going to present. Make sure they know why you are presenting it and why it is important for them to learn it.

2. Acknowledge learners who have some ability in this area.

3. Demonstrate the entire skills slowly and carefully.

4. Divide it into logical learning modules if the skill is a complex one. For example, the process of registering hospital patients is a complex one that can be taught in five logical modules.

5. Arrange an opportunity for participants to practice *each* of the five modules until they have reached a level of proficiency. Provide appropriate feedback on each of the modules to ensure mastery of the skills associated with it. For example, if a participant has difficulty entering the patient's name and address on the hospital computer system, let that person practice the skill until he or she is comfortable.

6. Arrange an opportunity for participants to practice the *entire* process from beginning to end.

7. Schedule practice sessions with appropriate feedback that enable the participant to demonstrate the entire skill *five more times*. The insurance broker will demonstrate the ability to process six separate claim forms.

A form based on this figure is provided as Figure B-25 in Appendix B.

would be "hardwired" into that participant's memory by Friday; if it were practiced every Monday at noon for six consecutive Mondays, it would be "hardwired" after six weeks. After each practice, the skill becomes more automatic.

The Whole-Brain Approach to Learning

Have you heard the expressions right-brained and left-brained? They refer to a scientific theory about the types of brain activity that happen in the right and left hemispheres of our brain. Although we all use both hemispheres of our brain, many people find that there is either a right-brain dominance or a left-brain dominance.

Right-Brain/Left-Brain Thinking

The *right brain* houses characteristics such as curiosity, socialization, experimentation, playfulness, artistry, risk taking, flexibility, creativity, and solution finding. The right brain welcomes opportunities; it's the hemisphere in which we envision the future and welcome change. The *left brain* houses logical thinking; activity in the left brain is more analytical and fact-based. Quantitative work, sequential thinking, planning, and detail work are all left-brain activities. Figure 3-12 compares the characteristics of the two brain hemispheres; Figure 3-13 gives some suggestions for stimulating both left-brain and right-brain behaviors.

Stimulating the Whole Brain

Because traditional learning is largely oriented to left-brain activity, it is often the right brain that is ignored. Because each of us regularly uses both hemispheres, you can enhance learning by using exercises that stimulate both sides. To stimulate both hemispheres, try using all the five senses:

- *Touch.* Give them pencils, games, balls, handouts, brochures, and stickers to place on their papers.
- *Sight.* Use flip charts, pictures, videos, and overheads.
- *Hearing.* Use discussion groups, music, fluctuation in voice tone, bells, and buzzers.
- *Taste.* Use snacks, cookies, soda, lunch, and coffee. Offer healthy snacks as rewards.

Figure 3-12.   Left-brain and right-brain characteristics.

Left-Brain Characteristics	Right-Brain Characteristics
- Prefers a step-by-step approach	- Arranges the parts to form a whole
- Looks at things one part at a time	- Follows hunches and feelings/takes leaps of logic
- Uses rational thinking to reach conclusions	- Deals with information on the basis of need or interest at the time
- Processes information logically	- Relates to concepts/information literally—as they are commonly known or understood
- Uses representational words—ones that stand for something other than their normal meanings	- Sees whole things and overall patterns
- Keeps track of time/thinks in terms of past, present, and future	- Uses imagery and responds to pictures, colors, and shapes
- Is comfortable with numbers	- Is oriented toward physical feelings
- Uses math to reach estimates	- Has little awareness of time
- Organizes, classifies, categorizes, and structures information	- Uses intuition to estimate and perceive shapes
	- Listens to music
	- Is interested in ideas and theories

Figure 3-13.   Suggestions to stimulate left-brain/right-brain behaviors.

How to Stimulate Left-Brain Behaviors	*How to Stimulate Right-Brain Behaviors*
▪ Verbal instructions and information	▪ Visual, kinesthetic instruction
▪ Evaluation of performance to a specific standard	▪ Learning through exploration and rewards for creative discoveries
▪ Systematic, logical problem-solving activities	▪ Subjective, intuitive problem-solving activities
▪ Critical, analytical reading/listening	▪ Teaching through demonstration
▪ Realistic stories	▪ Creative stories, fantasy, art, music, poetry
▪ Step-by-step approach in outline fashion	▪ Summarizing rather than outlining
▪ Well-structured assignments	▪ Open-ended assignments

▪ *Smell.* Have coffee ready—especially for morning sessions. Use scented markers. Give flowers as game prizes.

Understanding the differences in your right- and left-brain learners will be a significant key to success. If you use a number of the activities discussed in this chapter, you will be applying an area of knowledge that many other trainers have overlooked—the right and left hemispheres of the brain and the natural influences they have on adult learning.

Action Plan for Efficient Learning Transfer

In the space below, develop a plan that will ensure efficient transfer of learning from your participants' short-term memory to their long-term memory. Include learning transfer techniques, "hardwiring" techniques, and whole-brained learning activities you plan to use. Include, also, distractions you plan to avoid.

Learning transfer techniques:

"Hardwiring" techniques:

Whole-brained learning activities:

Distractions to avoid:

Notes

1. Michael F. Shaughnessy, "An Interview with Rita Dunn about Learning Styles," © 1998 Helen Dwight Reid Educational Foundation, *The Clearing House,* section 3, volume 71, page 141.

2. References to neurolinguistics and suggestions for effective teaching adapted from Bernadine P. Branchaw and Joel P. Bowman, *Instructor's Guide for Delmar Reference Manual,* © 1994, Delmar Publishers, Albany, New York.

3. Op cit., Michael F. Shaughnessy.

4. References to memory adapted from "Reducing Impositions on Working Memory through Instructional Strategies" by John D. Farquhar and Daniel W. Surry in *Performance & Instruction,* September 1995, pages 4–7.

5. Presentation by Jack M. Wolf, Ph.D., "Lifelong Learning Partners" at the Creative Problem Solving Institute, Summer 1998. For more information, contact wolfman73@aol.com.

Resources

Adult Learning

Knowles, Malcolm. *The Adult Learner, A Neglected Species,* 4th edition (paperback). Houston: Gulf Publishing, 1996.
————. *The Modern Practice of Adult Education: From Pedagogy to Andragogy,* revised edition. Englewood Cliffs, N.J.: Cambridge Book Company, a division of Simon & Schuster, Inc., 1998.

Learning Styles

Zielinski, Dave, editor. "Different Strokes: Learning Styles in the Classroom." In *Making Training Pay Off on the Job,* 3rd edition. Minneapolis: Minneapolis Lakewood Publications, Inc., 1996.

4

Evaluating the Training Process

How do you know your training was effective? Even if your participants leave the training room happy and give you high scores on an evaluation as they walk out the door, it does not necessarily mean your participants learned or can apply what they learned to the job. It may only mean that your participants enjoyed themselves for the half-day session that just took place because they were able to get away from work for a while.

Only a systematic, targeted approach to training evaluation will help you answer the question, Did participants learn? There are four levels to systematic training evaluation:

1. Reaction
2. Knowledge
3. Application
4. Business results (ROI)

Turning Training Into Learning gives you the opportunity to explore all four levels of evaluation and see how each is an important part of the learning process.

This chapter focuses on the first two levels: reaction and knowledge. Together they are referred to as *program evaluation* because they help you to assess the effectiveness of your training program both during and immediately after the presentation. You will learn how to tune in to the needs of your participants while the session is still in progress so you can make the adjustments necessary to keep your participants actively involved. You will also learn how to design, administer, tabulate, and interpret the end-of-course evaluations. To help you gauge the amount of knowledge your participants are able to retain in long-term memory, you will learn how to design and track pretests and postcourse knowledge checks (see Figure 4-1).

Chapter 9, *Natural Transition*, focuses on the next two evaluation levels—application and business results. Chapters 4 and 9 together give you the tools you need to develop a systematic, targeted approach to evaluation. The table in Figure 4-2 illustrates the four levels of the evaluation process covered in this book.

Figure 4-1.   Guide to Chapter 4.

Training Stage	*Process Steps*
4. EVALUATE 	**1. Midcourse Reaction Evaluations** ■ First-half reality check ■ Flip-chart feedback ■ Observation of obvious clues **2. Postcourse Reaction Evaluations** ■ Decide what you will measure ■ Select the evaluation tool/type ■ Determine how to calculate results ■ Decide how to use evaluation results **3. Measures of Knowledge Retained** ■ Pretest ■ Posttest ■ Postcourse performance test ■ Comfort-level evaluation **4. The Foundation for LEARN**

Midcourse Reaction Evaluations

You're leading a three-hour course on communication. The session is progressing as planned, and it's time for a break. As you exit the training room on your way to the rest room, one of your coworkers asks, "Well, how's it going?" This is a common scene in training programs everywhere. You give your coworker a two-second briefing and rush on.

There's only one thing wrong with this scene: The people who should be answering this question are your participants, not you. By the time the course is half over, they can provide you with valuable feedback that will help you keep them tuned in to the learning process. There are three simple ways to elicit this information: the first-half reality check, flip-chart feedback, and observation of obvious clues.

First-Half Reality Check

One way to find out how it's going is to ask. You can set the stage for this feedback by telling participants at the start of the session that you will be asking for their help in making sure that their needs are being met.

Five minutes before the break, you can ask the whole group a few simple questions:

Figure 4-2. The evaluation process.

Evaluation Element	When?	Why?	How?
Reaction— Chapter 4	During the course or immediately following it, before participants leave the classroom	To measure the effectiveness of the program content and delivery	Use the course evaluation form
Knowledge—Chapter 4	At the end of the training program, before participants leave	To measure the degree to which the training program was effective in delivering the message	Check pre- and posttest results and use the course evaluation form
Application—Chapter 9	1 to 60 days after the training occurred	To measure the degree to which the training has transferred and been utilized on the job	Review participant action plans/ buddy system; survey customers, colleagues, and managers whom the training participant interacts with
Business Results (ROI)— Chapter 9	3 months after the training occurred	To measure the impact of the training on business goals and objectives	Measure performance progress against business goals and objectives

- Is the session helpful to you so far?
- Am I moving too slowly?
- Am I moving too fast?
- Is anything unclear?

The one disadvantage of asking this type of question is that participants may feel obligated to tell you what they think you would like to hear. You can avoid this problem by using the anonymous technique described below.

Flip-Chart Feedback

Have four pieces of flip-chart paper available for participants at the end of the first half of the session. Label the sheets in large block letters using the following headings (see Figure 4-3):

- I wish you would stop . . .
- I hope you keep on . . .
- I don't understand . . .
- During the second half of the course, start . . .

Give each participant a pad of Post-it Notes.™ About five minutes before the break, ask participants to complete each of these sentences by writing the rest of the sentence on a Post-it and sticking it onto the appropriate piece of flip-chart paper. Explain that you will begin your break while they are providing feedback for you. *Then leave the room.*

Return a few minutes early from your break to receive your feedback. Don't panic if there are a lot of Post-its on the I-wish-you-would-stop . . . flip chart. These may be valuable items of feedback that you could never have received from the participants face-to-face. Some I-wish-you-would-stop items may include:

- Removing the slides too fast before I can copy them
- Blocking the screen so I can't always see it
- Generalizing
- Letting one person dominate the discussion

Your ability to adapt the second half of your session to the comments you have received may be a challenge, but it's worth the effort. You might want to begin the second half by reporting on some of your feedback to determine whether these comments express the opinions of a large portion of your group.

Observation of Obvious Clues

Often you will have an accurate sense of how well the session is going from the body language, alertness, and participation level of the group. If you sense that the session is missing the intended mark, you may be able to steer it back on course if you use one of the techniques described in this section

Figure 4-3.   Flip-chart feedback.

I hope
you keep
on . . . .

During the
second half
of the course,
start . . . .

I wish
you would
stop . . . .

I don't
understand . . . .

to diagnose the problem. Then you can devote the first portion of the second half of the session working with the group to address some of their issues.

Postcourse Reaction Evaluations

When the course is over, you have another opportunity to obtain feedback from the participants. The end-of-course evaluation that is handed out before participants leave the training room is sometimes referred to as the "smile sheet" because participants have a tendency to tell you what you want to hear—something that will make you smile—rather than tell you their true reactions to the course.

When evaluating your training efforts, you are probably most interested in finding out if the participants actually attained the learning objectives established for the course. You can use the reaction evaluation to ask them if they learned, and you can test their knowledge in the second level of evaluation (see the sections on pre- and posttest evaluations later in this chapter).

If you take time to plan the evaluation carefully, you will gather information that will help you both adjust this course to the needs of your participants and plan future courses. There are four basic steps to planning the postcourse evaluation:

1. Decide specifically what you want to measure.
2. Identify the evaluation tool you want to use.
3. Decide how you will calculate the results.
4. Decide what you will do with the evaluation results.

Decide What You Will Measure

Program evaluation allows you to gauge how useful the course *process* was (e.g., the length of the course, the materials provided, and the effectiveness of the instructor). Another major benefit of this evaluation level is that trainers have the opportunity to poll participants for new program suggestions. These data can be captured and analyzed to determine future broad-based course offerings.

Postcourse evaluations can include questions such as:

- Was the course the right length?
- Did the equipment work well in helping you learn course objectives?
- Were the materials presented clearly and concisely?
- Did the course meet your expectations?
- How relevant was the course to your job?
- How effective was the course overall?
- What additional needs do you have that were not addressed in the course?

In selecting the questions to include in your evaluation, concentrate on the ones that will provide the most relevant information for you. Theoretically, you can include as many questions as you can think of, but your participants have only a short time in which to provide the answers you are looking for. A few well-chosen questions will be of benefit to both the participants and you.

Select the Evaluation Tool/Type

There is a variety of evaluations available to you. You can use a quick generic evaluation or develop one specifically for your unique course. You can use objective questions that ask participants to select the most appropriate answers from those you have provided or open-ended questions that ask participants to supply the answers.

Figure 4-4 shows a generic, objective continuum evaluation that asks participants to position their responses somewhere on a line between two opposite opinions. Figure 4-5 shows a type of open-ended qualitative evaluation; it asks participants to specify what worked and didn't work during the training. You may want to custom-tailor an evaluation that combines this type of open-ended feedback with more structured feedback.

If you are asking participants to react to questions, you can use a five-point (Likert) scale or a scale with four or six points because the latter encourages participants to be more decisive in their answers, rather than rating down the middle (all threes, as in the five-point rating scale). Some large companies are now recommending the four- or six-point scale. You can use questions that ask participants to indicate their opinion of the training that took place or to report on their observations of the event.

Figure 4-6 shows an evaluation form that includes both open-ended questions and customized, structured questions based on a four-point scale.

Figure 4-4.   Continuum workshop evaluation.

_____

Please take a moment to evaluate this training session by placing a mark on each of the lines below to indicate your opinion of the training. Position your mark at the appropriate spot between the two statements.

　　I believe this workshop was . . .

		5　　　　　3　　　　　1	
A.	Time well spent	L-------------L-------------J	A total waste of time
B.	Relevant to me	L-------------L-------------J	Not relevant and I could care less
C.	Useful	L-------------L-------------J	Not useful at all
D.	Interesting	L-------------L-------------J	Boring me to death
E.	Stimulating	L-------------L-------------J	Putting me to sleep
F.	Able to involve me	L-------------L-------------J	Impersonal—the instructor didn't know I was here!
G.	Clear	L-------------L-------------J	Unclear—what was it about?
H.	Flexible	L-------------L-------------J	Rigid—the instructor wouldn't budge an inch

_____

A copy of this form is provided as Figure B-26 in Appendix B.

Figure 4-5.   Open-ended evaluation.

The three most useful parts of the course were:

1.

2.

3.

The three least useful parts of the course were:

1.

2.

3.

The course helped me understand how to _____.

The course could have helped me understand _____.

I would improve future courses by _____.

What I liked most about the course was _____.

What I liked least about the course was _____.

A copy of this form is provided as Figure B-27 in Appendix B.

This evaluation includes three questions, items 9, 10, and 11, that ask participants to specify their needs and preferences for future training.

Figure 4-7 shows a descriptive evaluation form that asks participants to be more specific in their responses by selecting one out of five descriptive answers to each question. The rating scale for this evaluation is the traditional five-point Likert scale.

Determine How to Calculate the Results

The most well-designed quantitative evaluation instrument will be of little value if you don't know how to calculate quantitative results. While you may use Excel or a similar spreadsheet program to do these calculations automatically, these manual calculations will help you understand the process. There are six steps to the calculation process:

1. Set up the worksheet.
2. Record the evaluations.
3. Verify your work.
4. Multiply the number of ratings by the rating value.
5. Add the totals.
6. Divide the numerator by the denominator.

Figure 4-6.　Evaluation form.

Concerning the content . . .
State your learning objectives and use the scale to measure the effectiveness of the learning objectives.

	Not at All			**To a Great Extent**
1. I understand how to develop a communication plan.	1	2	3	4
2. I understand how to select the appropriate communication channel.	1	2	3	4

3. As a result of this course, I will be able to use the following skills in my job:

_____

	Not Effective		**Very Effective**	
Concerning the process . . .				
4. How effective were the materials for the program? I would suggest _____	1	2	3	4
5. How effective was the length of the program? I would suggest _____	1	2	3	4
6. How effective was (were) the instructor(s)? I would suggest _____	1	2	3	4

7. What interested me most in the session was: _____

_____

8. What interested me least in the session was: _____

_____

9. To improve future training sessions, I would suggest: _____

_____

10. I would also be interested in learning about the following training (check all appropriate boxes):
    ❐ Written communication　　❐ Oral communication　　❐ Effective listening
    ❐ Project management　　　　❐ Leadership　　　　　　❐ Presentation skills
    ❐ Software applications　　　❐ Other suggestions: _____
    　　　　　　　　　　　　　　　　　　　　　　　　　　　_____

11. What training length do you think is most appropriate?
    ❐ 1 full day　　❐ ½ day　　❐ 2 one-hour segments　　❐ 2 full days　　❐ 1 week

---

A copy of this form is provided as Figure B-28 in Appendix B.

Figure 4-7.   Descriptive evaluation form.

1. Did the course content meet your expectations?				
(5) It exceeded my expectations. It was just what I needed. I'm glad I attended.	(4) It was what I expected and needed. I'm glad I attended.	(3) Some of it met my needs; I did not need other parts of the course. I have mixed feelings about whether I should have attended or not.	(2) Although a portion of it met my needs, it was not the course I expected. If I had known this ahead of time, I probably would not have attended.	(1) It was not what I expected, and it did not meet any of my needs in this area. Frankly, it was a waste of 3 hours.
Comments:				

2. As a result of the session, do you feel that you can write an effective business memo that will get results?				
(5) I'm confident that I can write much more effective memos than I used to. I'm sure they'll get results.	(4) I'm pretty sure I'll be able to write better memos than I used to.	(3) I'm going to try, but I'm not sure.	(2) I doubt it. I'm not sure I understood some of the concepts.	(1) Absolutely not! I didn't understand a word the instructor was talking about.
Comments:				

3. Will you be able to apply the communication skills you learned in your current position?				
(5) Absolutely! I'm going to start today.	(4) I think so. If I'm able to apply them, it will be helpful, so I'll try.	(3) I'm going to try, but I'm not sure.	(2) I doubt it, but I'll see if there is any way I can use them.	(1) Absolutely not! There is no way I'll be able to use this stuff.
Comments:				

4. Did the instructor present the materials in a way that helped you understand them?				
(5) Absolutely! I think the instructor really knew her stuff.	(4) Yes, I got all of it.	(3) I'm not really sure. Sometimes I thought she knew what she was talking about, and other times I wasn't sure she knew.	(2) Not really, I didn't understand.	(1) Absolutely not! She didn't have a clue.
Comments:				

5. Did the instructor capture and hold your attention throughout the session?				
(5) Always! What an instructor! I never felt bored.	(4) Yes, she did a good job of keeping me engaged.	(3) Sometimes, but I did daydream on occasion.	(2) Not really. I was thinking more about the work I would have to go back to.	(1) Absolutely not! My brain left a while ago.
Comments:				

A form based on this figure is provided as Figure B-29 in Appendix B.

Step 1—Set Up the Worksheet. There are five parts to setting up the worksheet (see Figure 4-8):

1. In the left column, number the rows to indicate the number of quantitative questions you have on your evaluation. In this example, you have six quantitative questions.
2. Now devote one column to each number on your rating scale. In this example, you are using a 4-point scale.
3. Title the last column of the table Total.
4. Count each of the evaluation forms you have received. The number of evaluation forms times the highest point on your rating scale equals the denominator. For example, you have 20 evaluation forms, and you used a 4-point rating scale for your numeric evaluations. If you multiply 20 by 4, the denominator is 80.
5. Add the denominator to all of your questions in the Total column.

Figure 4-8. Setting up a worksheet.

Evaluation Question	1	2	3	4	Total
1					/80
2					/80
3					/80
4					/80
5					/80
6					/80
Denominator formula: 20 evaluations × 4-point rating scale = 80					

A copy of this form is provided as Figure B-30 in Appendix B.

Step 2—Record the Evaluation. When your worksheet is ready and your denominator is in place, you can begin recording participant response (see Figure 4-9). For example, on the first evaluation form you are capturing, the participant rated the six questions as follows:

Figure 4-9.   Record evaluations of questions.

Evaluation Question	1	2	3	4	Total
1		I			/80
2		I			/80
3			I		/80
4			I		/80
5				I	/80
6				I	/80
Denominator formula: 20 evaluations × 4-point rating scale = 80					

Question	Rating
1	2
2	2
3	3
4	3
5	4
6	4

Continue recording ratings for each of the evaluations. Sometimes participants don't rate a question; if that is the case, make sure you subtract the rating scale (in this case, 4) for each unanswered question from the denominator. For example, if one participant left question 6 unanswered, you would decrease the denominator for that answer to 76 (19 evaluations times 4 points = 76). It is important to do this so the scores won't be calculated incorrectly.

Step 3—Verify Your Work. When you have captured all of the evaluations, your worksheet will look like Figure 4-10.

To make sure you have recorded all the evaluations correctly, count the number of responses for each question. In this case, you have twenty responses for questions 1 and 3–5, 17 for question 2, and 19 for question 6.

Step 4—Multiply the Number of Ratings by the Rating Value. Once you have all the ratings entered, multiply the number of ratings by the rating value at the top of the column. This step is highlighted in bold in Figure 4-11.

Figure 4-10.   Detail all evaluations.

Evaluation Question	1	2	3	4	Total
1	I	III	THL III	THL III	/80
2 (−3)		THL II	THL	IIII	/68
3		IIII	THL II	THL IIII	/80
4		IIII	THL III	THL III	/80
5	III	II	THL I	IIII	/80
6 (−1)	IIII	THL	THL	THL	/76
Denominator formula: 20 evaluations × 4-point rating scale = 80					

Step 5—Add the Totals. Once you have determined the calculation for each number and rating, add the total within each column across the row, by each question, to determine the numerator. This step is displayed in the chart in Figure 4-12.

Step 6—Divide the Numerator by the Denominator. When you have all the numerators calculated, you can begin scoring the rating. To score the final combined rating, divide the numerator by the denominator (from your Total column) and multiply the total by four (the rating scale; see Figure 4-13). For example, question 1 calculation:

$$63 \div 80 = .7875 \times 4 = 3.1 \text{ (final combined rating)}$$

Decide How to Use the Evaluation Results

Evaluations that are tabulated and filed in a drawer, never to be looked at again, are of no use to you or your organization. Examples of some of the many adjustments you can make to your training as a result of evaluation feedback include:

- Adding content needed to meet emerging needs
- Deleting content considered irrelevant by participants
- Finding a different way to explain and demonstrate concepts that participants find hard to understand

- Adding more exercises
- Adjusting the length of the course
- Working with outside vendors who received disappointing ratings from participants to improve their workshops

Evaluations that are used as a true source of feedback for improvement are worth the time and effort they take to create, administer, tabulate, and interpret.

Figure 4-11.   Multiply ratings by rating values.

Evaluation Question	1	2	3	4	Total
1	I $1 \times 1 = 1$	III $3 \times 2 = 6$	THL III $8 \times 3 = 24$	THL III $8 \times 4 = 32$	/80
2 (−3)		THL II $7 \times 2 = 14$	THL I $6 \times 3 = 18$	IIII $4 \times 4 = 16$	/68
3		IIII $4 \times 2 = 8$	THL II $7 \times 3 = 21$	THL IIII $9 \times 4 = 36$	/80
4		IIII $4 \times 2 = 8$	THL III $8 \times 3 = 24$	THL III $8 \times 4 = 32$	/80
5	III $3 \times 1 = 3$	THL II $7 \times 2 = 14$	THL I $6 \times 3 = 18$	IIII $4 \times 4 = 16$	/80
6 (−1)	IIII $4 \times 1 = 4$	THL $5 \times 2 = 10$	THL $5 \times 3 = 15$	THL $5 \times 4 = 20$	/76
Denominator formula: 20 evaluations × 4-point rating scale = 80					

Figure 4-12.   Add the totals.

Evaluation Question	1	2	3	4	Total
1	I **1 +**	III **6 +**	THL III **24 +**	THL III **32 =**	**63**/80
2 (−3)		THL II **14 +**	THL I **18 +**	IIII **16 =**	**48**/68
3		IIII **8 +**	THL II **21 +**	THL IIII **36 =**	**65**/80
4		IIII **8 +**	THL III **24 +**	THL III **32 =**	**64**/80
5	III **3 +**	THL II **14 +**	THL I **18 +**	IIII **16 =**	**51**/80
6 (−1)	IIII **4 +**	THL **10 +**	THL **15 +**	THL **20 =**	**49**/76
Denominator formula: 20 evaluations × 4-point rating scale = 80					

Figure 4-13.   Compute the final combined ratings.

Evaluation Question	Total	Final Combined Rating
1	63/80	**3.1**
2 (−3)	48/68	**2.8**
3	65/80	**3.3**
4	64/80	**3.2**
5	51/80	**2.5**
6 (−1)	49/76	**2.6**

Measuring Knowledge Retained

Instead of asking participants how well they liked the course, you can test their knowledge both before and after the course or ask them to give an honest reporting of their own knowledge before and after. Tools that will help you accomplish this include:

- Pretests
- Posttests
- Postcourse performance tests
- Comfort-level evaluations

Pretest

The learning objectives identified in the development phase (see Chapter 2) drive the learning you will be measuring with the pre- and posttests. During the pretest, you are trying to determine how competent the participants are on each of the learning objectives you have identified for the course.

If the course is skill-based, you might ask participants to actually demonstrate the skills you will be building so you can get a baseline competence measurement. For the pretest, they might use Excel to create a chart, write a business memo, give a one-minute speech, or demonstrate their abilities on whatever other skills you will be building.

Posttest

How much did participants learn during the course? Have they mastered the skills and abilities presented in the course well enough to apply them on the job? The posttest can ask participants to perform, for a second time, the same test you gave them for a pretest. The results from both the pretest and the posttest can be analyzed to determine the amount of performance improvement that occurred during the training.

The pretest identified a performance gap between the level of performance the participant was able to demonstrate and the level required. The comparison between the pre- and posttests is an effective way for you to summarize and measure training effectiveness.

Once you have calculated the results from the pre- and posttests, display them in a table similar to the one in Figure 4-14.

Postcourse Performance Test

To test your participants' knowledge of the system, you can ask them to actually perform the skills they have just learned:

- If participants have just learned to use the cash register, you can ask them to ring up a complicated sale.
- If participants have just learned to use PowerPoint, you can ask them to develop a set of overheads.

Figure 4-14. Sample evaluation of pretest/posttest results.

Evaluation Question	Pretest Results	Posttest Results	Improvement
1	1.5	3.5	2.0
2	2.2	3.0	0.8
3	1.7	2.9	1.2

- If participants have just learned how to register guests in a hotel and validate credit cards, you can ask them to register a guest using a simulated registration system at the end of the program.

The sample questions in Figure 4-15 represent a number of queries to be performed for the new Quester system. Participants would be given this performance test to show they can find specific information online after the function has been demonstrated during the training. If this test has also been used as a pretest, you can easily track the skills and knowledge participants have acquired during the training.

Figure 4-15. Sample postcourse performance test on Quester.

1. **From the Quing, generate a Kox query using Account #7803 and date range of 11/04/98–12/05/98.**

   Q: What is the permission number? *(Ans: LS2137)*

   Q: Who is the authorizing party? *(Ans: Terp37)*

2. **Select the account to view the Account Details.**

   Q: What is the first field in the top left-hand corner? *(Ans 370-2512 telephone number)*

3. **From the Demand window, select the Fame option and run a query using Customer Number 6913762.**

   Q: What is the field name and data in the first row of the third column? *(Ans: Effective: 9/28/98–5/6/99)*

   Q: What is the primary exchange code? *(Ans: KEISHA)*

   Q: Who is the authorizing party? *(Ans: Antoine Cooke)*

Comfort-Level Evaluation

Because adults have a vested interest in learning and being able to perform new skills on the job, you may want to ask them to complete a comfort-level evaluation (see Figure 4-16) at the end of each session of technical training. This type of evaluation can put participants at ease and make the learning process easier because they can ask for more instruction or more practice if they need it.

Figure 4-16.   Sample comfort-level evaluation.

Please take a minute to indicate how comfortable you are with the skills you learned in today's session.

Technique or Skill	Piece of Cake I didn't have any trouble with this and will be able to use it easily.	Let Me Practice I'm catching on, but I need more practice time.	Show Me Again I'm having trouble with this and need more instruction.
1. Using your password to sign on to the reservation system			
2. Locating the guest using reservation number			
3. Checking credit			
4. Verifying check-in and check-out dates			
5. Printing check-in form for guest signature			

A copy of this form is provided as Figure B-31 in Appendix B.

Chapters 1 through 4 form the foundation for the main event—LEARN. Part Two of *Turning Training Into Learning* will introduce the LEARN process, and give you the tools to put it into action.

PART TWO

The LEARN Process:

Linking Training to Learning

Here it is—the heart of this book—the LEARN process. It is the process we all experience as learners before we can own and use what we've received in a training situation. LEARN is an acronym that represents the five-step process participants follow as they take in, practice, apply, and internalize skills and concepts. LEARN is the secret for turning training into learning. Each letter of this acronym stands for an important part of the learning process (see Figure P2-1).

Figure P2-1. The LEARN process.

L	Listen and Understand—If you capture my attention and interest, I'll listen to what you have to offer and try to understand it.
E	Evaluate and Decide—When you help me see what's in it for me, I'll evaluate the competencies you've introduced and decide how I can use them on the job or in my life outside the job.
A	Attempt and Build—If you help me build my skills step-by-step in a safe environment, I'll make a serious attempt to learn.
R	Return and Apply—When I feel comfortable with the skills and abilities I've learned, I'll return to the job and actually use what you've taught me. I'll be able to apply them to my own situation.
N	Natural Transition—Now these skills and abilities are mine. I own them. I may pass them on to other people or take them to the next level and learn more on my own.

Chapters 5 through 9 are each devoted to one letter in the LEARN acronym (see Figure P2-2). The subtitle for each chapter is its secret to success because this is what the adult learner *really* wants. These chapters will lead you through the LEARN process and help you put yourself in the learner's shoes.

Figure P2-2.   Outline of Chapters 5–9.

Chapter	Acronym Letter	Meaning	Chapter Subtitle (Secret to Success)
5	L	Listen and Understand	Capture my attention and interest
6	E	Evaluate and Decide	Help me see what's in it for me
7	A	Attempt and Build	Help me build my skills step-by-step
8	R	Return and Apply	Send me back to use them on the job
9	N	Natural Transition	Now they're mine

Chapter 10, Putting It All Together, fits the pieces of the puzzle back together (see Figure P2-3) and reviews the entire process of *Turning Training Into Learning.* As we fit the pieces of the puzzle back together, we will discuss some of the pitfalls that may inadvertently occur in the training process and give you both some safety net solutions and tips to remember. We will also cover the training summary report.

Figure P2-3.   The training process puzzle.

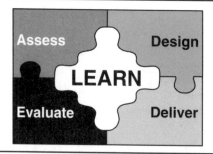

5

Listen and Understand

Capture My Attention and Interest

Well, here I am, on my way to Room 465 for a class called Effective Communication. I almost decided to skip it because I have a mountain of work on my desk, but I need to learn how to communicate better with my boss. Hope this class can help me. If the class isn't very good, I can always sneak out during the break and go back to work. Oh no, I just saw Joe Anderson walk into the room. I hope the instructor doesn't let Joe monopolize the class like he usually does. Well, I'm at the door and it's almost time for the class to start. Guess I'm going in.

Training is only successful when your participants have learned. If you don't capture your participants' attention and interest up front, you will be hard-pressed to capture it later.

The best way to start this process is by making an effort to understand your participants and their needs before you begin helping them learn. This effort can spell the difference between interested, responsive participants and class members who remain detached and uninterested for the entire session. The personal connection that comes with two-way communication between each participant and the instructor can play an important role in starting the class off on the right foot.

The tone, approach, and supporting tools you use to open your training will guide it from that point on. This chapter will provide you with the tools that will help you understand your learners before asking them to understand you. You will learn how to establish a safe environment, get to know your participants, establish ground rules, and set the tone for learning. You will also learn how to manage your participants' expectations by telling them what they can expect to learn as well as what they should *not* expect to learn during the training (see Figure 5-1).

Establish a Safe Environment

The first step in capturing the interest and attention of your participants is providing an opening that establishes a safe environment. It calls for providing a welcome, introducing yourself, and giving the lay of the land.

Providing a Warm Welcome

You have an opportunity to begin capturing the interest and attention of the learners from the moment they enter the room. This means that you need to be sure the training environment is ready for them when they walk in. Figure 5-2 includes some basic guidelines for being prepared to provide your participants with a warm welcome; Figure 5-3 gives directions for making table tents to display participant names. If the room is set up and you are ready for the session, you will have an opportunity to visit informally with participants before the session starts. Your informal welcome and sincere interest

Figure 5-1.   Guide to Chapter 5.

Learning Stage	Secrets to Success

LISTEN & UNDERSTAND 	**Capture My Attention and Interest**
	
	1. **Establishing a Safe Environment**
	
	  ■ Providing a warm welcome
	  ■ Getting to know you (facilitator introductions)
	  ■ Giving participants the lay of the land
	
	2. **Facilitating Participant Introductions**
	
	  ■ Basic introductions
	  ■ Creative questions
	
	3. **Establishing Ground Rules**
	
	4. **Selecting the Icebreaker and Setting the Tone**
	
	  ■ Organizational receptivity
	  ■ Group cohesiveness
	  ■ Link to training content
	  ■ Icebreaker samples
	
	5. **Give the Plan for the Day**

Figure 5-2. Guidelines for establishing a safe learning environment.

1. Arrive early and make sure you have all your materials and equipment.

2. Check the room temperature.

3. Check the refreshments. Unwrap the plates/trays from catering.

4. Check the overhead and other audiovisual equipment.

5. Set up the flip charts. Make sure there are markers and that they work.

6. Ensure that physical barriers have been removed so all participants have access to the room, especially those who have special needs.

7. Have a sign-in sheet (if you're using one) ready for participants to sign as they enter, or have it ready to circulate after participants are all seated.

8. Place your agendas and handouts on the table in front of each seat, or place them at the door for participants to take when they enter the room.

9. Fold paper into table tents and place one on the table in front of each seat. (See Figure 5-3 for table tent directions.)

10. Place enough markers on the table to provide easy access to them by all participants.

11. Verify that the clock in the room is working properly, or place a small clock at the front of the room for your use. (This will ensure that you don't have to keep looking at your watch to keep the session on target.)

12. Locate the nearest rest rooms, telephones, water fountains, and emergency exits if you are unfamiliar with the room. Be prepared to give participants the lay of the land at the beginning of the session. Make sure you know how to get help in case of an emergency.

A form based on this figure is provided as Figure B-32 in Appendix B.

Figure 5-3.   Table tent directions.

To prepare table tents, fold 8½-by-11-inch plain paper or card stock into thirds, as you would fold a letter for mailing. Crease each fold. Position the paper to form a tent on the table. Instruct participants to use the markers to write their first names on *both* the front and back sides of the table tent so those people sitting next to them as well as across the table from them will be able to see their names. If the session is a computer training session, you can instruct participants to position their table tents on top of the monitors.

in them as they arrive in the room can help to start your training off on the right foot.

Getting to Know You (Facilitator Introductions)

Taking the time to introduce yourself is essential for setting the tone, clarifying expectations, and establishing your credibility as a facilitator. As the facilitator, you should begin by introducing:

- The course name
- Your name and relevant experience
- Why you are facilitating the course
- Your own experience with learning the training topic

If you have a personal interest in the course content, this is the time to tell your participants. It's the portion of the course in which you are the seller and the participants are the buyers. It's your job to begin selling the content to them so they will evaluate the course and decide to participate in it. (Chapter 6, Evaluate and Decide, covers these areas.) The script outlined in Figure 5-4 is a sample you can follow to deliver your introduction to the course.

Figure 5-4.   Sample facilitator introduction script.

Good afternoon, and welcome to Effective Communication. My name is John Moore, and I've been a member of the Organizational Development staff here at Shannon Industries for six years. Before joining Shannon, I worked as a customer service manager at a large public relations firm.

Effective Communication is one of my favorite courses in the staff curriculum because the communications tools you're going to learn here today are so helpful and easy to use that I use them myself. I only wish I had mastered them a few years ago. They would have saved me a lot of time and effort in planning the communication I do every day.

Figure 5-5. Sample lay-of-the-land facilitator script.

In a minute I'm going to ask each of you to introduce yourselves, but we have some housekeeping to get out of the way. I'm going to pass this sign-in sheet around the room beginning here in the first row. Please sign in next to your name, and check to be sure that your phone number, office address, and e-mail address are correct. If you are the last person to sign, please be sure to bring the sheet up and put it here on the table. The course materials for today's session are in front of you. You should have an agenda [hold one up], a pack of course materials that looks like this [hold one up], and a case problem [hold one up]. For your convenience, your course materials include a copy of each of the overheads I'm going to show you today.

So we can learn each other's names, I'd like each of you to use a marker to write your first name on both the front and back of the table tent in front of you [demonstrate as you talk].

The rest rooms are at the end of the hall—women on the left by the elevator and men on the right by the staircase. The house phone is on the wall at the back of the room; there is a pay phone on the wall next to the elevator. This morning's session is scheduled to end at 12:30. We will take a ten-minute break about 11:00, but feel free to leave the room for a bathroom break when you need to. Now who has a question?

Giving Participants the Lay of the Land

Your participants will feel more comfortable if you give them some basic information about the location of essential facilities, such as the rest rooms and telephones. The script in Figure 5-5 is a sample for you to follow.

Facilitating Participant Introductions

When you have completed your introduction, you can ask your participants to introduce themselves to you and the rest of the group. These introductions give your learners a chance to begin involving themselves in the session from the start. They also give you an opportunity to gather some information about them.

Basic Introductions

The most common way to handle course introductions is to ask participants to state:

- Their name
- What department or company they are with
- What they hope to learn as a result of the training

When participants are providing this information, it's very important for you to pay close attention to each one of them. To show that you are listening, repeat the names of some of the departments and some of the reasons participants are attending the course. Occasionally someone may say, "I'm here because my boss said I have to attend. I don't really want to be here." You might answer, "Welcome. I hope that by the end of the morning, you'll feel that the session was worthwhile."

You may also want to ask participants to indicate how long they have worked for the organization. An effective way to establish participant credibility is by recording the number of years of experience participants have next to their course expectations.

Figure 5-6 is a list of these questions. You might want to use it as an overhead to remind participants of the questions as they are waiting for a turn to answer.

It is important to record your participants' responses (excluding name and department) on the flip chart. This helps to establish learner expectations and allows the entire group to review, validate, and/or modify their expectations as the course progresses. When you have completed the introduction, you can total up the years of experience of the entire class (see Figure 5-7) and let the participants know that you value their years of experience. You might say:

> As you see, we have thirty-five years of experience in this room. Your knowledge and experience are just as valuable as the content presented in this training class. So I would encourage you to add your experiences and lessons learned whenever you feel they might be relevant.

Not only do you set the tone for interactive participation, you also demonstrate respect for your participants' knowledge and experiences—a valuable concept! Since you have positively reinforced their knowledge and experiences, they will feel more comfortable sharing their insights.

Creative Questions

You may want to add a question to the basic introduction that asks participants to demonstrate a bit of creativity. These questions can give you an

Figure 5-6.   Questions for participants.

Participant Introduction

Name:

Department:

I have been with the company _____ years.

In this course, I hope to learn _____.

A copy of this form is provided as Figure B-33 in Appendix B.

Figure 5-7. Sample flip chart of participants' responses.

Years	*What I Hope to Learn Today*
5	1. How to write clearer business memos
11	2. How to do a better job of expressing myself when I talk with my boss.
3	3. How to state what I need without being offensive
2	4. How to use grammar more accurately
14	5. How to get my staff to come to the point when they are talking with me so I can save time
35	

opportunity to learn a little more about them and the way they think. The creative questions described below are useful if the course is longer (more than four hours in length) and if your participants will be interacting with each other as they learn. They are also helpful if you will be challenging learners to master soft skills such as leadership or coaching.

Pictorial Introduction. You can select several symbols and put them on a page. You might want to have at least four to eight symbols so there is a variety to choose from. Provide participants with a copy of the selected symbols; ask them to choose a symbol that best describes them and to state why. You can be as creative as you want in selecting the symbols. Some may be easily accessible from the clip art in your word processing program. Sample symbols you might want to use are displayed in Figure 5-8.

The way in which your participants describe their choice of symbols will give you an insight into the self-image that each one has. Participants might respond with statements such as: "I chose the figure who is kicking up his heels because that's how I feel this week. I'm leaving for vacation on Friday." "I chose the bull's eye because that's the way I feel most of the time—like I have a bull's eye on my shirt. When there's extra work to do, I'm an easy target. I'm the first one everyone picks."

Figure 5-8. Sample symbols for creative introduction.

Select a symbol that best represents you and explain why.

A copy of these symbols are provided as Figure B-34 in Appendix B.

You might want to use these symbols to help you form teams for in-class activities. You might put all the bull's eyes on the same team; you also could decide that each team should include people who have selected each of the four symbols.

Movie Reference Introduction. You may want to ask all the participants to add a movie reference to the basic introduction information they are giving you. You might say: "Name a movie that describes you (or that you relate to) and explain why." The movies your participants name will give you some insight into the way each one thinks and the type of references or examples that might appeal to that person. If you've seen the movie yourself, you might want to refer to scenes from it.

A participant might say, "I really relate to *Braveheart* because life is really a series of challenges that call for going forward and beating the odds." If this person is in a leadership course, he or she is showing a positive attitude and a lot of drive or initiative. Another who relates to *Star Wars* may show a spirit of adventure and a good imagination. The participant who relates to *The Game* may thrive on problem solving. The one who relates to *You've Got Mail* or *Sleepless in Seattle* may be optimistic and have a very positive attitude about the future.

Ideal Vacation Introduction. You might ask your participants to describe their ideal vacation. As with the movie introductions, the descriptions you receive will give you some insight into what appeals to each person and what references might be readily understood and recognized by them. As participants tell you about their preferences for backpacking, canoeing, and hiking; safaris in Africa; or days on the beach in St. Martin or Maui, they will be opening up to the idea of participating in the session. This information will give you additional opportunities to reference items of interest to participants.

Paired Introduction. You can ask participants to split up into pairs and have them take five minutes to give each other an introduction (based on the criteria you outline). Once they have completed this exercise, you can have them come together as a group and ask each person to introduce the other person he or she interviewed.

This exercise will give participants a chance to become comfortable with each other at the start of the session and will give you an opportunity to hear each one in a presentation mode.

Establishing Ground Rules

Establishing ground rules up front is an important, and often overlooked, process. Because you are shaping the behavior parameters you expect from participants, the time for ground rules is immediately after introductions. These rules of conduct can help to shape a successful learning event. They establish the behavior parameters that you can expect from participants, what they can expect from you, and what they can expect from each other. If you post them in an easy-to-see location (the front of the training room), you can use them as a reference point for facilitating group dynamics.

You can begin the process of establishing ground rules by presenting the group with a set of sample rules on a flip chart. You can review these with the group to reach consensus on them; you can also let participants add to or modify the list as they wish. If you have difficulty reaching consensus on the ground rules, modify the language until all your learners agree. Sample ground rules might include the following statements:

- Start on time, stay on time, and stop on time.
- Listen to each other, and let everyone speak.
- Share experiences and ideas—no idea is a bad idea.
- Be focused—avoid side conversations.
- Other [have your group add or modify the list, then reach consensus].

If the session is one in which participants may express opinions or display emotions, you may want to add this simple rule: What is said in this room stays in this room. If this rule is firmly established and adhered to, your participants may feel they can be more honest with their comments and more open to learning what they need for themselves, and trust the learning environment.

If the session will include participants from different levels in the organization, and if these levels have no impact on the learning to be accomplished, you may want to add one more rule: Check your titles at the door—all participants are equally important in this session.

Selecting the Icebreaker and Setting the Tone

The icebreaker will help you set the tone and encourage participants to open up to the participation process. Three considerations to keep in mind when selecting an icebreaker for your session are organizational receptivity, group cohesiveness, and link to training content.

Organizational Receptivity

Understanding the receptivity of the organization and the particular group of participants you will be working with can help you select an appropriate icebreaker that can set the tone for all the activities you introduce during the training session. In an organization such as a bank or an investment corporation, where both participants and the culture may be more reserved, you will probably want to avoid icebreakers that resemble games (e.g., Bingo Beginnings or Scavenger Hunt Scramble). A better selection might be an icebreaker that asks participants to differentiate true statements from false ones, such as Two Truths and a Lie.

Group Cohesiveness

If your participants are a group of people who already know each other, you will want to avoid icebreakers that are designed for the purpose of learning names, such as Name Tag Mixer or Name Association. Many of the other icebreakers that ask participants to identify facts about each other (e.g., Bingo Beginnings) might be appropriate even if the group does know each other because they may not know the type of information contained in these activities. (Who has a cat? Who reads *Time* magazine? Who likes to dance?) If your participants do not know each other, any of the icebreakers will be appropriate.

Link to Training Content

Unless you are selecting a simple introductory activity, you will want to try to select an icebreaker that is relevant to the training course so you can make a seamless transition. By doing this, you will avoid responses from your participants such as, Why are we doing this? In a communications course, you might use an activity based on words. In a team-building course, you might use an activity that requires participants to work in teams. In a time management course, you might use a timed activity.

Icebreaker Samples

A collection of nine icebreakers are shown in Figures 5-9 to 5-17. As you read these activities, you will see that you can develop variations on each one to give you a wide range of activities to choose from.

(text continues on page 116)

Figure 5-9. Bingo beginnings.

Objective: To enable participants to meet as many people as possible in a short time.

Procedure: Develop a bingo card on which each space is filled with a way to describe participants. Give the cards to all participants; have them walk around the room seeking other people's names for each description. Even if someone fits more than one category, that person can only sign a participant's card once. The first person who has a bingo wins. If you have a short session, the winner can be the first person to complete a horizontal, diagonal, or vertical row. If it is a longer session, the winner can be the first person to fill the entire card. Remember, if you want participants to complete the entire card, you can't have more spaces than participants.

Has been at the company less than one year	Rides a bicycle	Plays golf	Has two children	Walks to work
Has four children	Enjoys scuba diving	Drives a Buick	Takes the train to work	Has a cat
Has a dog	Plays tennis	FREE	Speaks Spanish	Has tropical fish
Drives a Ford	Has been at the company more than five years	Speaks French	Reads *Time* magazine	Drives to work
Likes football	Hates football	Likes to dance	Enjoys swimming	Hates broccoli

A copy of this card is provided as Figure B-35 in Appendix B.

Figure 5-10. Name-tag mixer.

Objective: To help participants who do not know each other learn the names of other participants.

Procedure: When participants enter the room, ask them to sign in and hand them a name tag—but make sure the name tag belongs to *someone else*. When all participants are in the room, have them move around the room looking for the person whose name tag they are holding. When the participant meets the person who is listed on the name tag, he or she is responsible for interviewing that person. When the group sits down, each participant introduces the person he or she interviewed.

Figure 5-11.   Scavenger hunt scramble.

Objective: To give participants an opportunity to meet each other and determine simple facts about each other. This activity is similar to Bingo Beginnings, but participants are encouraged to find a participant for each item on the list (participants may be different in each square).

Procedure: Develop a list of simple facts that could be used to describe participants; provide a signature line after each item. Distribute the list to all participants. At the beginning of the session, encourage all participants to begin the scavenger hunt by filling in their cards with first names as they interview other participants. Each person is allowed to use a participant's name only one time.

Scavenger Hunt Fact   **First Name**

 1. Speaks Spanish   _____

 2. Plays chess   _____

 3. Likes skiing   _____

 4. Has two sisters   _____

 5. Plays racquetball   _____

 6. Likes crossword puzzles   _____

 7. Goes to the movies often   _____

 8. Reads mysteries   _____

 9. Has three children   _____

10. Has a dog   _____

11. Has a cat   _____

12. Traveled to Europe last year   _____

13. Likes ballroom dancing   _____

14. Plays the piano   _____

A copy of this form is provided as Figure B-36 in Appendix B.

Figure 5-12. Team résumé.

Objective: To help a newly formed team build team pride. This activity is particularly good to use during a time of reorganization when new teams are asked to attend training as a team.

Procedure: Ask newly formed teams to sit as a group and work as fast as they can (in brainstorming fashion) to complete the team résumé. Each person should be encouraged to add as many entries as possible. The completed résumé can serve as a source of team pride.

Team Résumé Worksheet

1. Our team has held the following jobs:

2. Our team has experience in:

3. Our team likes to do the following extracurricular activities:

4. Our team . . .

A copy of this form is provided as Figure B-37 in Appendix B.

Figure 5-13.   Five fast facts.

Objective: To give participants an opportunity to learn simple facts about other participants in the session and to give them an opportunity to talk informally with each other.

Procedure: Give each participant a blank stick-on name tag. Ask them to write their first names on the top line and to list five words or brief phrases about themselves. These phrases should be something that can be used as conversation starters. When you have completed the introductions, give participants five minutes to meet at least ten other participants.

```
                        ANDREW

              1. Jets fan

              2. Likes jogging

              3. Collects baseball cards

              4. Has twin daughters

              5. Going scuba diving next month
```

Figure 5-14.   Name association.

Objective: To help each participant provide a means of helping other participants remember his or her name. This is a good activity when there is a reason for participants to remember other participants' last names.

Procedure: Ask each participant to introduce himself or herself and give a rhyme, story, or sound-alike word that can help others remember the name.

I'm Sheila Furjanic ("fur" like a fur coat, "jan" like the girl's name, and "ic" like awful-tasting medicine)

I'm Laurie Trotman (to remember my name, think of a man at the racetrack leading a trotter around the track)

I'm Janet Weston (think of my friend Wes carrying a ton of packages)

I'm Joe Fredrickson (think of my friend Fred and his son Rick)

Figure 5-15.   Playing-card mixer.

Objective: To give participants an opportunity to mix with each other and get acquainted. This works well with a large group of participants, some of whom know each other and some who don't.

Procedure: Remove all the cards below the jack from several decks of cards and place the high cards in a bowl. As participants enter the room, ask each one to draw a card. When you give the signal, they move around the room and attempt to combine their cards to form a good poker hand. The best hand wins a prize.

Figure 5-16.   Mystery money mixer.

Objective: To give participants, especially new ones, an opportunity to mix with the rest of a group.

Procedure: This exercise works best when there is a large group of participants. Before the session starts, ask one person, secretly, to be the mystery money person. Give this person 20 one-dollar bills. When the session starts, announce that there is one person in the audience who is a mystery person. If you introduce yourself to the mystery person during the break, he or she will give you a dollar.

When it's time for the break, you wil see a lot of activity as everyone tries to figure out who the mystery person is. This exercise works well when there is a group of about 200 participants and there is enough activity in the room for the mystery person to be hidden in the crowd.

Figure 5-17.   Two truths and a lie.

Objective: To enable participants to get to know each other and test their perceptions of the other participants.

Procedure: Instruct each participant to write on a piece of paper three facts about himself or herself. Two of these facts should be true, and one should be a lie. (For example: I speak French—truth; I ride a motorcycle—truth; I ran in a marathon last month—lie.)

When all facts have been recorded, call on the first participant and ask him or her to read the three facts. The challenge for the rest of the group is to determine which two facts are true and which one is a lie.

Give the Plan for the Day

When you have captured participants' attention, they need to know the plan for the day. What's in store for them and what can they expect to learn? In addition to distributing a hard copy of the agenda, you may want to create a copy that can be displayed on a flip chart so it can be reviewed during the course of the training in order to remind participants of the course's objectives and to manage their expectations. Figure 5-18 shows a typical training agenda. Figure 5-19 shows the learning objectives for an effective communications course. Notice they include two types:

1. Objectives the participants can meet at the completion of the training course
2. Objectives the participants can meet after practicing the skills they learn in the course for several weeks

When you have captured your participants' attention and sparked their interest, it's time to tell them what the course can do for them. Chapter 6 will help you give participants the experiences and information they need to make the decision that this course is worth participating in and learning from.

Figure 5-18.   Sample training agenda.

Timing	Agenda
8:45–9:00	Breakfast
9:00–9:15	Getting to Know You
9:15–9:30	Introduction to Effective Communication Basics
9:30–10:30	The Communication System
10:30–10:45	Break
10:45–12:00	Practicing the System
12:00–12:15	Using the System on the Job/How to Get More Practice
12:15–12:25	Summary
12:25–12:30	Evaluation

Figure 5-19.   Sample course objectives.

At the end of this session, you will be able to demonstrate your ability to plan clear, concise communications that are just right for your audience.

When you have practiced the skills you learn in this course for two or three weeks, you will be comfortable with your ability to plan clear, concise communications that are targeted to the needs of your audience.

6

Evaluate and Decide

Help Me See What's in It for Me

> *I'm still here in Room 465 in the Effective Communication class. The first few minutes were fine. The instructor seems OK, and I even got a chance to say why I signed up for class. I hope she paid attention because I'm NOT going to sit here and listen to a boring lecture for three hours. I've got better things to do—even back at work. Our break is coming up at 10:30, and if it doesn't look like the course has anything for me, I'm out of here. Or maybe I'll stay right here and draft that report I have due tomorrow. I'll bet the instructor will never know what I'm doing.*

As soon as you have the attention of your participants (see Chapter 5), you face a double challenge: (1) creating an active learning situation that can involve your participants in the learning process and (2) convincing your learners that they should actively participate in the learning process.

Before you can engage your participants in any type of learning process, they have to *decide* to participate. Without active engagement by the learner, no learning can possibly take place, because learning is an active process, not a passive one. This chapter presents a road map for the important process of getting your learners on board to learn. It begins with a communication technique that will help your participants realize the value of the course material. The chapter includes an easy-to-use system for beginning the process of communicating with your participants, and techniques for handling questions—even the tricky ones. A series of easy-to-use activities is included to help you encourage participation. The chapter concludes with the big decision your participants will be making, Is this for me? (See Figure 6-1.)

Figure 6-1. Guide to Chapter 6.

Learning Stage	*Secrets to Success*
EVALUATE & DECIDE	**Help Me See What's in It for Me**

1. Introduce Your Course

- Create situational questions
- Tell a personal story
- Admit your own vulnerability
- Sell the course benefits

2. Manage Participant Expectations

3. Link Learning to What Participants Already Know

- Use creative imagery to understand your participants
- Begin where your participants are
- Progress step-by-step to where you want participants to be

4. Generate and Guide Discussion

- Ask the right questions
- Don't be afraid of silence
- Encourage more than one response
- Acknowledge everyone who responds
- Field unsolicited questions—even the tricky ones

5. Encourage Continued Participation

6. The Big Decision—Is This for Me?

- Check-in, checkout point
- Physical/mental exit point

Introduce Your Course

As a general rule, it is better to ask than to tell. Just about anything that can be stated to adults by a facilitator can be *asked* by that facilitator. You can relate to participants and make them think by turning declarative statements into questions. Thinking is driven by questions, not statements. If you know how to create situational questions and guide discussion, you can begin helping participants see what's in it for them.

Create Situational Questions

Situational questions ask participants to recall situations in their own experiences that are directly related to the course content. The questions usually introduce problems that could be solved by implementing the competencies that will be presented in the course. Here are a few examples of situational questions:

- Have you ever had a conversation with someone and found out later that you each had a different idea about what was said?
- Did you ever find your mind wandering when you were talking with someone and admit that you only heard about one-third of what was said?
- How many times have you had a conversation with someone and found that you were too embarrassed to admit you didn't understand what the other person was talking about, so you pretended to understand?
- When is the last time you finished the workday with more items on your to-do list than you had at the start of the day—even though you worked every minute of the day?
- Do you sometimes look up a phone number and find that you've forgotten it before you have a chance to dial the number?

Did these questions pique your interest? They are a form of situational questioning that can pull the participants in and engage them in the learning process. Situational questions help participants recall (or envision) times when they have been in similar situations and help them realize that they can benefit from the training. These questions also provide an opening for you to make a connection between the question and the concepts or skills participants will be acquiring in the session. You can use the simple four-step process in Figure 6-2 to develop situational questions.

Tell a Personal Story

Everyone likes to hear a good story. When you are introducing the course, you have the perfect opportunity to tell participants a story that can involve them in the learning process. The best type of story is one that involves your own personal experience because you give your learners a real point of reference, one you can fully describe. See Figure 6-3 for an example of a personal introduction to a communication course.

If you had doubts about the value of the course content when you first learned it, let participants know about your doubts and your current opinion of the value of that content. When you tell a sincere story that involves your own experiences, it gives your participants an opportunity to relate to you and the content they're about to receive in a much more personal way. Figure 6-4 shows an example of a personal introduction to a course on quality management tools.

If you don't have a personal story to tell, you can borrow one from a past participant (with that person's permission, of course). Figure 6-5 is an introduction to a public speaking course that highlights the success of a previous participant.

For an even stronger way to launch the course, you may want to use live

Figure 6-2.   Four-step situational questioning process.

Step 1.	**Identify a concept or skill that participants will be learning in the session.**
Concept:	Communication is a two-way process—both giving and receiving messages.
Step 2.	**Recall a realistic situation in which the concept applies.**
Situation:	You were talking with your neighbor Bill about his job as a stockbroker a couple of weeks ago and were too embarrassed to admit you didn't have any idea what most of the terms he was using really meant. So you pretended that you understood and were interested in what he was talking about.
Step 3.	**Determine the link between your example and the concept.**
Link:	If you had been honest and admitted that you didn't understand what he was talking about, you would have had some valid two-way communication. You would also have learned something about his job as a stockbroker.
Step 4.	**Write a question asking participants if they have ever been in a similar situation.**
Question:	"How many times have you had a conversation with someone and found that you were too embarrassed to admit you didn't understand what the other person was talking about, so you pretended to understand?"

A form based on this figure is provided as Figure B-38 in Appendix B.

Figure 6-3.   Sample personal experience introduction.

"When I first heard about the RACE Communication System, I didn't think it could be any better than all the others I'd learned about in the past. But this one is different. It's something I use every time I have an important letter to write, report to prepare, or conversation to get ready for. I even used it to prepare for this class."

testimonials. Invite a past participant to give the course introduction and endorse the content of the course.

Admit Your Own Vulnerability

Because you are in a position of authority as facilitator of the session, it's very important for you to establish an atmosphere that enables participants to admit and overcome their fears of learning. These fears are very common in technical training situations. If you had difficulty learning the same technical programs or systems, your introduction might sound something like the one in Figure 6-6.

Figure 6-4. Sample personal subject matter introduction.

"If you had told me a year ago that I would be using quality management tools like the ones you are going to be learning about today to help me save money, I would have told you that you were crazy. But the Pareto chart alone helped our department save about $15,000 this year by helping us figure out which problems to fix in order to get the most benefit from our process improvement efforts. This morning we're going to take a quick look at three of these tools—the fishbone diagram, the histogram, and the Pareto chart. This afternoon you're going to have a chance to practice using them until you feel comfortable with all three of these tools. Trust me, they aren't hard to learn, and they are worth the effort."

Figure 6-5. Sample past participant recommendation.

"How many of you know Nancy Smith from Plant Maintenance? When she participated in Seminar for Speakers, she was so reluctant to talk in front of people that she was afraid to open her mouth in class. Nancy wants you to know that the techniques she learned in this class helped her to begin conquering her fear of speaking in public. This was the first of three courses she took here at the Training Department. If you attended the recent Town Hall meeting in the auditorium, you had a chance to see and hear Nancy onstage in front of a group of 200 people. She was calm and confident. Nancy wants you to know that if she can do it, so can you."

Figure 6-6. Sample vulnerability introduction.

"I know some of you might be thinking, 'Oh no! I'll never be able to master this stuff.' But don't worry. I felt the same way. The first time I sat through a demonstration of the entire Insurance Questionnaire System, I thought I was never going to be able to learn it, let alone be here teaching it to you. But a surprising thing happened when I forced myself to listen and try. It wasn't as bad as I thought it would be. Sure I made mistakes. But little by little, I mastered it well enough to use it myself and pass it on to you. Now I use the Insurance Questionnaire System every day without even thinking about it. I think it's a great system for entering patient insurance because it has built-in editing features that won't let you make stupid mistakes. I promise that all of you will be able to learn it, too."

Sell the Course Benefits

A classic marketing statement is "Sell the sizzle, not the steak." This refers to converting the feature of a product or service into a benefit that can be experienced by the buyer. In your training sessions, the participants are your buyers. It's your job to turn the course features (content) into benefits that your participants will use to their own advantage (both on the job and in their personal lives).

Participants in a time management course aren't just learning to create better schedules and prioritize their time (features), they are gaining extra hours in the week, creating a working environment that is less stressful, and gaining approval from their supervisors (benefits). For each item or feature within the course content, there is a corresponding participant benefit. Figure 6-7 shows some features and the associated benefits for typical training/learning situations.

Manage Participant Expectations

When participants introduced themselves (see Chapter 5), they were asked to answer this simple question: What do you hope to learn as a result of this training? If you find out that participants hope to learn concepts or skills that you are *not* planning to include in the course, you need to be very clear about the fact that these topics will *not* be covered. The participant who is expecting PowerPoint training and is in an Excel class will be disappointed if he or she is not informed, as will the participant who expects communication skills training and has somehow enrolled in a memory improvement course. You may want to refer misplaced participants to a course that does contain material they are seeking; you can use the requests from these participants as the basis for developing additional training sessions/courses. But you need to be clear about the fact that the desired content will not be presented at *this* time.

Here's what you might say: "When we introduced ourselves a few minutes ago, you gave me quite a list of things you hope to learn as a result of today's training. Before we begin, I want to make sure that you know what you can expect to learn and what we will *not* be covering today." At this point, you should refer to the flip chart on which you recorded the subject areas your participants hope to learn.

As you point to items on the flip chart, you can say, "This course *will* focus on oral communication skills. It will help you learn how to talk more easily and effectively with your boss, coworkers, and staff. It will also help you run more effective meetings. But today we *won't* be working on writing letters and memos or on preparing formal presentations. If you are interested in learning how to write better letters and memos, you should be sure to sign up for the Effective Letter Workshop on [give date]. To learn to prepare formal presentations, you can sign up for Preparing Powerful Presentations on [give date]. We hope you will all stay and be part of today's class even if you were originally looking for one of the topics we will not be covering. The skills you will learn in today's session will help *everyone* who reports to someone else." See the section titled "The Big Decision" at the end of this chapter for suggestions about options you might offer these participants.

Sometimes participants are frustrated because they can't identify their needs and express them either to you or to their managers. Figure 6-8 is a classic poem written by a participant who is expressing this frustration.

Figure 6-7. Sample training features and benefits.

Transforming Features Into Benefits		
Course	*Feature (Content)*	*Benefits*
Public Speaking	Overcoming stage fright	▪ Respect ▪ Authority ▪ Confidence ▪ Poised presence at meetings when you have to speak in front of coworkers and superiors
..ership Skills for Supervisors	Providing feedback and constructive criticism	▪ Ability to transform your staff into a more productive and efficient team ▪ Respect from your superiors ▪ Increased profit
Memory Skills	Learning techniques for remembering names and faces	▪ Freedom from embarrassment ▪ Ability to be more productive ▪ Closer releationship with people who feel you care about them enough to remember their names
Excel Basics	Calculating using basic formulas	▪ Reclaimed time ▪ Accuracy ▪ Speed in making decisions dependent on calculations
PowerPoint Basics	Using basic design for presentations	▪ Professional presentations that are convincing ▪ Respect from recipients of your presentations

A form based on this figure appears as Figure B-39 in Appendix B.

Figure 6-8.   Participant's poem.

There Is Something I Don't Know

There is something I don't know
     that I am supposed to know.
I don't know what it is I don't know
     and yet am supposed to know,
and I feel I look stupid
     if I seem both not to know it
          and not know what it is I don't know.
Therefore I pretend to know it.
     This is nerve-racking
          since I don't know what I must pretend to know.
Therefore I pretend to know everything.

I feel *you* know what I am supposed to know
but you can't tell me what it is
Because you don't know that I don't know what it is,

You may know what I don't know, but not
     that I don't know it,
and I can't tell you. So you will have
to tell me everything.

Author Unknown

Link Learning to What Participants Already Know

One of the best ways for you to help participants learn is to begin by relating to what they already know. This means that, as a facilitator, you need to figure out what's going on in your participants' minds before you try to fill those minds with what you have on your mind.

Use Creative Imagery to Understand Your Participants

If you do not have some opportunity to talk with participants before the start of the course, you can use another technique to understand them and their needs. *Creative imagery* helps you analyze your participants by thinking, or imagining, that you are looking at the training as they would look at it. There are three basic steps in the creative imagery process. It calls for you to imagine what your participants might be thinking about the course based on the information you know about them and their departments.

Creative Imagery Process

Step 1: Determine the makeup of your participant group. Review the course registrations and look for common demographic characteristics (front-line employees, union workers, supervisors, directors, staff members predominantly from one or two departments).

Example: In a communications course, participants are made up of front-line staff members from the food service, security, and customer service departments.

Step 2: Look for similarities in the participant makeup. Identify common needs with regard to the subject.

Example: Almost all the participants have to communicate on a regular basis with their bosses, coworkers, and customers. It's important for them to be able to get their ideas across to the people they are talking with and to understand what others are trying to tell them.

Step 3: Imagine the attitudes, questions, motivations, etc., of typical participants.

Examples: (Purposeful) Several of the participants are working for a manager who is known to be difficult to talk with and work with. They are probably thinking, "I signed up for this course so I can figure out how to talk to my boss. Sometimes I feel as if we're speaking different languages. Sure hope I can get some pointers here. I'm tired of feeling like she doesn't get it."

(Under stress) Volume in the customer service department has been increasing, while the staff has been shrinking. The staff has been under pressure to serve more customers per hour while appearing to be ready and willing to solve customer issues. Customer service representatives may be thinking, "How can we be nice to customers when we're under the gun to take more calls? I need help talking to the customers and my boss."

(Reluctant/insulted) "My boss signed me up. Said I'd probably like the course. I think I talk just fine. I really don't want to be here."

(Reluctant to talk in public) "I hope I won't have to get up in front of everyone and talk. I hate that."

(Proud/defiant) "I've been communicating with the people in the restaurant for a *long* time. I'll bet I can teach *our instructor* a thing or two about the subject—especially about people who are hungry, tired, and cranky."

(Recommended by previous participants) "Glad I'm here. If the course is as good as Jack says it is, I need this."

Begin Where Your Participants Are

Because you have a limited amount of time to pack your participants' heads with everything they need to know, you may be eager to begin teaching them what they need to know as soon as the introductions are over. *Resist the temptation!* One of the easiest ways to lose your participants is to begin presenting concepts without linking them to what your participants already know.

When your introductions are over and your participants are ready to begin the learning process, it is important for you to remember what they are probably thinking and begin there. Build a bridge from where your participants are to where you want them to be:

- If you are teaching participants a new system for recording sales, begin by relating it to the system they already know.
- If you are teaching flowcharts, begin by describing and charting the flow of steps in a process everyone knows (starting the car, getting out of bed, brushing teeth).
- If your session is on customer service, begin by asking your participants to describe a time they received excellent customer service and to list the characteristics that made the service excellent.

For every session and every topic, there is a way to link it to the participants' current level of understanding. Your challenge as a trainer is to find that link. One facilitator found the link for an ergonomics presentation by saying, "I know what you're thinking—you're saying to yourself, 'Oh, no. Here comes a boring lecture on ergonomics.' Well, I'm here today to give you something that can help you feel better and perform better. First, I want all of you to take a minute to be aware of the way you are sitting in your chair. . . ."

Progress Step-by-Step to Where You Want Participants to Be

When you have established a firm link with the participants' current experience and understanding, your next challenge is to progress step-by-step from what your participants already know to what you want them to know. Figure 6-9 shows you a seven-step process for accomplishing this.

Generate and Guide Discussion

When you have established the necessary connection in your participants' minds by beginning where they are, you need to get them involved. Active engagement by the learner is essential because learning is not a passive activity—it's an active one.

Generating and guiding in-class discussion is an important facilitation skill. When you ask open-ended questions that call for participants to relate what you are saying to their own experiences, training becomes real for them. Adult learners come to training with a wealth of practical, on-the-job, and personal experiences. If you can get participants to recall these experiences and relate them to the topic you are discussing, the training becomes relevant to them. Generating and guiding class discussion calls for asking the right

Figure 6-9.   Bridge-building process.

Build a Bridge From Where Your Participants Are to Where You Want Them to Be

How do you get there?

1. Get into the minds of your learners and try to understand what they are thinking about the subject at hand.

2. Begin by addressing their thoughts and feelings.

3. Explain where you want them to be.

4. Involve them in designing the plan for getting there.

5. Move in logical steps from what they know to what you want them to know.

6. Keep them involved.

7. Give them lots of feedback.

A form based on this figure appears as Figure B-40 in Appendix B.

questions, allowing silence, encouraging multiple responses, recognizing everyone who responds, and answering unsolicited questions.

Ask the Right Questions

Ask open-ended questions that require participants to think back to their own experiences:

- When has listening been a particularly important skill for you on the job?
- I want you to take a minute to picture in your mind the best boss you have ever had. It could be the one you have now or any boss you have ever had. When you have the picture clearly in your mind, I want you to write down three words or phrases that describe why this boss is good.

Don't Be Afraid of Silence

Don't be afraid to let participants think. Silence is a good thing; you shouldn't rush to fill it by answering your own questions. The first time you allow the room to be silent after you have asked a question, it will feel uncomfortable. But if you force yourself *not* to provide the answer, you will find that your participants *will* respond. Inexperienced facilitators are quick to fill any gaps by answering their own questions. After this happens several times in a row, the participants learn that they don't have to think of the answers because the facilitator will provide them all.

Encourage More Than One Response

If you ask the entire group a question rather than directing the question to one participant, you will engage more of your participants in the learning process. When you do have an answer, even if it is the right answer, you can ask for examples, explanations, and other opinions. You might say something like, "That's good. What else should we consider?" or "That's good. Now who can give me an example?"

Acknowledge Everyone Who Responds

Try to acknowledge every response, even the wrong ones. If you don't want participants to be afraid to offer responses that are less than perfect, you will need to ensure that there is a safe environment for discussion. You can acknowledge correct answers with a positive response such as "Good" and incorrect answers with a response such as "That's interesting," "Let's come back to that in a minute," or "Thanks, Sam." In recapping the discussion, you can summarize the fact that there are a lot of opinions about the subject. Then you can explain the correct answer in detail.

Field Unsolicited Questions—Even the Tricky Ones

Your learners' decision to participate will, in part, be determined by your responses to their questions. You can't anticipate every question that will be asked by participants, but you can develop a strategy for answering them. You will probably have to deal with several types of difficult questions.

Questions That Depart From the Subject at Hand. You are leading a discussion on negotiating union contracts and mention the recent results of a negotiation that modified the vacation days available to union members. The next five questions from your participants are requests for clarification about their vacation days and other related benefits. Because you don't want to turn your training session into a general union benefits session, you can use the "parking lot" described in Figure 6-10 to store these questions until you can deal with them—probably after class.

Figure 6-10. The "parking lot."

Participants will appreciate the fact that you use the "parking lot" to acknowledge the fact that you have heard all their questions, even if you have to delay answering some of them until a later time.

What Is It?

The "parking lot" is a convenient technique for both storing and having access to questions you need to postpone answering. It calls for using a flip chart, whiteboard, or other visible area where you can list each of the questions you want to delay answering.

How Does It Work?

When a participant asks a question that is a candidate for the parking lot:

1. Acknowledge the response. "Sam, that's an interesting question and I don't want to lose it." (While you're talking, repeat the question or ask the participant to repeat it.)
2. Move to the "parking lot" and begin writing the question as you explain, "I don't want to lose your question, but we need to stay on track timewise. We will have to discuss it later."
3. Keep the "parking lot" questions displayed for both you and the participants. If there is an appropriate time to answer one of the questions, work it into the session.
4. If there is not an appropriate time to answer the questions, invite participants to talk with you at the break or after the session about them.
5. If you don't know the answers or if they are clearly out of the realm of the course, refer them to another resource for an answer.

Requests for Confidential or Inappropriate Information. Questions about salary, layoffs, downsizing, disciplinary actions, etc., are clearly inappropriate. Similarly, gossip from participants concerning these topics is inappropriate. As the facilitator, it is your responsibility to set a tone of professionalism in your courses and sessions. Often a simple statement, such as "Let's not get into that" or "Let's not go there," is all that is necessary to discourage this type of discussion. If participants do not respond to these simple suggestions, you will have to be more direct with your statement. You might say, "I have to ask you to refrain from discussing salary issues in the session." Maintaining control of the nature of the discussion will help you create an environment in which your participants feel safe and able to learn.

Encourage Continued Participation

Sometimes your participants will be reluctant to participate. Yet, the best learning situations for adults involve open discussions in which participants can express their opinions, relate experiences to the content, and engage in problem solving. All these activities call for them to participate in the session rather than just sit back and listen. If you have difficulty engaging your participants in discussion, you may want to use one of the following techniques for generating participation:

- Volunteers
- Round Robin
- Answer Box
- Brainstorming
- Rotating Flip Charts
- Silent Pass
- Penny for Your Thoughts

Volunteers. Chances are you will have at least one vocal participant who will elect to volunteer. Although sometimes this person will dominate the group, asking for a volunteer often gets the ball rolling and encourages other participants to share their thoughts with the group. It is also a nonthreatening way of encouraging participation. You can simply ask, "Are there any volunteers who would like to share their experience?"

Round Robin. If one participant is dominating your group and stifling other participants' ideas, you can use the round robin technique to ensure that all your participants have an opportunity to share their ideas. You ask a question and tell your participants that after they think for a moment, you will begin soliciting responses, one at a time. To begin the process, you can ask for a volunteer; then proceed around the room, one person at a time, asking each one to talk. Although some participants may feel somewhat uncomfortable, this is an effective way of ensuring balanced participation.

Brainstorming. Brainstorming is an effective technique that generates a lot of information in a short period of time. Ask participants to generate suggestions as quickly as they can, and not to analyze or criticize the information. Capture the suggestions on a flip chart so participants can view their work in progress. This helps foster additional ideas and solutions. Emphasize that no idea is a bad idea, and tell them to think outside the box. Usually, this technique generates a great amount of ideas and creative thinking. However, you have to facilitate this process carefully to allow everyone's ideas to be heard because your loudest and most active participant may try to dominate the activity.

Answer Box. Another way to ensure balanced participation is to ask a question or suggest a problem that needs solving and ask participants to write their answers on an index card. Once you have given them a couple of minutes to write, collect the index cards and ask a participant to volunteer to read all the responses while you capture them on a flip chart or an overhead. This is a nonthreatening approach and allows you to give everyone the opportunity to be heard while remaining anonymous. If everyone submits a card, those participants who are quieter will have the same opportunity to be heard as those who usually dominate the discussion. When you are posting ideas, you should remember to follow the rule that no idea is a bad idea.

Rotating Flip Charts. Another more interactive approach involves the use of flip charts. It is a good way to get participants up and out of their seats and to generate a lot of ideas quickly. Before class, write a single topic on each flip chart. Place a generous supply of markers on the table and ask participants to move quickly around the room, jotting their ideas regarding the topic on each flip chart. Give them five seconds for each flip. Assume, for example, that you are running a session in which you are trying to generate as many ideas as you can that may be used in creating a new line of business. Before class, you can prepare the flip charts by writing on each one the name of a newspaper section. Ask participants to pretend that it is five years in the future; then have them move from one flip chart to another writing headlines for articles about your successful business. Figure 6-11 is a sample of the rotating flip chart approach.

Silent Pass. This technique is also useful because you encourage everyone to participate in a nonthreatening way. It is similar to brainstorming but is done silently and on paper. Have all participants begin with a blank sheet of paper; assign each one a different aspect of a problem or project. For example, if you are discussing plans for an upcoming conference, the topics might be:

- Speakers
- Location
- Promotion
- Lodging
- Materials
- Entertainment

- Telecommunications
- Refreshments

1. Ask each of the participants to write a different topic at the top of the blank piece of paper. (If there are more participants than topics, two or three participants can have the same topic.)
2. Ask the person who records the topic on the paper to begin by writing three ideas about that topic. (For example, for Speakers, the first person might write the names of three speakers.)
3. When everyone has had time to add ideas and notes to the paper, ask everyone to pass their papers to the right. The participant who receives the paper reviews the list, adds two suggestions or comments, and passes to the right again. (For example, the person who receives the paper about Speakers might add the name of a speaker, comment on one of the names on the list, or add a topic for which a speaker needs to be found.)
4. When they have completed the final silent pass, ask the person who started the paper to summarize the comments and add them to a flip chart for all to see and discuss.

Figure 6-11.   Sample rotating flip charts.

Newspaper Headlines for New Business Line
Five Years Into the Future

Finance	Technology	Community
We are the market leaders!	ABC Company has the newest and fastest technology in the industry.	ABC Company offers a $20,000 scholarship for the most dedicated community service student.

Penny for Your Thoughts. This is a technique that will help you achieve more balanced participation if you have a group in which a few people do all the talking. Give each participant three pennies. Ask everyone to display their pennies in clear sight on the table in front of them. During class discussion, participants spend a penny each time they speak. When they are out of pennies, they have to wait until all other pennies are spent before they are replenished.

The Big Decision—Is This for Me?

Each individual in your session who decides to open up and participate is subconsciously making the big decision: "This is for me, and I want to learn." The big decision has two important parts—the check-in, checkout point and the physical/mental exit point (see Figure 6-12).

Figure 6-12.   The big decision.

Check-In, Checkout Point

You can greatly increase the probability of check-in if you relate honestly to your participants from the moment they walk into the room. Make an effort to understand their thoughts and feelings, and begin by relating the subject at hand to those thoughts and feelings instead of launching into a presentation. You will be able to sense check-in or checkout by being alert to reactions you are receiving from your participants. If you establish two-way communication with them at the beginning of the session and maintain that connection throughout the entire session, your participants will easily be able to decide that this session is for them.

Physical/Mental Exit Point

For the few participants who clearly should not be in the session because it is not for them, you may want to consider offering them the opportunity to exit gracefully. If you establish this fact early in the session, you might allow a moment after the introductions for participants to elect to leave the room. Your goal should be for all remaining participants to be present both physically and mentally because learning involves active participation on your part and on the part of each and every learner.

7

Attempt and Build

Help Me Build My Skills Step-by-Step

> *This Effective Communication course definitely relates to my job—especially the part about being able to talk to my boss so she'll really understand what I'm saying. I hope the instructor has enough sense to let us practice until we get it. This is something I definitely need to learn.*

If the purpose of training is learning (and the application of that learning on the job), it is essential that participants remember what they have learned and value it enough to *want* to apply it on the job. More importantly, participants need to be proficient and relatively comfortable with using their new skills before they attempt to use them back at work. You will learn how to add activities to your presentation that will help participants remember what they have learned, realize the value on a personal level, and build the skills they need so they can apply them on the job. The ancient Chinese proverb in Figure 7-1 confirms this premise and sets the tone for this chapter. In this chapter, you will learn how to show your participants the skills you expect them to learn so they will remember the skills and involve them so they understand how to use those skills on the job (see Figure 7-2).

Figure 7-1.   Ancient Chinese proverb.

Tell me and I'll forget.
Show me and I may remember.
Involve me and I'll understand.

This figure is provided in Appendix B as Figure B-41.

Help Your Participants Remember

Your participants will have an easier time remembering what they have learned if you both use techniques that are relevant and integrate demonstrations of these techniques. Some useful learning techniques that should be incorporated into your training sessions include demonstrations, metaphors, movie and TV clips, games, and colored dot highlights.

Demonstrations

If you show them, they have a better chance of remembering. In fact, participants will probably remember your demonstrations before they remember what you've told them. If you use creative activities as a catalyst for learning and transition those into demonstrations, the learning will stick in your participant's minds. Examples of demonstrations that have been effective in helping participants remember are discussed in the text and depicted in the figures that follow.

Paper Creations Demonstration. The paper creations demonstration in Figure 7-3 can be used in both communication and leadership courses. It demonstrates the importance of two-way communication and the way that communication can be interpreted differently by different people. When you use this demonstration, it is almost impossible for your two volunteers to create the same final product.

As you lead the discussion following the activity, you should expect (or lead) participants to provide these answers:

1. Ask the paper folders why their creations do not match.
   Possible answers include (a) You didn't let us ask questions, (b) what you told us to do was hard to understand, (c) there are a lot of ways to interpret what you told us to do.

Figure 7-2. Guide to Chapter 7.

Learning Stage	Secrets to Success
ATTEMPT & BUILD 	**Help Me Build My Skills Step-by-Step** **1. Help Your Participants Remember** ■ Demonstrations ■ Metaphors ■ Movie and TV clips ■ Games ■ Colored dot highlights **2. Help Your Participants Relate** ■ Imaging ■ Real-life reference ■ Role-play props **3. Let Your Participants Practice, Practice, Practice** ■ Mastering each step ■ Creating a safe environment for practice ■ Offering training at the right time **4. Make it Real** ■ Case problems ■ Role playing ■ Simulations ■ Goal-based scenarios ■ Theater-based learning ■ Videotapes

2. Ask them what would have made the process easier.
   Possible answers include (a) being able to ask questions and (b) being able to see the other paper folder.
3. Ask the rest of the group to share their observations about how the instructions were interpreted.
   Possible answers include (a) observations about when the two paper folders began to interpret the directions differently and (b) comments about how the two creations differ.
4. Ask how the lessons from this demonstration can be applied to the communication that occurs every day on the job.
   Important points to stress include (a) two-way communication is an essential ingredient of every job; (b) remember that when you communicate a message to another person, that person may interpret it differently from the way you intend it to be interpreted; and (c) the

Figure 7-3.   Paper creations demonstration.

Course Topic:	Communication Skills
Purpose:	To show (a) the importance of two-way communication and (b) the way communication can be interpreted differently by different people.

Demonstration:

1. Ask for two volunteers from the group.

2. Ask them to stand back to back in front of the group so the group can see both of them but they can't see each other.

3. Hand each one an 8½ × 11 piece of paper.

4. Tell them that they are to follow all your instructions but are not allowed to ask questions.

5. Instruct them to:

   - Fold the paper in half.
   - Fold it again in thirds.
   - Rip off the right corner.
   - Unfold the paper and rip off the left corner.
   - Fold the paper in half again and rip a V-shaped notch in the top of the paper.
   - Unfold the paper again and rip a V-shaped notch in both the left and right sides of the paper.

6. Have your two participants face the group and show their creations. There is very little chance that they match each other.

Discussion:

1. Ask the two paper folders why their creations do not match.

2. Ask them what would have made the process easier.

3. Ask the rest of the group to share their observations about how the instructions were interpreted.

4. Ask how the lessons from this demonstration can be applied to the communication that occurs every day on the job.

As the trainer, you should review the discussion points so that you can process out the key learning points from the exercise.

only way to tell if your message was received and understood as you intended it to be is to let that person ask questions and to provide feedback based on those questions.

Leadership Demonstration. The leadership demonstration in Figure 7-4 uses a simple rope demonstration to show the importance of leading staff by being a role model and "pulling" staff rather than "pushing" them to perform.

As you lead the discussion following this activity, your participants should note that when you pushed the rope, it bunched up and was difficult

Figure 7-4. Leadership demonstration.

Course Topic:	Supervision and Leadership
Purpose:	To demonstrate why it is more effective to lead your staff than to push them to work
Materials:	Soft, pliable rope that is about 18 inches long
Demonstration A:	1. Place the rope on the table.
	2. Grasp the end of the rope and push it forward, causing the rope to bunch up on the table.
Discussion:	What happened when I *pushed* the rope? If the rope represents your staff, what happens if you push them into performing without leading the way by serving as an example? Chances are they will not be able to lead the way without your guidance.
Demonstration B:	1. Place the rope on the table.
	2. Grasp the end of the rope and pull it forward.
	3. Pull the rope around the table showing that it is easy to handle without having it bunch up.
Discussion:	What happened when I *pulled* the rope? If the rope represents your staff, in what way is it more effective if you lead their activities instead of pushing them to perform?

to move. You made virtually no progress in moving it to the desired destination. But when you pulled it, it was easy to move to the desired destination. If the rope represents your staff, it is more effective to lead their activities instead of pushing them. As a leader, you can demonstrate the ability to serve as a role model by maintaining the attitude that "We are in this effort together." Rather than having an "I want you to do xxx" attitude, the leader who is demonstrating the ability to "pull" the staff will have a "We're all in this together, and we make a great team" attitude.

Teamwork Demonstration for Retreat Setting. Not all learning takes place in the classroom. This activity (see Figure 7-5) is designed for team-building retreats that are held off-site, in a camp setting.

This demonstrates the importance and power of working as a team instead of as separate individuals. When you separate the logs in one campfire, they all go out. When you keep the other fire intact, it continues to burn. The

Figure 7-5. Teamwork demonstration for retreat setting.

Course Topic:	Team Building
Purpose:	To represent the importance and strength that come from working as a team
Materials:	Two small campfires built next to each other in a fire-safe area
Demonstration:	1. Explain that the fires represent two teams.
	2. Using fire tongs, carefully spread the logs from the first fire until they are separated from each other.
	3. Keep the other fire intact.
	4. Instruct participants to return to the fire area in one hour to check the status of the fires.
Follow-Up:	At the end of the hour, the fire that is intact should still be burning, while each of the logs that has been separated should have stopped burning and gotten cold.
Discussion:	What happened when the team disbanded and members went their own way? Why is the team that never separated still burning? How does this demonstration relate to teams in the work setting?

analogy is that the burning fire represents the power of teams and teamwork. They can keep an effort moving, and they seem to energize each team member. When a team disbands and members go their own separate ways, an effort may not keep going because there is no longer group energy.

Change Perception Demonstration. This demonstration (see Figure 7-6) uses a simple in-class demonstration that involves changing things about one's appearance to demonstrate that change is usually viewed as a negative event.

In leading the discussion following this activity, point out that most people automatically remove something rather than just moving it from one position to another because they subconsciously interpret change to mean giving something up.

As more and more organizations are undergoing changes, this activity can be a valuable introduction to a discussion about approaching change with a positive attitude.

Figure 7-6.   Change perception demonstration.

Course Topic:	Accepting Change
Purpose:	To show that people often have a negative perception of change
Demonstration:	1. Instruct participants to pair off, face their partners, and observe each other.
	2. Instruct them to turn around with their backs to each other.
	3. Instruct all participants to change three things about their appearance.
	4. Ask participants to turn around, face their partners, and try to determine what has been changed, while relatively few modify the position of an item.
Usual Result:	The majority of your participants will remove something—a piece of clothing, a watch, a ring, glasses, a pin, etc., when they have been asked to change something, while relatively few modify the position of an item.
Discussion:	How many of you removed something instead of simply changing the position of it? Most people automatically associate change with giving something up instead of doing something differently. How can this negative perception be overcome in today's rapidly changing organizations?

Metaphors

Advertisers have known for many years that they can create long-lasting images by using words and expressions that readily bring images to your mind. Metaphors help you to take advantage of this image-creating ability by using words or phrases as substitutes for others. A popular anti-drug ad shows an egg frying in a pan. The voice-over says, "This is your brain on drugs." Instant coffee has been said to "stir your soul." In a concert ad, announcer Tom Brokaw is quoted as saying, "Mostly Mozart is a crown jewel in any New York summer."

According to management consultant Thomas Davenport, the extra few moments it takes to interpret metaphors makes them stick like linguistic bugs on our mental flypaper. Davenport says that metaphors are particularly appealing because they call out for attention, are dense with meaning, and have a long cognitive shelf life.

He quotes Peter Silas, chief executive of Phillips Petroleum, who used a powerful, long-lasting metaphor when he spoke of the company's competitive challenge by saying, "We cannot afford to wait until the storm has passed. We must learn to work in the rain."[1]

Figure 7-7 shows four rules Davenport suggests for using metaphors. These rules can help you as you create or adopt metaphors to use in your training sessions.

Movie and TV Clips

An effective approach to demonstrate learning topics, build your participants' memory, and help them relate to the learning in a different way (especially when the session is over) is to use short clips from commercial movies

---

Figure 7-7.   Rules for using metaphors.

1. **Use metaphors that move.** Your participants will be able to picture the movement if you use words such as sprint, soar, fly, climb, or even brawl.

2. **Relate to your audience.** Be careful not to use hunting metaphors with animal rights activists or war metaphors with pacifists. If metaphors are part of your usual conversation, you may have to "scrub" them for sensitivity to your audience.

3. **Avoid clichés.** They have a tendency to come to mind too easily and often are easy substitutes for original thinking and expression. If you're "tickled pink" with a "tried but true" expression, it probably is "old hat" and should be "avoided like the plague."

4. **Be sure your metaphors are truthful.** Avoid expressions such as "employees are our most important asset" in a time of widespread organizational downsizing.

Adapted from Thomas O. Davenport, "Metaphorical Management," *Strategy & Leadership,* Volume 26, Number 3, July/August 1998. Used with permission.

or television shows. When you select a movie or TV show your participants are already familiar with, you gain the benefit of relating your material to a known, and often enjoyed, story or character.

Your job as facilitator is to (1) select clips that relate to the topic at hand; (2) introduce each clip by asking participants to watch for a particular interaction, conversation, expression, etc., while they are watching; (3) watch the clip with your participants; and (4) process out the clip by discussing the message of the clip and how it relates to the topic. Figure 7-8 provides a few suggested movies and classic TV shows that are good, popular candidates for clips that will impact your participants.

Figure 7-8. Suggested movie and TV clips.

Movie or TV Show	Clip	Use
A Few Good Men	Scene on the witness stand	▪ Leadership style
Apollo 13	Assembling the breathing mechanism	▪ Problem solving ▪ Teamwork
Big	Management meeting about new building/robot	▪ Communication ▪ Listening ▪ Understanding
Dances with Wolves	Discussion around the fire	▪ Respect ▪ Communication skills
Dead Poets Society	Seize the day (standing on the desk)	▪ Change ▪ Motivation
I Love Lucy	Ricky's time management chart	▪ Time management
Lean on Me	Students helping each other study/planning for the exam	▪ Teamwork
Mr. Holland's Opus	Clarinet player and instructor	▪ Coaching ▪ Not giving up
Norma Ray	Shutting down the plant	▪ Leadership
Teen Wolf	Coach not paying attention to student with problem	▪ Listening ▪ Communication
9 to 5	Copy machine breakdown and scolding by the manager	▪ Giving directions ▪ Leadership ▪ Handling criticism

Games

Games can be used to help your participants move the concepts you have presented from short-term memory into long-term memory (see Chapter 3). Almost any concepts that are taught can be molded into games that will help participants remember. Although the terms game and simulation are sometimes used synonymously, they have different basic purposes and structures; Figure 7-9 shows those differences. *Games* generally ask participants to recall facts and demonstrate the basic ability to apply these facts. While games can liven up a session and help participants to remember what they have learned, they are not designed to provide realistic practice of complete skills.

Television game shows can provide inspiration for the development of games that participants enjoy and will easily understand. A *Jeopardy* board can be designed to support any number of subject areas. For example, the same basic rules can be used to help participants learn technical terms or to help them demonstrate their understanding of a complex performance measurement program before it is implemented. Typical game materials include a large bulletin board to use as the master game board, play money, score sheets, bells or buzzers, and prizes. Alternatively, you can use a game software package that enables you to design and/or deliver games electronically.

Selecting Games. Factors to consider in selecting (or developing) games for your sessions are presented in Figure 7-10. Games that reinforce learning do not have to be elaborate or time-consuming to create.

Card Flash Game. One simple game that provides an opportunity to help participants remember concepts that might be considered by many trainers as dull or boring is the card flash game. It can be used as a comprehension check for any subject matter. The game calls for participants to respond to comprehension or application questions in unison by showing one of two prepreprared cards. This particular game has been successfully used many times, and participants rarely find it boring. One of your authors used it to describe a series of dry and unexciting billing regulations issued by Medicare. Steps in preparing the game are described on page 146.

Figure 7-9.   Basic differences between games and simulations.

	Input	*Performance*	*Outcome*
Games	The result of chance	Symbolic	▪ Winning ▪ Losing
Simulations	Realistic	Realistic roles	▪ Measurement against goals ▪ Feedback on performance

Figure 7-10. Factors to consider in selecting a game.

Question	Yes	No
1. **Does the game relate to the objectives of the course?** The game should help participants master concepts that relate to the ultimate objectives of the course. The lowest level of game that should be used is one that tests vocabulary terms against the meaning of those terms. A game that should **NOT** be used is a word finder that asks participants to simply circle words without indicating that they have an understanding of what those words mean.	❒	❒
2. **Has the game been tested for consistency in directions/rules/ scoring?** The game may sound good on paper, but you can't anticipate difficulties participants might have in understanding the directions, rules, and scoring if you don't test the game before you use it. An easy way to test a new game is to round up coworkers and offer them a pizza lunch for participating in your trial run. Directions that seem perfectly clear are often identified as confusing during this trial run and can be rewritten before the game is used in class.	❒	❒
3. **Can the game rules be taught in order to facilitate playing?** Sometimes game rules are, of necessity, somewhat complex. It's a good idea to practice teaching them to prospective players during your trial run. Often the way that rules are explained and demonstrated can get a game off and running correctly with no false starts.	❒	❒
4. **Does the strategy for winning correspond with the learning objectives of the session?** Make sure that the participants who show the best command of the course content are the ones who have the best chance of winning. This means that you will have to test several game scenarios to make sure that lucky participants who show little or no understanding of the content can't win.	❒	❒
5. **If the game calls for physical movement by the participants, does this movement work within the physical limitations of your room?** Here again, the trial run is important. If participants have to move around and are hampered by chairs that can trip them or tables that force them to squeeze by sideways, the game is not an appropriate one for the room. You should either change rooms or use another game. When designing these games, you should also consider the needs of disabled participants.	❒	❒
6. **If the game calls for using bells, buzzers, or other signaling devices, will these devices be accepted (or tolerated) by**	❒	❒

(continues)

Figure 7-10. (Continued)

---

occupants of surrounding classrooms and offices? If the room you are using for your class is in close proximity to other classrooms or offices, you can be a very unpopular person if your game interferes with the work of others. Bright-colored signs that are raised by the participants can be used as substitutes for noisy signaling devices if noise is a problem. You may also want to alert your "neighbors" that the class may become a little loud even if you are using noiseless signaling devices, because enthusiastic game contestants can easily forget that they are in class.

7. **Are all players allowed to actively participate?** Games that call   ❏   ❏
   for one representative from each team to compete while the rest watch should be modified to allow everyone a chance to participate on a rotating basis. The disadvantage of using a rotation is that participants who know they will not be participating for several turns can lose interest. An alternative technique is to put the names of the participants from each team in a hat and draw them at random for each round. Then all participants have to stay alert because they never know when they will be called on.

8. **Will the time invested in the game yield a worthwhile amount**   ❏   ❏
   of learning, or can the concepts be better taught in another way? Concepts can almost always be taught in another way, but games provide an opportunity to help participants master knowledge that might be harder to master through simple discussion and study. Because games take more time than discussion, it's important to make sure the concepts that are taught and tested through games are the ones that are the most important as participants master the goals of the course.

A copy of this form is provided as Figure B-42 in Appendix B.

1. *Analyze the content and develop a series of questions* that have only two possible responses. For example:
   a. Location of merchandise within a small store (answer: first floor/second floor)
   b. Business English sentences being checked for grammar (answer: correct/incorrect)
   c. Medicare case examples for billing (answer: bundle/don't bundle)
   d. ADA or sexual harassment situation (answer: complies/does not comply)
2. *Prepare overheads or flip charts* with the questions you have decided on.
3. *Create a set of answer cards* for each participant or team of two participants. Use $8^1/_2 \times 11$ pages with the answer choices in 48-point type

with an easy-to-read typeface such as Ariel or Times Roman. Fasten each page on a card stock backing (half of a file folder words well) to prevent participants from reading other people's answers through the back of the page.

4. *Develop a set of rules.* For example: This activity will give you a chance to check your knowledge of the grammar rules we have just been discussing. As I flash sentences on the overhead projector, you are going to tell me whether they are grammatically correct or grammatically incorrect:

    a. When a sentence appears on the screen, you have 10 seconds to decide whether it is correct or incorrect.

    b. You all have two answer cards. One says "correct," the other "incorrect." As soon as you see a sentence, decide which of the two cards you will show and place it on top of the table with your hands on either side of the card.

    c. When I ring this bell, raise your cards.

    d. You will get one point for each correct answer.

    e. The participant(s) with the most correct answers will be the winner(s) and receive a prize.

    Alternate ending: The participants with the most correct answers will have an opportunity to compete in the final round by rewriting each of the incorrect sentences. The participant with the most correctly rewritten sentences is the winner.

5. *Add interest to the questions you are preparing* by using names of television celebrities, cartoon characters, recording artists, or film stars. For a grammar game, you might use the following items:

    a. Meg Ryan and Kevin Bacon decide to film their next movies on the moon. (correct/not correct)

    b. Miss Piggy plans to show voters she can run for congress and win. (correct/not correct)

    c. Ricky Martin can make a fan lose inhibition and dance in the streets. (correct/not correct)

6. *Prepare a scoring sheet.*

7. *Facilitate the game and award prizes.*

Colored Dot Highlights

Another way to help participants remember concepts they learn and identify them for implementation on the job is the use of colored dots. These dots are available in most office supply stores. At the start of the session, supply each participant with a collection of small, yellow, red, and green dots. Instruct participants to use the dots to annotate handouts and notes using the guide in Figure 7-11. (This technique can also be used for group decision-making activities.)

Help Your Participants Relate

Another way to help your learners prepare to implement the skills and concepts you are presenting is to help them relate to the material in a different way. Imaging, real-life reference, and role-play props serve this purpose.

Figure 7-11. Colored dot highlights.

Dot Color	Code
Yellow	I have some questions I need to ask about this idea/area.
Red	This idea/skill is important! I'll definitely use it on the job.
Green	This idea/skill sounds as if it has promise. I might use it on the job.

Imaging

When you use imaging, you can either ask participants to recall their own past experiences as a basis for learning or let them imagine the images you create. You can also ask them to use imaging (that is, mentally visualize something) to help them picture the successful application of the skills they have learned in your class when they return to the job. Images can include any or all of the following experiences:

- Visual images (seeing colors, shapes, people, scenery, etc.)
- Images of smells (smelling a flower, a pine branch, a turkey dinner, a fresh baked pie)
- Tactile images—shaking someone's hand, running, climbing, swimming, feeling rain on your face, feeling sand between your toes)
- Food images (tasting and feeling the texture and cold sensation of your favorite ice cream)
- Kinesthetic images (riding in a plane, experiencing a roller-coaster ride, driving a car)
- Auditory images (hearing music, a baby's cry, the sound of the ocean, rustling of the trees, someone singing)

Done properly, this can be a powerful learning tool because it enables each participant to personalize the learning needs and the desired outcomes.

The imaging exercise in Figure 7-12 asks participants to recall their own past experiences with a boss they admired. It can be used to develop a list of leadership characteristics to launch a discussion of leadership.

Although it might seem unusual, the imaging exercise in Figure 7-13 can be helpful in personal goal setting. It asks participants to go with you as you take an imaginary walk in the woods and retrieve a message. As part of the exercise, each participant retrieves a personal message. Because the exercise helps participants get in touch with their subconscious thoughts, participants often find that they receive messages about their own personal goals and direction that they might otherwise have found difficult to get in touch with.

Real-Life Reference

A less complex, but equally powerful technique for helping participants relate to materials or learning topics is the use of real-life reference. If you were presenting a customer service class to experienced customer service representatives, you would do them a disservice if you ignored their cumula-

Figure 7-12.   Leadership imaging exercise.

Many of us can easily pull up examples of bosses we did not like. But each of us also has images of the boss we admired and respected—the boss we wanted to work hard for, the one who made coming to work a pleasure. Do you all have this boss in mind? Now I want you to close your eyes and go back in time to when you worked for this person.

Imagine that you are at your old work location, in your old job—the one you enjoyed doing because of this boss. You see your boss and are ready to have a conversation. Spend a moment hearing your boss's voice and seeing his or her smile. Imagine a conversation and listen to the words. Feel the atmosphere—what sounds did you hear? Where was the desk, chair, computer, printer? Enjoy being there again.

While you are there, try to determine what it is about this situation that motivates you, gives you pleasure, and makes you want to do your best. [Pause for approximately two minutes.] Now I want you to return to the classroom. When you are ready, slowly open your eyes and rejoin the class.

Processing questions:

1. Who wants to share their image with us? Who was your boss? What type of business did you work in together?
2. What is it about this person that motivated you and made you want to work?
3. What does this person say to you when you do a good job?
4. What does this person say to you when you make a mistake?

Outcome:
As participants describe the characteristics of good bosses, create a list on the flip chart for use in a discussion about leadership.

tive years of experience. Instead of lecturing, you might ask these reps to pair up and hand each pair a piece of paper that contains a picture of a telephone receiver and cord. This is meant to symbolize the customer on the phone. Then you could challenge the pairs: "Remember the most difficult customer you dealt with last month. What made this situation difficult? What did this customer want? Why was the request difficult to fulfill? What did you do? What barriers did you have to overcome? Would this situation have been easier to handle if something were different? Explain."

After fifteen minutes of discussion time, you could ask participants to provide you with a list of challenges and solutions. This could be the foundation for an interesting class discussion based on the wealth of knowledge in the room.

Role-Play Props

Another technique that will help your learners relate involves the use of simple props, such as cotton and Vaseline, to create a situation that can help

Figure 7-13.   Goal-setting exercise.

Spend a moment getting comfortable and relaxed. Close your eyes and take a deep breath. Let it go slowly. Breathe in again and exhale. Place your feet on the floor and fold your hands in your lap. As you breathe slowly, let your feet relax. Now feel all the tension flowing out of your legs, your torso, your arms, your neck, your back, your neck. Slowly move your head from side to side as you enjoy feeling relaxed.

Now imagine that you are at the edge of the woods. The trees are so dense that the light from the sun is obscured, but you aren't afraid. There is a clear path surrounded by wildflowers. Breathe in and smell the pine, the wildflowers, the fresh air. As you walk on the path, watch the butterflies floating gently from one tree to another. Hear the crunch of the leaves and pine needles as you enjoy your walk. The temperature is perfect. There is a gentle breeze. Touch a leaf and run your fingers along its surface. Feel the dew on the bottom and the sun-baked surface of the top. In the distance, you see a beautiful pond. The trees are reflected in the water to form a beautiful, serene picture.

As you walk along the edge of the pond, you notice a small wooden cabin tucked into the edge of the woods. As you get closer, you notice that the door is open and the sun is streaming through the open window, inviting you to enter. As you step into the cabin, you smell the wood that forms the wall. It has worn smooth with time. Inside the cabin, you see a table, and on the table is an object that is meant just for you. It has a message for you. You carefully lift the object and receive the message. You have been waiting for this message. You spend as much time with the object and message as you need to. Then you gently replace the object and slowly exit the cabin. The woods are even more beautiful than they were when you entered. The butterflies lead the way as you enjoy your leisurely walk back down the path and out of the woods. You don't have to feel bad about leaving the woods because you can return to this place at any time. Everything will be exactly as you left it, and you will feel peaceful and rested whenever you return.

Now, when you are ready, feel the chair you are sitting on. Feel your feet, your legs, your arms, and your head. Slowly open your eyes. Now take a deep breath. Does anyone want to share with us the object you found in the cabin and the message it had for you?

learners develop empathy for their customers. Customer service representatives often deal with senior citizens who have some difficulty with both their eyesight and hearing. To help the reps experience these problems, you can ask them to role-play a customer service interaction, both on the phone and face-to-face, while their glasses are smeared with Vaseline and their ears are stuffed with cotton. This helps your learners feel what the customer feels and is a powerful way of simulating the customers' experience. Some of your participants may not be too happy smearing Vaseline on their glasses, so you might want to supply them with some inexpensive imitation glasses they can use to practice this exercise.

Let Your Participants Practice, Practice, Practice

Unfortunately, many training sessions are designed to pack four hours' worth of learning into three or to squeeze three hours' worth of learning into two. When the training session is packed with wall-to-wall content, there are often only a few minutes left for practice. When this happens, the concepts, skills, and procedures that are being presented don't move from short-term memory to long-term memory. Instead, they evaporate shortly after participants leave the session. Participants need to master each step, put them all together, and practice until it is natural so they can apply them on the job. So be realistic in covering your learning objectives; minimize course content to cover only what you can demonstrate and practice during the training. If you have additional material, you can condense it into a user guide handout and give that information to your learners as supplemental reading. The objective is to ensure that you are providing your learners with a learning opportunity, so don't make the common mistake of cramming too much material into a short period of time. You will definitely overload your learners and risk having them walk away with too much that equals nothing!

Mastering Each Step

This is probably the least practiced and most critical step in ensuring that training skills are actually mastered in order to apply them at work. When sports skills, musical skills, acting, film making, and a host of other areas are taught, learners expect to master each step before practicing the whole event. Yet when skills are taught in the typical training session, particularly soft skills, learners are expected to absorb all they are taught and master these skills in their entirety before returning to the job. Right before the learners leave the room, they may even prepare an action plan and promise that they will apply what they have learned when they return to work. Unfortunately, there is nothing to apply because the skills have not been learned! It is virtually impossible to learn a skill by listening to a presentation, discussing, watching a demonstration, playing a game, and participating in one or two hurried role plays. Can you learn to play the guitar by going to concerts? Probably not.

The Skill-Building Procedure. To ensure that your participants learn the skills you want them to apply, they need to have the opportunity to practice *and master* each step before putting them all together. The template in Figure 7-14 shows the procedure to follow in helping participants practice, practice, practice.

Your participants can build their skills step-by-step only if they have a crystal-clear understanding of the skills they are supposed to build and the freedom to practice those skills until they are mastered.

A skill-building example begins on page 153.

Figure 7-14.   Template for ensuring practice, practice, practice.

Step	Explanation
1. **Explain the skill in words**	Take time to explain the skill or procedure in words so the learner knows what is expected and why.
2. **Demonstrate the whole skill**	Show the learner how to use the *entire* skill or how to conduct the procedure while you explain it again.
3. **Divide the skill into steps**	Divide the skill into logical steps that can be practiced separately.
4. **Demonstrate step 1**	Demonstrate step I and again explain it to the learner as you demonstrate.
5. **Drill step 1 to mastery**	Let the learner practice step 1 until it is mastered, providing a variety of examples to practice on. Provide encouragement and feedback.
6. **Demonstrate step 2**	Demonstrate step 2, linking it to step 1 and explaining it as you demonstrate.
7. **Drill step 2 to mastery**	Let the learner practice step 2 until it is mastered, providing enough examples, encouragement, and feedback.
8. **Demonstrate step 3**	Demonstrate step 3, linking it to step 2 and explaining it as you demonstrate.
9. **Drill step 3 to mastery**	Let the learner practice step 3 until it is mastered, providing encouragement and feedback.
10. **Continue demonstrating and mastering each step until the entire skill is learned**	Demonstrate each of the remaining steps and let the participant practice them to mastery.
11. **Practice the entire skill**	Instruct the learner to practice the entire skill, providing feedback as needed.
12. **Repeat practice with feedback**	Arrange an opportunity for the learner to practice the entire skill again, providing feedback as needed.
13. **Follow up**	Periodically check the learner's progress and be available for retraining as necessary.

A form based on this figure is provided as Figure B-43 in Appendix B.

Skill-Building Example

Course. Communications course for customer service representatives

Goal. Mastery of a basic communication technique that will help them communicate with coworkers, supervisors, and customers

Preparation. To facilitate the necessary practice, you need to prepare a sheet that contains at least ten communication situations similar to the one below.

Sample situation. You are working the front counter of a small pharmacy that is affiliated with a much larger pharmacy 15 minutes away. Mrs. Adams came from her doctor's office an hour ago (at 4:00 P.M.) and dropped off a prescription. Her doctor told her she *must* begin taking this medication by 6:00. It's now 5:00, and she is at your counter to pick up the medication. She reminds you that she must begin taking it by 6:00. When you look in the bin where her prescription should be, you can't find it. You talk with a pharmacist who tells you that it is in stock at your other location. It can either be sent here by 5:30 or delivered to Mrs Adams's home by 6:00.

1. **Explain the skill in words.** Now it's time to begin the communication technique I promised you. There are six steps to the process. We are going to practice each of these steps separately, but when you master them, you'll see that they become seamless and automatic.
   a. Start with a noncontroversial statement about your topic. It should be one that the person you are talking to will agree with.
   b. Explain what has occurred regarding your topic to create a reason for this conversation.
   c. Present your main message. It should be straightforward and easy to understand.
   d. Structure the rest of your conversation to support your message.
2. **Demonstrate the whole skill.** Describe the situation regarding Mrs. Adams's prescription. She is still standing at the counter, and you need to say something to her.
   a. *Start with a noncontroversial topic Mrs. Adams will agree with.* "I realize how important it is for you to begin taking your medication by 6:00, and we're going to make *sure* you have your medication before 6:00 so you can do that."
   b. *Explain what has occurred regarding your topic to create a reason for this conversation.* "But I'm sorry that it's not ready right now. We do not have that medication at this location right now, but we do have it at our main pharmacy on Grand Street."
   c. *Present your main message. It should be straightforward and easy to understand.* "Mrs. Adams, you have a choice: You can either wait here or return home and we will have your medication delivered. If you decide to wait here, we will have your medication sent right over and you'll have it by 5:30. If you return home, you'll have it by 5:45."
   d. *Structure the rest of your conversation to support the main mes-*

sage. Mrs. Adams elects to stay and wait for her prescription. "Because of this inconvenience, we'd like to buy you a cup of coffee at our coffee shop [hand her the money]. I'll be sure that the prescription is here for you when you return at 5:30." You follow up with the Grand Street pharmacy to tell them about her choice and ask about a way to track the arrival of the messenger.

3. ***Divide the skill into steps.*** This communication technique is already divided into four basic communication steps. List these steps on a flip chart and review each one.

4. ***Demonstrate Step 1.*** This is what you might say as you demonstrate step 1. Think of a noncontroversial statement that the person you are talking to will agree with. "In trying to find a noncontroversial statement Mrs. Adams will agree with, I tried to think of what is going on in her mind. The most important thing to her right now is that she must have her medication by 6:00. If I approached the counter and told her that her medication wasn't here, what would she say to me? [Pause for answers.] That's right, she would tell me that she must have the medication by 6:00. This is something we can agree on. She *must* hear me say that she will get it before 6:00 in order for her to accept anything else I have to tell her."

5. ***Drill Step 1 to Mastery.*** Ask the class to work in pairs. Distribute the situation sheets you have prepared. These situations will be used as drills. First, Participant A selects a situation for Participant B to work on. Then Participant B selects a situation for Participant A to work on. This process continues until each person has created at least five noncontroversial statements that are acceptable to the other member of the pair.

   At the conclusion of the exercise, ask for examples of these statements, using a flip chart to record the answers. Ask volunteers to explain their rationale for developing the statements they have used.

6. ***Demonstrate Step 2.*** This is what you might say as you demonstrate step 2, which is to explain what has occurred regarding your topic to create a reason for this conversation.

   "Now that you are sure Mrs. Adams knows you are on the same page as far as getting this prescription to her on time, she is probably ready to listen to your explanation of what has occurred.

   " 'But I'm sorry that it's not ready right now. We do not have that medication at this location right now, but we do have it at our main pharmacy on Grand Street.' "

7. ***Drill Step 2 to Mastery.*** Ask your participant pairs to work on developing statements for this step in the process. Each one will develop at least five statements. At the conclusion of the practice time, ask for volunteers and record some of these statements on the flip chart.

8. ***Demonstrate Step 3.*** This is what you might say as you demonstrate step 3, which is to present your main message. It should be straightforward and easy to understand. "Now you are able to offer Mrs. Adams a choice. Both options will result in a win-win situation for

her, but you have to be sensitive to the fact that she is being inconvenienced. The main message to her is that the medication is available and she is able to choose how she receives it.

" 'Mrs. Adams, you have a choice: You can either wait here or return home and we will have your medication delivered. If you decide to wait here, we will have your medication sent right over and you'll have it by 5:30. If you return home, you'll have it by 5:45.' "

9. ***Drill Step 3 to Mastery.*** Follow the procedure established in Steps 1 and 2.

10. ***Demonstrate Step 4.*** This is what you might say as you demonstrate step 4, which is to structure the rest of your conversation to support your message. "Because Mrs. Adams elects to stay and wait for her prescription, you will have more control over the outcome of the situation. First, you need to help Mrs. Adams deal with the wait time. Then you need to follow up to make sure the medication will arrive.

" 'Because of this inconvenience, we'd like to buy you a cup of coffee at our coffee shop [hand her the money]. I'll be sure that the prescription is here for you when you return at 5:30.' You follow up with the Grand Street pharmacy to tell them about her choice and ask about a way to track the arrival of the messenger."

11. ***Practice the entire skill.*** Have teams of two practice the entire skill using the situations they are already familiar with.

12. ***Repeat practice with feedback.*** Ask for volunteers to role-play an entire situation from the practice sheet in front of the group. Ask members of the group to provide feedback. Continue as long as time allows.

13. ***Follow up.*** Arrange to be available to members of the class for any necessary retraining as they apply this communication technique on the job.

Creating a Safe Environment for Practice

When it comes to learning a skill, mistakes are OK! They are valuable because they become lessons learned. Participants need to know that it is OK to make mistakes, as long as they learn from them and correct their actions in their next attempt to practice the skill. Your participants also need to be free to admit that they don't understand, ask for more help, and experiment with the skills or procedures until they feel comfortable enough with them to be able to perform them automatically.

Offering Training at the Right Time

An important and easily overcome reason for failed training efforts is the timing of the training. If too much time elapses between the training and the implementation of that training, the training becomes ineffective. Even when participants have mastered new skills, and are ready and eager to implement them, waiting time can be deadly. After a period of several weeks, a refresher course is needed to again prepare participants for implementation. On the other hand, when training is completed and skills are mastered just in time for them to be implemented, training is more likely to be effective.

Make It Real

When participants have mastered each of the skills step-by-step that they will be implementing, they need to practice in a realistic setting. Case problems, role playing, simulations, goal-based scenarios, theater-based learning, and videotapes all enable the participants to taste reality within the safe setting of a classroom.

Case Problems

Case problems can be based on either real events or simulated events. They present a situation in enough detail to enable the participant to step inside a problem, analyze it, and determine a solution. The Case of the Harried Horoscope Department (see Figures 7-15 and 7-16) was developed to help participants gain practical experience using a six-step problem-solving process. While obviously fiction, it provides a problem for participants to solve using the six-step process.

A valuable case problem provides information that is relevant to the learner. You want to research the case scenario to provide accurate information for the case problem so that it will be perceived as a real and relevant job scenario. You can have fun developing these scenarios, but you need to ensure that you are not having so much fun that the material is not relevant to your learners. You also need to know your audience. If your audience includes multiple levels from various departments, you want to give a generic example (like the Harried Horoscope Department), so that in one way or another all your learners will be able to relate to the material.

Another benefit of the case problem is that you are providing a real example in a safe environment. So, for example, in the problem-solving case problem you have given your learners, the methodology (the context) and the case problem provide the content to practice the methodology you have given your learners.

Figure 7-15.   The case of the harried horoscope department.

It's 5:00 Friday afternoon, and you are glad to see this week coming to an end—now you have time to reflect.

Three months ago you were hired as manager of the Horoscope Department at Services Unlimited. The department has been in existence for a little over a year.

(text continues on page 163)

You were brought in to replace the first manager, Rainbow Adams, when she left very suddenly to accept an exciting position with the Psychics of Pompeii. Adams left on August 1, and you moved into the position on August 10.

You report to the Vice President for Special Services, Phyllis Jillman. Because you have had extensive horoscope experience, Phyllis turned the department over to you with very little direction. Now you have begun to see some of the mounting problems within the department. Although you have asked Phyllis for her opinion on several issues, she has made it clear to you that she wants you to take charge and solve the problems in the department by yourself. So the future of the department is in your capable hands—for better or worse.

Mission of the Department

The mission of the Horoscope Department is to support Services Unlimited by providing horoscopes to all customers who request them. Your staff is responsible for securing accurate, timely horoscopes from the two company astrologers and supplying horoscopes on a weekly basis to the customers who request them.

It is your goal to provide the most accurate horoscopes possible, not written months in advance like the ones in the newspaper.

Orders and Methods of Delivery

Horoscope requests come into the department and horoscopes are delivered via several methods:

Requests In	Orders Out
Phone	Interoffice mail
Interoffice mail	Mail
Mail	Fax
Fax	E-Mail
E-Mail	
In person	

(continues)

Figure 7-15.   (Continued)

Policies and Procedures

1. Orders are valid for one week's worth of horoscopes from the day after the order is placed. The entire week's worth of horoscopes are delivered at one time.

Request Received	Days Covered in Order
Monday	Tuesday through Monday
Tuesday	Wednesday through Tuesday
Wednesday	Thursday through Wednesday
Thursday	Friday through Thursday
Friday	Monday through Friday

2. The deadline for the next-day service requests is 12:00 noon of the day before.
3. The department does not accept standing orders for horoscopes. A new order must be placed each week.
4. All calls come into the department through the direct horoscope line at 555-STAR. This is also the main line for the department. There are 8 hunt lines connected to the main number.
5. All STAR reporters have e-mail. The interoffice mail is collected and delivered twice a day, at 11:00 A.M. and 3:00 P.M. U.S. mail is delivered and picked up once a day.

Your Staff

There are six people on your team—five STAR reporters and one student assistant. The staff is shown in the Table of Organization (see Figure 7-16) and described below.

Wendy Goldberg	Experienced horoscope reporter recruited from the local horoscope hotline. Joined the staff when the department opened 2 years ago.
Ted Wong	Experienced horoscope reporter recruited from an upstate newspaper. Joined the staff when the department opened 2 years ago.
Alberto Ruiz	Services Unlimited employee for many years. Transferred to the department from Special Events about 1 year ago.
Don Thompson	Services Unlimited employee for many years. Transferred from Financial Services about 1 year ago.

Anjali Shama   Recent college graduate who joined the department just 6 months ago.

Kimberly O'Malley   Student assistant who works 25 hours a week.

Plant and Physical Layout

Because there is a shortage of office space, your STAR reporters do not all have offices in the same area. Wendy, Ted, and Alberto have offices at one end of the floor. Your office is with the rest of your staff at the other end of the floor.

One plain-paper fax machine is located between Wendy's and Ted's offices. According to Wendy, there has never been a formal training program in the department, and there is no procedures manual. STAR reporters learn by doing.

Signs of Trouble

Your volume of customer complaints has been increasing. Sometimes people even stop you in the hall to give you their complaints. You decide that it's time to focus on identifying some of the problems in your department. First, you decide to find out if these complaints are new or if they have always been there. So you ask Wendy for the complaint resolution file for the two years before you joined the department.

"Complaint file?" says Wendy with a puzzled look. "I don't think we have any kind of file. When Rainbow ran the department, she took care of complaints herself."

Not to be deterred, you ask Ted for the same information.

"We've always had a slew of complaints," says Ted. "But as far as I can see, we're doing the best we can."

"Is there any kind of record or file of the complaints?" you ask.

"Nope," he answers. "Rainbow always took care of it herself."

Sitting in the STAR Reporter's Seat

Because you have been unsuccessful in gathering any solid information about the complaints in the department, you decide to go right to the front lines—and answer the STAR phone for an hour yourself. Out of the 21 calls you answered, 5 bothered you.

Call One

"It's about time," sneers the caller. "I've been on hold for hours."

"I'm sorry," you answer. "What can I do for you?"

(continues)

Figure 7-15.   (Continued)

"I'm tired of waiting around for you people to do your jobs. I've talked with several people, and you have a real problem with your service. I would really appreciate it if I could get my horoscopes faxed to me. I've made this request over and over, and so far it hasn't happened. Instead, they come in the mail. But I'm on the road and I don't GET my mail every day. WHAT DOES IT TAKE to get my horoscopes faxed to me? Is your machine broken or something?"

Call Two

"Hello," says the next caller. "Is this the horoscope line?"

You introduce yourself and ask, "What can I do for you?"

"I'm tired of getting the runaround," says the caller. "Your department is all screwed up."

"I'm sorry you feel that way," you say. "Can you explain what you mean?"

"DEFINITELY! EVERY TIME I call in, your line is BUSY—and I mean EVERY TIME! Then when I finally get through, I am put on hold immediately. Then three different people proceed to ask me the same question—what's my sign. Why do three different people ask me the same question? Because they all answer the call! And to top it all off, I NEVER GET MY HOROSCOPE! What kind of department is this anyway?"

Call Three

"Is this the astrology line?" says the next caller.

You introduce yourself and ask him, "What can I help you with?"

"This is the fourth call I've made to your department in 15 minutes. What's wrong with you people? I keep getting cut off."

Call Four

"It's about time," says the caller. "I'm tired of being put on hold."

You introduce yourself and ask her, "What can I help you with?"

"I'm tired of getting the run-around. I've been on hold for 18 minutes and 36 seconds, and I'll probably get cut off when your staff picks up. I have an important decision to make, and I MUST have my horoscope NOW. PUT ME THROUGH TO THE ASTROLOGER IMMEDIATELY!"

Call Five

"EXCUSE ME!" says the caller. "This is Sky Saunders. Remember me—I'm one of the astrologers who makes your little department work. I GIVE YOU THE PREDICTIONS FOR THE WEEK—REMEMBER!"

"Hello, Sky," you say as you introduce yourself. "Having a bad day?"

"You could say that! We need to talk NOW," sneers Sky. "I can't keep working under these conditions—due to YOUR lousy telecommunications systems, I can't get MY job done. WE HAVE TO TALK. When can we meet?"

Collecting Complaints

You decide to ask your staff to monitor calls for a three-day period—Wednesday, Thursday, and Friday—to see if you were in the STAR reporter's seat on a lousy day or if there really are serious problems in the department.

At your meeting the following Monday morning, you learn the results of the three-day survey:

Average calls per day	1,250 calls
Average complaints per day	325 complaints
Percent of incoming calls with complaints	26%

Your Assignment

Use the six problem-solving steps to analyze the problems in the Horoscope Department and develop a solution.

Figure 7-16. Table of organization for Figure 7-15.

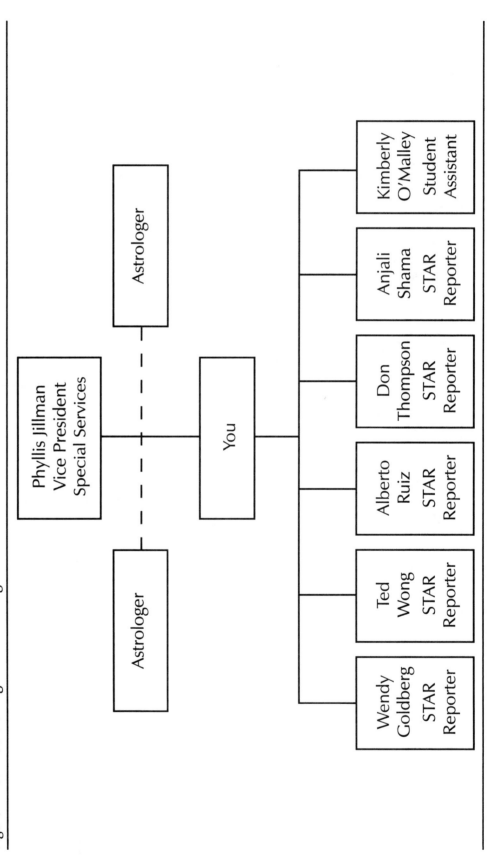

Role Playing

Another technique to use as you attempt to create realism in your classroom is role playing. An effective way to create a situation in which each participant is creatively involved in the role-playing process is to develop hidden-agenda role plays. Each participant receives a role and prepares for the discussion that is about to occur by reading the background information and rationale provided. Figure 7-17 shows a hidden-agenda role play for two participants that was used in a communications course. Figure 7-18 shows another hidden-agenda role play, also for a communications course (this one requires three participants.) These two exercises provide your participants with the opportunity to review their roles from the designed perspective. It also allows them to put themselves into a different perspective, and generates communication that can be viewed from opposing sides.

Role plays are shorter, less complicated ways of depicting a job-related function or situation. Less preparation is required in developing role plays versus case problems or simulations.

Simulations

One of the most reliable techniques for bringing realism into the training class is the simulation, which involves realistic input, working conditions,

Figure 7-17.   Sample hidden-agenda role play for two participants.

First Communicator (Pat)

It's 7:30 Tuesday morning, and Randy Johnson's dog has done it again! You put the garbage cans out half an hour ago. Now, when you're ready to leave for work, you find Sparkie spreading the contents of the cans all over the lawn. You've been on good terms with the Johnson family since you moved into the neighborhood 5 years ago, and you've been comfortable with the fact that Sparkie has been allowed to run freely like all the other neighborhood dogs. This didn't seem to be a problem before this week, but now that Sparkie is about 6 months old, he is growing quickly. Unfortunately, he has just learned how to charge your garbage cans hard enough to knock them over. When it happened last week, you picked up the trash and made a mental note to talk with your neighbor, but you never got around to it. Now you're really angry. This has to stop! You've just called Randy and asked for a minute of his time. Take the next 5 minutes to plan your discussion with Randy. Then have the actual conversation.

Second Communicator (Randy)

You and your two children have lived on Windsor Terrace for 7 years. Your neighbor Pat Dyce has lived down the block for 5 years. Pat has just called and asked to see you for a minute. Last year Pat collected for the National Cancer Society, and you suspect that he is collecting again. You locate your checkbook and wait for Pat to ring the doorbell.

These role-playing assignments are provided as Figures B-44 and B-45 in Appendix B.

Figure 7-18.   Sample hidden-agenda role play for three participants.

First Communicator (Mark)

It's 3:30 Thursday afternoon, and you're overloaded with work. You report to two directors, Ashley and Jennifer. They are equal in level and title. Yesterday they both gave you high-priority projects that are due tomorrow afternoon. You realize now that you will have to stay late tonight just to finish one of them by the deadline. You might be able to get some help from your coworker, Angela, but one of the directors will have to rearrange Angela's workload. If she does help you, there's about a 50 percent chance that you will be able to meet both deadlines. If you can only get one project done by tomorrow afternoon, you don't know which one it should be.

Because both directors have asked for a status report, you've decided to talk with both of them at the same time. Take the next 5 minutes to prepare what you will say. Then meet with them.

Second Communicator (Ashley)

Mark is one of the brightest and best workers in your office. You have given him an important report to prepare before the end of the day Friday. Because this report contains politically sensitive information, you want it on Friday so you can make any necessary changes before you present it at a meeting next Wednesday. When you ask Mark how the report is coming, he says he wants to talk with you for a moment in the conference room. Go there now and talk with him.

Third Communicator (Jennifer)

Mark is one of the brightest and best workers in your office. You have given him a complex project that absolutely *must* be ready tomorrow at 5:00. You are leaving for Washington at 9:30 Friday evening and are scheduled to make a presentation, using the information in the report, on Saturday morning. When you ask Mark how the report is coming, he says he wants to talk with you for a moment in the conference room. Go there now and talk with him.

These role-playing assignments are provided as Figures B-46, B-47, and B-48 in Appendix B.

interactions, standards, and goals. Many of the more realistic simulations are made better through creative software or online access. However, simulations do not have to be computerized to be realistic. Figure 7-19 provides a template for you to use in evaluating possible simulations for use in your training.

Unlike role plays, simulations tend to be longer and more complicated in development. They are more time-consuming to develop and execute, but they are an effective way of demonstrating a series of real job-related activities in a safe environment.

Goal-Based Scenarios

One very effective type of simulation is the goal-based scenario. It calls for presenting to teams of participants challenging tasks similar to those they are

Figure 7-19. Template for evaluating simulations.

Question	Yes	No
1. Are the educational objectives for each role or position clearly defined?	❐	❐
2. Do the objectives relate directly to the course objectives?	❐	❐
3. Do the objectives relate to the real world?	❐	❐
4. Are participants asked to make decisions that approximate real-life decisions?	❐	❐
5. Are participants given feedback on the results of their decisions?	❐	❐
6. Do the required activities correspond with the educational objectives of the simulation?	❐	❐
7. Do the required activities within the simulation correspond with the activities of the real world?	❐	❐
8. Are the directions easy to understand?	❐	❐
9. Is the amount of necessary preparation time realistic for your situation?	❐	❐
10. Will the time invested in the simulation yield more worthwhile learning than if the concepts involved were taught in another way?	❐	❐

A copy of this form is provided as Figure B-49 in Appendix B.

likely to encounter on the job. These tasks are embedded in a problem situation that is realistic, carefully created, and sequenced to teach specific skills and lessons. Throughout the training, coaches are available to reinforce the learners' understanding of what they are doing, provide feedback, and help participants relate the training to what they will experience on the job.

Theater-Based Learning

Traditionally, in-class attempts at realism are hampered by the fact that participants have no realistic customers, employees, clients, etc., against which to role-play. Participants who are involved in the beginning stages of learning the concepts at hand often lack the sophistication and confidence to inject realism into the role of the person on whom the learner is practicing newly developed skills. That's where theater-based learning comes into play. It is an approach that uses professional actors who can assume any role needed to facilitate realism in the training classroom. If you do not have a formal theater-based program, you may be able to work with a local college or community theater to recruit actors who are willing to help. This approach can be costly and time-consuming, but it definitely has its advantages.

Videotapes

Another way to help make it real is to videotape your participants as they are doing role plays and simulations. These tapes can be used for nonthreatening feedback and discussions. Often learners are their own best critics when they see themselves on tape. If a participant commits to improving a technique, he or she can derive a great deal of satisfaction out of watching a second tape in which this improvement is evident.

Note

1. Adapted with permission from Thomas O. Davenport, "Metaphorical Management," *Strategy & Leadership,* Volume 26, Number 3, July/August 1998.

8

Return and Apply

Send Me Back to Use Them on the Job

Hey, those exercises were pretty good! Now I've tried the new communication system and it works—at least here in the class-room. But what happens when I return to the job? I hope I get some help figuring out how to apply this system when I get back to work. I need it.

To effectively transition your participants from "Now I've tried it" to "I'll return and apply it" calls for planned follow-up activities as well as tools to assist your learners in achieving training results that are applied on the job. The process of getting learners ready to actually apply what they have learned is often overlooked because many trainers think their job resides within the training initiative itself. This could not be further from the truth. If you commit the time and effort to support your learners when they leave the classroom, as well as give them the tools to apply their training, you will dramatically increase the probability that they will be able to use what they have learned to achieve results on the job.

This chapter begins by introducing a return and apply model, which highlights the elements that are essential to achieving results when partici-pants return to work (see Figure 8-1). It shows you how to build a variety of easy-to-use support tools into your training that will help you send your participants back to their respective jobs ready to apply what they have learned. It also features follow-up techniques to use several weeks after the

Figure 8-1.   Guide to Chapter 8.

Learning Stage	*Secrets to Success*

RETURN & APPLY	**Send Me Back to Use Them on the Job**

1. Create a Method to Support Learning on the Job

- The return and apply model
- Training support
- On-the-job management support
- Participant commitment
- OD steering committee

2. Training Support Tools

- Quick reference cards
- Job aids
- Users' guides
- Cueing Signs
- Message products

3. On-the-Job Management Support Tools

- Training contract verification
- Supervisor action plan
- Supervisor feedback form
- Case scenario meetings
- Learner recognition

4. Participant Commitment and Support Tools

- Action plan
- Buddy system
- Case scenario journals
- Participant networking

5. Follow-Up Tools

- Newsletters
- Dear Trainer column
- Participant feedback form

training has concluded, as well as forms for summarizing and reporting the results of your training efforts.

Create a Method to Support Learning on the Job

If there is no plan in place when participants return to work, the learning that happened in the training room may never be applied or achieve business results. By adopting the return and apply model, you can ensure that there is a plan in place to apply learning and achieve results.

The Return and Apply Model

The return and apply model in Figure 8-2 highlights three elements that are critical to the success of your training efforts—continued training support, on-the-job management support, and participant commitment. It also shows a suggested element that can help to ensure that the application of training is supported on an organization-wide basis—the OD steering committee. Each of these elements is described below with a list of the tools you will find in this chapter to help you implement the return and apply model in your own organization.

Figure 8-2.   Return and apply model.

Training Support

If you give participants tools to help them remember and apply what they have learned and show them how to use these tools, they will be more likely to actually implement what they have learned. *Tools in this chapter* that will help your participants remember what they have learned and facilitate the implementation of their new skills include:

- Quick reference cards
- Job aids
- Users' guides
- Cueing signs
- Message products

On-the-Job Management Support

If you are following the LEARN process, you already engaged management support when you assessed the need for training (see Chapter 1) and entered into a training contract with each participant's supervisor (see Chapter 2) prior to the start of training. As training concludes, you will want to identify specifically what is required of these supervisors in order to help learners apply newly acquired skills on the job. Because it is unlikely that either the managers or the supervisors were part of the actual training, it is important for you to establish a partnership with them by keeping them informed and working closely with them to ensure that you can maintain the buy-in you established during assessment. You will also want to prepare a formal training summary report to keep the participants, supervisors, and managers informed of the training results. Tools in this chapter that will help you maintain on-the-job management support include:

- Training contract verification
- Supervisor action plan
- Supervisor feedback form
- Case scenario meetings
- Learner recognition

Participant Commitment

Just because your learners have been committed enough to actively participate in the training session does not necessarily mean they will try to implement what they have learned when they return to work. Some of them may even consider training to be a vacation from the job instead of a vital link to improved job performance. You can help to ensure the commitment of participants by making sure they *understand* and can *use* each of the training support tools you have provided by implementing the following participant commitment tools:

- Action plan
- Buddy system
- Case scenario journals
- Participant networking

OD Steering Committee

Although it is not an essential element in the return and apply process, an OD steering committee comprised of representatives from various departments and levels—representing a cross-section of the organization—will help not only the return and apply process but the entire LEARN effort. This group can guide and monitor OD initiatives. The committee understands the training and development needs throughout the organization and tracks the progress of initiatives designed to meet these needs. The committee sponsors, supports, and records the bottom-line results of OD initiatives from an organizational perspective.

Training Support Tools

Tools can help participants recall what they have learned and make it easy to complete a step-by-step process without having to ask for help. They can mean the difference between learning that is applied and learning that never happens. Training support mechanisms are tools that are made available to the learner to ease the return and apply process and to keep that process active until the learners "own" the skills themselves.

Quick Reference Cards

At the conclusion of your training, you can provide participants with wallet-size quick reference cards that summarize the steps they will need to follow to apply the learning. Participants sometimes keep these cards in their wallets for years—hopefully as a reminder of the course content and its application on the job. Figure 8-3 shows both sides of a sample quick reference card for a communication course.

Job Aids

Job aids are at-a-glance versions of the procedural steps you covered in your training. These aids should be no longer than two sides of an 8½ by 11 sheet of paper so they can be slipped into clear plastic sheet protectors and posted near the workstation where they will be used. They should be easy to see and read at a glance, with no extraneous words. Often job aids are all that are needed to be sure that employees are able to perform a process successfully with no intervention from a supervisor or coworker when they return to the job. You can provide participants with electronic versions of the job aids. They are readily available when needed, and can be updated easily.

You may even elect to use job aids as a *substitute* for actual training. If the employees you are working with are already familiar with a process, you might call a meeting and explain a variation in that process. This is a common occurrence when the flow of the computer screens needed to input customer information is changed. You can provide all staff members with a job aid that will provide them with an at-a-glance view of that part of the process that has changed.

Figure 8-4 shows the first few boxes of a job aid used as a follow-up

(text continues on page 174)

Figure 8-3.   Sample quick reference card.

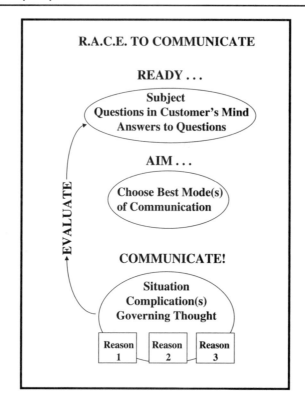

R.A.C.E. COMMUNICATION SYSTEM

1. READY—Plan your communication
        Why. Why communicate?
        Topic. Name your topic.
        Questions. List the questions your audience will have.
        Answers. Answer each question.

2. AIM—Decide how and when to communicate
        Analyze **emotions** of audience.
        Assess clarity and **tone** of message.
        Choose **channel(s)**.
        Select **time(s)**.

3. COMMUNICATE--Deliver the message
        Situation. Make a noncontroversial statement.
        Complication(s). The problem(s).
        Governing Thought. What you hope to accomplish.
        Message. Base your message on the Governing Thought.

4. EVALUATE—Assess your communication's effectiveness
        Seek Feedback. Questions answered? Move on.
        Try Again. If questions not answered.

Figure 8-4. Sample job aid.

Direct Admit Inpatient

COMMANDS AND HINTS

COMMANDS		HELPFUL HINTS
Unlock the Keyboard	Left [Ctrl]	Wait until Cursor is Red to type
Move Cursor Forward	[Tab] or →	To see more information on Complax, type "right"
Move Cursor Backwards	[Shift][Tab] or ←	
Go Back to DELAINA	[F3]	To fix an error, type "M" in SEL Column of Summary [Ctrl]
Go Back One Screen (in Summary Screens)	[F7]	To Logoff, press [F12], type "i" to inactivate open sessions, type "F" to logoff TXP menu
Exit New Notes Screen	[F3]	Press [F3] to return to TYX Screen
Exit AL	Type "End"	
Go to AL Notes (from RRICKI)	Type "AL"	To post Social Security #, type "SS#" [Ctrl]
Return from Master Screen	[F12]	To go to another screen from Master, type "C dire" [Ctrl].
Erase a line of type	[End]	On next screen type name of screen you want to go to [Ctrl]
Delete one character	[Delete]	To exit from a list of companies or insurances, type "end"

(Start) ▶

DELAINA Menu

Type "BXG" [Ctrl]

Complax Screen

Type Patient's Name [Ctrl]

Complax Name Inquiry

1. Find Patient's Name (Type "Right" for more info)
2. Type SEQ# [Ctrl]

Master Screen

1. Right Patient? (Check Address, SS#, Birthdate)
2. If Patient has Medicare, type # and change MCR ELIG from D to C
3. If Patient has Medicaid, type #
4. If Patient has Blue Cross, type # [Ctrl]

Coverage Verification Menu

Type "OMB" to verify Medicare [Ctrl]
Type "MEV" to verify Medicaid [Ctrl]
Type "BEV" to verify Blue Cross [Ctrl]
To continue without verifying coverage, type "BXG" [Ctrl]
(You have a second screen for MEV and BEV verifications)
Type "END" to exit

technique for entering patient information using a new computer system. Each box represents a full page from the users' guide. It also includes a section called PBAR Commands and Hints. PBAR is the patient billing system, and this section includes common instructions on how to navigate through this complex system, moving from one screen to another.

Users' Guides

Complex skills that are taught in training classes can easily become less clear as soon as the training ends. Carefully prepared users' guides will help to ensure that there is a resource available for learners who need to know each step in a complex process.

If you need to prepare a guide that involves the process of keyboarding information into screens, you can capture images to include in your guide using most standard software packages. In Microsoft Office software, follow these six steps:

1. View the first screen you are going to teach on your computer monitor.
2. Press the [Print Screen] key on your computer.
3. Open a new blank slide in PowerPoint or document in Word.
4. Select the "paste" option to make a slide of the screen you viewed on your monitor.
5. Use the drawing features to annotate the screen. You can create white text boxes with instructions, number the steps in your procedure, draw arrows, and more.
6. Print the slide or page for your users' guide.

Figure 8-5 shows one page from a computer users' start-up screen.

Cueing Signs

Because we all go on automatic pilot when we perform the steps in a process we are familiar with (see the section titled Psychomotor Learning in Chapter 2), it's often hard to break a habit when something changes. This is particularly true when the process involves entering information into a computer.

When the process for entering patient information at a large rehabilitation clinic changed, staff members found they had to alter their automatic-pilots mind-set and enter one additional piece of patient information—the patient record number—before pressing [Enter] and submitting the information to the computer system. If they forgot to enter this information, the entire transaction would have to be voided. To help the staff remember this new process, the cueing card in Figure 8-6 was printed on fluorescent paper and taped to each computer terminal the morning the system change went into effect. As an added incentive not to make mistakes, the staff was promised lunch at the end of the first week of using the changed system if fewer than 2 percent of their transactions had to be voided because they forgot to key in the patient number before pressing [Enter]. Surprisingly, the staff

Figure 8-5. Sample users' guide page.

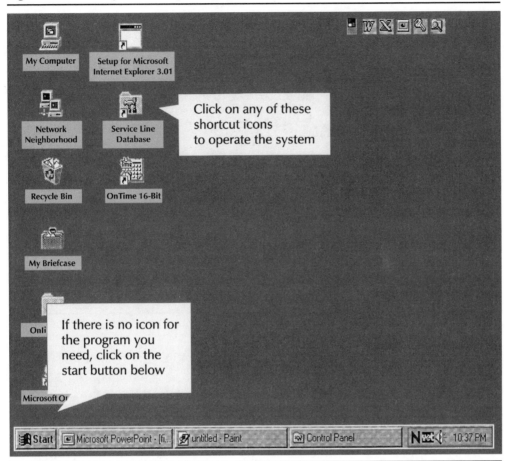

Figure 8-6.   Sample cueing sign.

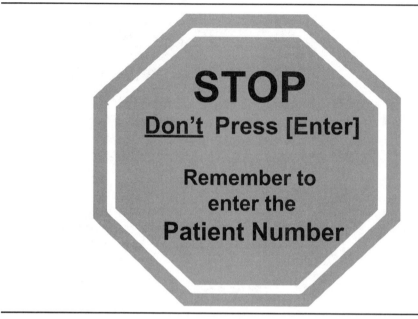

earned their party with room to spare. There wasn't a single error; all patient transactions included the patient record number.

Message Products

Another type of training support tool is a small gift with a message printed on it. This gift can be a ruler, bookmark, pen, paperweight, cup, glass, key, ball, ring, mirror, etc., with a message printed on it. One customer service course presented participants with stress balls that held the slogan, The Customer Comes First.

   One unique product that can contain several messages is a rotating message pen, which is a colorful plastic pen with a plastic viewing screen on it (see Figure 8-7). When the pen is clicked repeatedly, a series of six short messages can be viewed on the screen. The pen can be used to remind participants of specific techniques learned during the training. For example, your pen can list the six-step model for billing:

1. Identify billing code.
2. Verify customer name.

Figure 8-7.   Sample rotating message pen.

3. Verify customer address and telephone number.
4. Determine billing amount.
5. Record billing amount in AC section.
6. Forward billing information to BC rep.

On-the-Job Management Support Tools

Although it is the responsibility of the manager who requested the training to support the effort and the responsibility of the supervisor to serve as a mentor for the participant when he or she returns to work, it is *your* responsibility to facilitate this effort. The tools in this section will help you to facilitate on-the-job management support.

Training Contract Verification

This is the time to remind the manager and supervisor of the contract you prepared during the assessment process. Make a copy of the contract; add the dates of the actual training sessions, names of the participants who attended, and brief comments about the sessions (see Figure 8-8).

Supervisor Action Plan

The supervisor action plan shown in Figure 8-9 should link to the training contract. You can work collaboratively with the supervisor to complete a blank action plan template that indicates a time frame for the implementation of skills on the job. This plan can be particularly important if participants have acquired skills in the training session that they may not have an opportunity to implement in the course of their current positions. A skill that is not implemented can easily evaporate from the participant's skills. If training is to produce the results that are expected for the organization, the requester, the supervisor, and the participant must agree to implement them promptly.

Supervisor Feedback Form

This form will help you maintain an open line of communication with the supervisors who are helping participants return and apply the skills they have learned in the training session. It is human nature to give more attention to those matters for which we have accountability. You can establish this accountability by asking supervisors to use a feedback form similar to the one shown in Figure 8-10 to report the outcome of participants' attempts to implement skills learned during training on a regular basis. If the form identifies retraining or new training that is needed to help participants master skills, it will help you to succeed in maintaining a collaborative relationship and to achieve results. The results from the supervisor feedback form will be incorporated into the training summary report in Chapter 10.

Figure 8-8.   Sample completed training contract.

Training Contract	
Requesting Department: Refreshment Stand **Sponsoring Manager:** Dave Martin (requester) **Date:** March 1, 2000	**Telephone Number:** 555-555-3070 **Fax Number:** 555-555-5050 **E-Mail Address:** David.Martin@lcmall.com

Background Information
- Identify *why* training is needed (to improve customer service/reduce complaints)
- Identify relevant events that prompted the training request (demand from theater manager)

Training Goal
- Identify the *overall goal* for the training program (improved customer satisfaction; reduced complaints because currently receive complaints about 25% of employees)

Training Learning Objectives
- Identify the *learning objectives* to be achieved during the training (see Figure 2-8)

Key Performance Measures
- *How will you know training has been successful?*
  (customer service complaints will decrease gradually over the next two months; by that time, there will be complaints on no more than 5% of employees)
- What changes are required?
  (increased skill in register handling, customer service, and pricing)
- Complete the Measuring Business Results form.

Target Audience(s)
- Identify the *participants/audiences* you are targeting for the training (100% of refreshment stand staff)

Requirements
- List any requirements the requester would be responsible for performing prior to and during training
  (provide a list of staff members, their positions, and their hours)

Budget/Cost *(only applicable for internal chargebacks)*
- Identify any cost/budget requirements (N/A)

Manager Follow-Up Activities
- Identify follow-up activities the requesting sponsor (management) needs to perform (weekly meetings/rewards for improved performance)

Approval	
I agree with the terms of this contract. *David Martin* Requester Approval	I agree with the terms of this contract. *Patricia Dunn* Training Department Approval

Dates of Actual Training: 3/15/00 – 3/30/00

Participants: *See attached list of participants*

Comments: *23 of the 25 staff members successfully mastered all required skills. Additional cash register training is scheduled for Angela Perey and Bill Smithson.*

Figure 8-9. Sample supervisor action plan.

Training course: Active Listening	**Date delivered:** October 15, 1999
Department request: Employee Relations	**Participants:** 21 Employee Relations Reps
Activity:	**Date Due:**
1. I will conduct weekly case scenario meetings on . . .	**Frequency:** Every Thursday **Start date:** 12/3 **Time:** 2 P.M.
2. I will hold the following recognition programs: Employee-of-the-month award	**Frequency:** monthly **Start date:** November
3. Other activities I will perform include: Lunch with the director Give tickets to a Broadway show	**Frequency:** 6 times a year **Start date:** December

Activity Description

1. Supervisor holds weekly case scenario meetings to illustrate positive and negative customer experiences.

2. Supervisor identifies recognition programs that support the learned behaviors from the training.

3. Supervisor identifies additional training support activities that will be conducted after the training was completed.

Case Scenario Meetings

If learners are asked to document instances in which they were able to use newly learned skills and instances when they attempted to use them but were not able to, the supervisor providing mentoring support for the training can conduct weekly or biweekly case scenario meetings. At these meetings, employees can share their experiences and determine why the skills learned in training were or were not transferable to job-related situations. The manager should end a session by emphasizing the lessons learned and action steps to be taken before the next meeting. Figure 8-11 shows an agenda for a case scenario meeting; Figure 8-12 shows a sample case scenario meeting.

Figure 8-10. Supervisor feedback form (application and results assessment).

How is your employee doing? Please take a minute to rate your employee's ability to apply the objectives learned during the training on the job, using the scale below.

Learning Objectives	Applied on the Job	Frequency*	Level of Success**
Learning objective A	❑ Yes ❑ No	0 1 2 3	1 2 3 4 5
Learning objective B	❑ Yes ❑ No	0 1 2 3	1 2 3 4 5
Learning objective C	❑ Yes ❑ No	0 1 2 3	1 2 3 4 5

*Frequency scale: 0 (never), 1 (once), 2 (often), 3 (all the time).
**Success scale: Not successful, 1—very successful, 5.

As a result of the training, my employee has been able to . . .

What can the training department do to assist you in supporting your employee in applying the skills on the job?

❑ Call me; I need help supporting my employee's application.
❑ I'm doing just fine.
❑ The support tools are not working because _____

_____

_____

❑ Give me more information on _____

❑ I would suggest *(please describe)* _____

Overall, I believe my employee's performance has improved:

Not at all				Significantly
1	2	3	4	5

A copy of this form is provided as Figure B-50 in Appendix B.

Figure 8-11. Case scenario meeting agenda.

5 minutes	Welcome, purpose of meeting.
3 minutes	Ask for volunteers to share their attempts to return and apply.
15 minutes	Ask each volunteer to indicate what skill(s) he or she attempted to apply and what happened.
30 minutes	Discuss the outcome of the scenario, using the case scenario template (see Figure 8-12) to record what went well, what did not go well, lessons learned, and action steps.
3 minutes	Schedule the next meeting and remind participants to collect more case scenario examples.

Learner Recognition

There is no doubt that employees are motivated when they are recognized; so often they are not recognized for a job well done. To reinforce and reward improved performance that occurred as a result of training, your role as a trainer is to identify ways this can be done in the classroom and on the job. Although you can only control rewards in the classroom, you can influence both informal and formal rewards outside the classroom. Figure 8-13 includes some strategies for informal and formal recognition, awards, and celebrations that managers and supervisors can use to recognize employees who have returned to the job, applied what they learned, and achieved results. You may also want to refer to two books by Blanchard Nelson that are helpful in motivating and recognizing employees; *1001 Ways to Reward Employees* (1994) and *1001 Ways to Energize Employees* (1997).

The follow-up form in Figure 8-14 enables you to assess the effectiveness of the case scenario meetings and learner recognition programs. The output from this form will tell you if the support programs are being used and how effective they have been. This form will provide data for future course modifications and validation of the program. You should collect the data and summarize the findings to be incorporated as post-training documentation.

Participant Commitment and Support Tools

The participant commitment and support tools listed in this section will help your participants formalize their plans to apply the skills they acquired when they return to work.

Action Plan

An action plan will help participants make definitive plans to implement the skills they acquire in your training sessions. A typical plan includes both what the participant plans to do and when. See Figure 8-15 for an example.

Figure 8-12.   Sample case scenario meeting.

Volunteer: Mary Morris

Course: How to Handle Difficult Customers

Scenario: Last week I had a really difficult customer. She received a bill with a charge of $2,500 she did not make. This lady was so upset that she began screaming at me the minute I answered the phone. The tips I learned in the course for how to handle difficult customers really helped. [Mary continues to describe the situation.]

Group Discussion:

The group discusses outcomes, what went well, what did not go well, lessons learned, and action steps.

Outcome	What Went Well (Pros)	What Did Not Go Well (Cons)	Lessons Learned
▪ Charge was eliminated from the bill. ▪ Customer was satisfied with the result.	▪ I didn't react negatively to the irate customer. ▪ I apoligized for the customer's problem. ▪ I resolved the customer's problem.	▪ I did not have a current list of the billing representatives and their phone numbers. ▪ The customer was impatient when I was searching for the right person to talk with.	▪ It helps to remain calm, emphathize with the customer, and offer a sincere apology. ▪ It's important to have the current list of contact names and numbers on hand.

Action Steps: Get a current list of the billing representatives and their phone numbers. Post it in a place near the phone.

A copy of this form is provided as Figure B-51 in Appendix B.

Buddy System

The buddy system is an effective approach to help support participants. To set up a buddy system, you can either randomly pair up your participants so they will have a contact buddy at the end of the training or allow them to select their own buddies. The system enables your learners to have a support person to share experiences and successes with after they leave the training program. The table in Figure 8-16 highlights some advantages and challenges associated with implementing both types of buddy systems.

Once you have paired up your participants in the buddy system, have them review the sample buddy contract in Figure 8-17 and add to or change

Figure 8-13. Strategies for learner recognition.

Recognition Strategy	*Component*
1. Informal recognition	■ Verbally recognize improved performance to the individuals and their colleagues.
	■ Host a surprise luncheon.
	■ Invite employees to participate on a new team.
	■ Ask employees what special assignment/project they want to work on.
	■ Provide comp time off.
2. Formal recognition	■ Identify the performance achievement in the company newsletter.
	■ Post the achievement on a Web site.
	■ Conduct small-group and large-group performance-based recognition meetings.
	■ Invite senior management to deliver the recognition messages (note, phone call, e-mail, or in person).
3. Awards	■ Distribute formal plaques, certificates, or trophies.
	■ Provide gift certificates.
	■ Provide prizes, trips, theater tickets, sporting event tickets, etc.
4. Celebrations	■ Let your employees decide how they want to celebrate performance achievements and give them a budget to do so.

A checklist based on this form is provided as Figure B-52 in Appendix B.

the contract as they see fit. Emphasize that the contract is used as a guide only to get them started. The intention is to provide the structure for a contract that both can agree on, outlining some types of activities they'll want to conduct, but let them take control and own the relationship from there.

Case Scenario Journals

We previously discussed the value of case scenarios as one of the management support tools. To prepare participants for their case scenario meetings, you can encourage them to keep a journal detailing their experiences as they attempt to implement new skills. Each week they might document:

■ What went well
■ What did not go well
■ Lessons learned
■ Action steps for next week

Figure 8-14.   Support activities follow-up form.

Manager/Supervisor Support Activities Follow-Up Plan		
Question	*Yes*	*No*
1. Have you conducted weekly case scenario meetings?	❏	❏
2. If yes, how effective were the meetings?		
3. If you answered yes to question 1, did you use the weekly case scenario planning form?	❏	❏
4. Have you conducted any recognition programs?	❏	❏
5. If yes, how effective do you believe these programs were in reinforcing performance?		
6. Have you conducted any support activities other than the weekly case scenario meetings or recognition programs?	❏	❏
7. If yes, describe the activity you conducted.		

8. On a scale of 1 to 5, how would you rate the overall
    effectiveness of weekly case scenario meetings? (please circle)

Not Effective   *Very Effective*

1   2   3   4   5

9. On a scale of 1 to 5, how would you rate the overall effectiveness of recognition
    programs? (please circle)

Not Effective   *Very Effective*

1   2   3   4   5

10. What would you suggest to improve performance support programs?

A copy of this form is provided as Figure B-53 in Appendix B.

Figure 8-15.   Sample participant action plan.

Training course: _____	Date delivered: _____
Department request: _____	Participants: _____ _____ _____ _____ _____
Activity:	**Date Due:**
1. Prioritize my work each week so I can make sure to devote enough time to the highest-priority projects (Learning Objective A).	Frequency (daily, weekly, etc.): ____ Start date: _____
2. Make a to-do list each afternoon before I leave work so I can start right in the next morning (Learning Objective B).	Frequency (daily, weekly, etc.): ____ Start date: _____
3. Set aside 20 minutes each day and file all accumulated papers that are sitting on my desk (Learning Objective C).	Frequency (daily, weekly, etc.): ____ Start date: _____

A copy of this form is provided as Figure B-54 in Appendix B.

By sharing both successes and challenges with each other, the participants are able to learn from their own experiences and the experiences of others.

Participant Networking

If you provide each participant with the name, department, phone number, fax number, and e-mail address of all the group members from a workshop or training group (see Figure 8-18), you will help facilitate open communication among the group after the course has ended.

Follow-Up Tools

If you forget about participants, they may forget what they have learned. But if you stay in contact with participants through the tools suggested in this

Figure 8-16. Buddy system table.

Buddy Selection Type	Advantages	Challenges
Trainer selects buddies	<ul><li>This is an objective viewpoint and approach.</li><li>Participants are exposed to new and different perspectives.</li><li>Pairs can be formed using selection criteria (department, level, etc.).</li></ul>	<ul><li>Participants may not have an affinity with their buddy.</li><li>Participants may feel forced into the pair.</li></ul>
Participants select their own buddies	<ul><li>Participants have control.</li></ul>	<ul><li>Participants may gravitate toward friends who have similar perspectives and who are not as objective.</li><li>Participants familiar with each other may not complete follow-up activities due to other priorities.</li></ul>

section, they will have a better chance of remembering and applying the learning and you will have a better chance of receiving valid feedback to track the results of the learning.

Newsletters

As technical training is being implemented, feedback often alerts trainers to additional information that the learners need (e.g., system upgrades). Instead of issuing a memo that includes the updates learners need to know, you can produce a newsletter with short news items that will catch the attention of the learners. If you print each issue of a training update newsletter on a different bright-colored paper, your learners may even look forward to receiving these additional pieces of information.

The newsletter in Figure 8-19 was one of a series of five that were used to update participants who had learned and implemented a new patient billing system.

Dear Trainer Column

A feature you can add to a series of newsletters is a Dear Trainer column. If you receive the same question from several different participants when they

Figure 8-17.   Sample buddy contract.

Training course: Effective Problem Solving	**Training course date:** December 15, 1999

Participant A's name: Kristine Smitt **Telephone #:** 212-555-7803 **E-mail address:** ksmitt@obly.com **Fax #:** 212-555-1234	**Participant B's name:** Daniel Ramirez **Telephone #:** 212-555-7991 **E-mail address:** dramirez@obly. com **Fax #:** 212-555-8768

Guiding Principles

- We will share our experiences and lessons learned.
- We will offer to help each other whenever necessary.
  Others . . .

Next Steps

Over the next month, we will:
- Meet at least 2 times to discuss our progress to date.
- Brainstorm alternative solutions to the problems we have encountered.
- Implement alternative solutions identified.

Signature   Signature

Kristine Smitt   *Daniel Ramirez*

Participant A: Kristine Smitt   **Participant B:** Daniel Ramirez

A copy of this form is provided as Figure B-55 in Appendix B.

---

are in the process of applying what you have taught them, you can encourage one of them to write you a Dear Trainer note for use in the newsletter. When you print the question and your answer to it, you can provide the same answer to all the participants who read your newsletters.

Participant Feedback Form

When participants have been back at work for approximately three weeks, you can contact them directly or ask their managers to assist in having them complete an additional evaluation form detailing their success in implementing what they learned and achieving results. See Figure 8-20 for a sample evaluation form of this type. The results of this evaluation form can be used in the training summary report described in Chapter 10.

Figure 8-18.   Sample contact list.

Course Name: Effective Problem Solving			**Facilitator:** Helene Saunders
Date Attended: January 20, 2000			

Participant Name	Department	Telephone/ Fax	E-Mail Address
1. Lisa Barnable	Editing	87803 73464	lbarn@xyz.com
2. Melissa Betancourt	Legal	86330 77868	Mbeta@xyz.com
3. Robert Bradley	Finance	86685 76656	rbrad@xyz.com
4. Donna Dean	Human Resources	85524 72232	ddean@xyz.com
5. Yvette Lam	Administration	89194 74966	yvlam@xyz.com
6. Delroy Owen	Engineering	86463 75213	dowen@xyz.com
7. Vanessa L. Sanders	Communications	89573 79433	vsand@xyz.com
8. Jonathan Rankin	Business Planning	83546 70522	jrank@xyz.com
9. Laura Williams	Human Resources	87991 78136	lwill@xyz.com
10. Don Whitney	Technology	87377 71314	dwhit@xyz.com

A form based on this figure is provided as Figure B-56 in Appendix B.

Figure 8-19.   Sample newsletter.

S.T.E.A.M. INTERFACE ENGINE
NEWS FOR TODAY
Thursday, June 26

YOU'RE DOING A GREAT JOB
Congratulations again. Everyone seems to be gaining more confidence on the Insurance Questionnaire. And as your confidence grows, your speed will increase.

ADDITIONAL LOGON HINTS
Your password must be changed every 30 days. One good way to remember your password is to use two favorite words or names and alternate back and forth between them. Your password ***does not*** have to be a specific number of characters. Names of children, spouses, friends, etc., are easier to remember than other words. Remember, if you DO get locked out, call the help desk at 5535 to have your password reset.

EXPANDED INSURANCE TABLE
As you may have noticed, the insurance table has been ***updated*** since we went live on Saturday with more choices for Blue Cross New Jersey, Blue Cross Out of State, Cigna, and Healthsource.

BLUE CROSS "OTHER"
If you can't figure out which Blue Cross code to pick from the table (and can't find the plan/product line on the Managed Care Company ID Matrix Randy distributed), you can use ***Blue Cross Indemnity*** as the "Blue Cross Other" choice.

LIVING WITH S-L-O-W RESPONSE TIME WRITING BACK TO HIS
The clinical areas have priority when it comes to writing information to HIS, so if there's high activity in HIS, the write-back time will be slow. If you're waiting to print a patient's record that includes the insurances, you can look at the record in Patient Retrieval. The insurance information won't print out until you can find it in the HIS Patient Retrieval.

STATUS CODES FOR YOUR "DETECTIVE WORK"
We've attached a list of status codes you can use in detecting the problems that cause errors on your summary screens and correcting them. These codes are the ones the system is looking for in the status code area. Sometimes an error will disappear if you enter the right code.

MEDICAID PENDING FOR NEWBORNS/WORKERS' COMP FOR INPATIENTS
More binder pages—hot off the press. Here are pages that will show you how to do Medicaid Pending for newborns and Workers' Comp for Inpatients. If you still haven't received your binder, call Andy (5011).

Keep up the good work! More news later.

Note: You can also post newsletters online.

Figure 8-20.   Sample participant feedback form (application and results assessment).

How are you doing? Please take a minute to tell us whether you have been able to use the skills you learned in the Time Management course on the job. If you prepared an action plan, let us know how you did on each of the activities in your plan.

Action Plan Activities	Applied on the Job	Frequency*	Level of Success**
1. *Prioritize my work each week so I can make sure to devote enough time to the highest-priority projects.* (Learning Objective A)	❏ Yes ❏ No	0 1 2 3	1 2 3 4 5
2. *Make a to-do list each afternoon before I leave work so I can start right in the next morning.* (Learning Objective B)	❏ Yes ❏ No	0 1 2 3	1 2 3 4 5
3. *Set aside 20 minutes each day and file all accumulated papers that are sitting on my desk.* (Learning Objective C)	❏ Yes ❏ No	0 1 2 3	1 2 3 4 5

*Frequency scale: 0 (never), 1 (once), 2 (often), 3 (all the time).
**Success scale: Not successful, 1—very successful, 5.

As a result of the training, I have been able to keep the clutter on my desk to a minimum.

What can the training department do to assist you in supporting your skill application on the job?

❏ I'm doing just fine.
❏ Call me; I need help applying the skills on the job.
❏ The skills I learned are not working because _____
❏ Call my manager; I think he/she needs help in supporting me.
❏ Give me more information on <u>time management</u>.
❏ I would suggest (*please describe*) _____

Overall, I would say that this course helped my performance on the job improve:

Not at all				Greatly
1	2	3	4	5

A copy of this form is provided as Figure B-57 in Appendix B.

9

Natural Transition

Now They're Mine

> *The communication system I learned in that course makes so much sense that I use it with my friends outside of work. I even taught a few of them how to use it. I wonder if we'll ever hear from the instructor. I think she said she was going to follow up to see if the course made a difference on the job. You know what—this course did!*

The ultimate results of successful training extend beyond application on the job and business results—they actually make a difference in the permanent skill set of the learner. This type of transition is easy to see in a technical training situation in which the learner has just mastered a technical program related to a software application such as Excel, PowerPoint, or Access. However, this transition is harder to achieve and harder to see when the skill is in a softer behavior-based area such as communication, supervision, leadership, or team building.

This chapter begins by helping you understand the natural transition process. Then the chapter completes the discussion of formal training evaluation that began in Chapter 4 with reaction and knowledge. The remaining two levels of evaluation—application and business results (ROI)—are presented in this chapter (see Figure 9-1).

Figure 9-1.   Guide to Chapter 9.

Learning Stage	*Secrets to Success*
NATURAL TRANSITION LEARN	***Now They're Mine*** **1. The Natural Transition Process** ▪ The four stages of natural transition ▪ How the process works **2. Completing the Evaluation Process** **3. Application** ▪ Participant feedback form ▪ Supervisor feedback form ▪ Coworker feedback form ▪ Customer feedback form **4. Business Results (ROI)** ▪ Reviewing the goal ▪ Measuring progress toward the goal ▪ Tabulating the results ▪ Presenting the results

The Natural Transition Process

When training has been truly successful, a natural transition takes place. As a successful trainer, you will be fortunate enough to guide some of your learners to become masters. They will own the skill you are teaching so well they may even outdo their master (you). This is your ultimate reward. If knowledge is power, you can celebrate the fact that you have shared this power. It is now being duplicated throughout the organization.

Think back to how you acquired the skills you now own—the ones you are passing on to your learners. You probably acquired these skills from others; you subsequently molded them to meet your own needs as a learner. As you internalized this knowledge, you continued to share your skills with other official or nonofficial trainees. Now both you and those you have shared the learning with own it.

The Four Stages of Natural Transition

One interesting theory describes the process of natural transition and growth.[1] It suggests that learners follow a four-step process (see Figure 9-2);

1. Gather information, knowledge, and skills from other people and sources.

Figure 9-2.   Four stages of natural transition.

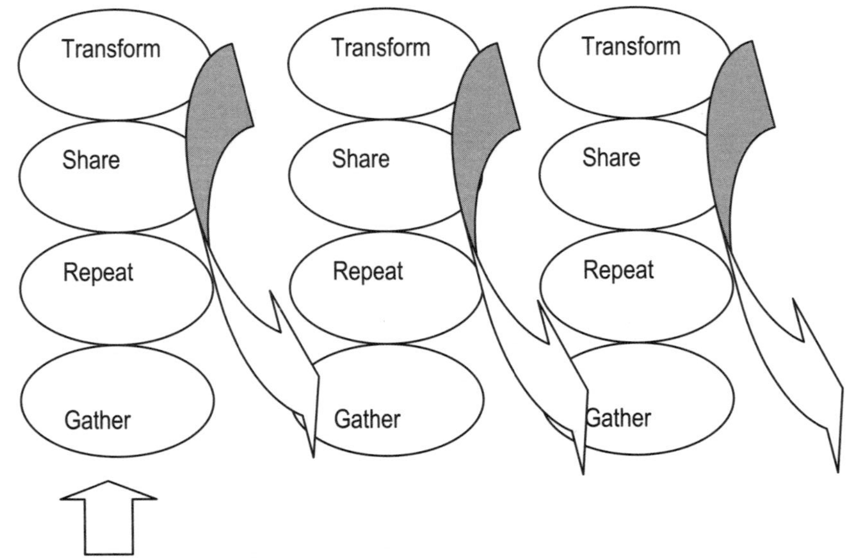

2. Repeat the information, knowledge, and skills in your own context.
3. Share what you've learned with other people.
4. Transform to a new level of understanding.

How the Process Works

To demonstrate this process, let's assume that you work in a large organization and have just been promoted to your first supervisory position.

Gather *information, knowledge, and skills from other people and sources.* You are happy about your promotion to supervisor and eager to learn how to do your new job well. You sign up for supervisory courses, talk with other experienced supervisors, and even read a few articles you found in a leadership magazine pertaining to the topic. When you're not actually working with your staff, you feel like a sponge, soaking up supervision tips from anywhere you can find them. You even engage in conversations with your family members and friends who have supervisory experience to gather additional thoughts, knowledge, and tips.

Repeat the information, knowledge, and skills in your own context. You try out many of the skills you have learned with your own staff, particularly the skills you like and feel comfortable using: When something works well, you use it as is without changing a thing; when something almost works, you adjust it until it is right for you; when something doesn't work at all, you forget about it and develop something else. Over a period of time, you find that you are creating your own style of leadership and supervision based on a combination of information, knowledge, and skills you have gathered from other people.

Share *what you've learned with other people.* When you begin realizing some success as a supervisor, you feel more confident about speaking up at all types of meetings. As you share your ideas and hear what other supervisors are doing, you really enjoy being able to help your colleagues learn some of the techniques that are working well for you. When new supervisors are hired, you are asked to go to lunch with them to share your supervision tips, and you really enjoy it. Most importantly, you feel as if your knowledge and expertise are valued.

Transform *to a new level of understanding.* After you have been a supervisor for a number of years, you are considered somewhat of an authority on practical techniques that work well for you. Often you are asked to create a formal training course for new supervisors. As time progresses, you write an article about the supervision approach you have been using. Now you've reached a point in your career when you have outgrown your role as a supervisor, and it's time for a new challenge. You are ready to become a department manager with new and broader responsibilities, which include goal setting, planning, budgeting, and forecasting. As soon as you take the job as department manager, there has been a transformation. You begin the gathering phase all over again (e.g., you sign up for courses on goal setting, planning, budgeting, and forecasting, and you talk with other managers, who share their ideas with you). The cycle continues.

Completing the Evaluation Process

Although a natural transition is the ultimate outcome of truly successful learning experiences, it is difficult to measure and evaluate. In most training situations, we have to rely on the traditional evaluation techniques that were introduced in Chapter 4; to complete the discussion of evaluation, we will spend the rest of this chapter looking at the two remaining evaluation levels—application and business results (see Figure 9-3).

In essence, you want the answers to two basic questions: (1) Was the training applied (application)? (2) Did it accomplish the goals that were established before the training began (business results)?

Application

As a trainer, you want to ensure that your training has led to learning that has been applied on the job. You also want to determine how often these newly acquired skills have been applied and what happened when they were used. Were they attempted once and forgotten, or have learners and their supervisors been making an honest attempt to integrate these new skills into everyday business practices? Have coworkers and customers noticed the intended results of this learning? There are a variety of tools that can help you make this determination:

- Participant feedback form
- Supervisor feedback form
- Coworker feedback form
- Customer feedback form

A more formalized approach to obtaining feedback from these sources is referred to as a 360-degree evaluation. The term 360-degree refers to the number of degrees in a circle. The 360-degree feedback process calls for soliciting feedback from the complete circle of people who work with the person being evaluated. The 360-degree feedback surveys are carefully crafted instruments that are customized for the organization and the situation. This book provides suggested tools for obtaining feedback but does not provide a complete 360-degree model.

Participant Feedback Form

When participants leave the classroom, most of them have every intention of applying what they have just learned when they return to the job. But, as you well know, life sometimes interferes with our plans and changes them. Your first step in measuring application is to follow up on the specific tools that were used in the course you are evaluating. If the participants created action plans, have they followed up on the actions specified in those plans? What

Figure 9-3.   The evaluation process.

Evaluation Element	When?	Why?	How?
Reaction—Chapter 4	During the course of immediately following it, before participants leave the classroom	To measure the effectiveness of the program content and delivery	Use the course evaluation form
Knowledge—Chapter 4	At the end of the training program, before participants leave	To measure the degree to which the training program was effective in delivering the message	Check pre- and posttest results and use the course evaluation form
Application—Chapter 9	1 to 60 days after the training occurred	To measure the degree to which the training has been transferred and utilized on the job	Review participant action plans/buddy system; survey customers, colleagues, and managers the training participant interacts with
Business Results (ROI)—Chapter 9	Three months after the training occurred	To measure the impact of the training on business goals and objectives	Measure performance progress against business goals and objectives

were the results? If they committed to participate in the buddy sytem, have they made contact with their buddies and scheduled meetings? What have they accomplished?

Figure 9-4 provides you with a template you can use to collect information from participants. It helps you capture three types of information for each action plan activity: (1) whether it was applied on the job, (2) how often it was applied, and (3) how successful it was. The more specific you can be in identifying the activities participants should be applying on the job, the better the quality of information you will receive. The form also includes a section that enables you to capture specific support needs that the participant might have at this time. You can collect information by mail or e-mail, in face-to-face interviews, or over the phone. Use the method that will be most effective for you.

This feedback form is a valuable source of information as you prepare future courses. When you invite participants to request additional support in applying what they have learned, you need to be prepared to provide that support. If several participants are experiencing the same challenges, you may want to plan some informal brown-bag lunch sessions so your participants can share their experiences with you and each other as well as brainstorm solutions.

Supervisor Feedback Form

Polling the participant's supervisor will help you determine the supervisor's version of what happened when the skills were applied on the job. Figure 9-5 provides you with a template that mirrors the one you are using for participants. It includes a section that invites the supervisor to request support from you. Just as with the participant feedback process, you can collect information by mail or e-mail, in face-to-face interviews, or over the phone. Use the method that will be most effective for you.

When you receive participant feedback forms and match them with the supervisor feedback forms, you will begin to gain a more complete picture of the success of the application process.

Coworker Feedback Form

The learner's coworkers are another group that should be targeted for feedback. Because they work with the learner, they can witness changes in performance. Since this group is often overlooked, we recommend that you solicit their feedback to gain another perspective of the learner's performance. The feedback form can be a simple one that poses no threat to the participant; you may even want the participant to distribute the survey. Be aware that participants may distribute the survey to their friends, so you can encourage them to do it anonymously. See Figure 9-6 for a suggested format.

(text continues on page 200)

Figure 9-4.   Participant feedback form (application and results assessment).

How are you doing? Please take a minute to tell us whether you have been able to use the skills you learned in _____ on the job. If you prepared an action plan, let us know how you did on each of the activities in your plan.

Action Plan Activities	Applied on the Job	Frequency*	Level of Success**
1. \<Insert action item for Learning Objective A\>	❏ Yes ❏ No	0 1 2 3	1 2 3 4 5
2. \<Insert action item for Learning Objective B\>	❏ Yes ❏ No	0 1 2 3	1 2 3 4 5
3. \<Insert action item for Learning Objective C\>	❏ Yes ❏ No	0 1 2 3	1 2 3 4 5

*Frequency scale: 0 (never), 1 (once), 2 (often), 3 (all the time).
**Success scale: Not successful, 1—very successful, 5.

As a result of the training, I have been able to . . .

What can the training department do to assist you in supporting your skill application on the job?

    ❏ I'm doing just fine.
    ❏ Call me; I need help applying the skills on the job.
    ❏ The skills I learned are not working because _____
    ❏ Call my manager; I think he/she needs help in supporting me.
    ❏ Give me more information on _____
    ❏ I would suggest *(please describe)* _____

Overall, I would say that this course helped my performance on the job improve:

Not at all				Greatly
1	2	3	4	5

A copy of this form is provided as Figure B-57 in Appendix B.

Figure 9-5.   Supervisor feedback form (application and results assessment).

How is your employee doing? Please take a minute to rate your employee's ability to apply the objectives learned during the training on the job, using the scale below.

Learning Objectives	Applied on the Job	Frequency*				Level of Success**				
<Insert Learning Objective A>	❏ Yes ❏ No	0	1	2	3	1	2	3	4	5
<Insert Learning Objective B>	❏ Yes ❏ No	0	1	2	3	1	2	3	4	5
<Insert Learning Objective C>	❏ Yes ❏ No	0	1	2	3	1	2	3	4	5

*Frequency scale: 0 (never), 1 (once), 2 (often), 3 (all the time).
**Success scale: Not successful, 1—very successful, 5.

As a result of the training, my employee has been able to . . .

What can the training department do to assist you in supporting your employee in applying the skills on the job?

  ❏ Call me; I need help supporting my employee's application.
  ❏ I'm doing just fine.
  ❏ The support tools are not working because _____

  _____

  ❏ Give me more information on _____
  ❏ I would suggest *(please describe)* _____

Overall, I believe my employee's performance has improved:

Not at all				Significantly
1	2	3	4	5

Since the training, I would rate employee impact on the job as:

No impact				Significant impact
1	2	3	4	5

Since the training, I believe my employee's performance has had an impact on the department by . . .

A copy of this form is provided as Figure B-58 in Appendix B.

Figure 9-6.   Coworker feedback form.

Dear <insert name of coworker>:

As you may know, I recently attended a course on <insert training course date> and have been trying to improve my <insert training topic> skills.

As a follow-up requirement from that course, I am asking several coworkers for their feedback. Please take a minute to complete this form and send it to <insert return address information>.

<Insert participant's signature>

Learning Objectives	Applied on the Job	Frequency*	Level of Success**
Learning Objective A	☐ Yes ☐ No	0 1 2 3	1 2 3 4 5
Learning Objective B	☐ Yes ☐ No	0 1 2 3	1 2 3 4 5
Learning Objective C	☐ Yes ☐ No	0 1 2 3	1 2 3 4 5

*Frequency scale: 0 (never), 1 (once), 2 (often), 3 (all the time).
**Success scale: Not successful, 1—very successful, 5.

Since this training, I notice that you:

A copy of this form is provided as Figure B-59 in Appendix B.

Customer Feedback Form

Ultimately the learner's performance impacts and affects customers. Whether these customers are internal or external, gaining their opinion enables you to measure the ultimate results of the training. Often this perspective is not included in the measuring performance, but nothing ties more directly to it. Figure 9-7 provides a template for obtaining customer feedback.

Targeting participants, supervisors, coworkers, and customers will enable you to assess the application of learning on the job, but it will not tell you whether bottom-line results were achieved. The next section, Business Results, will describe how you can measure business results.

Business Results (ROI)

Business results are sometimes referred to as a return on investment (ROI). To report business results for the training, you will need to refer back to the training contract example (see Figure 2-2). This contract, which was created

Figure 9-7.   Customer feedback form.

Dear <insert customer name>:

<Insert department name> Department is committed to providing the best service for our customers. Please take a moment to fill out this survey and tell us how we're doing.

<Insert department manager's signature>

	Performance *(Not satisfied = 1 to very satisfied = 5)*
1. On-time service	1 2 3 4 5

Comments:

2. Problem solving	1 2 3 4 5

Comments:

3. Courtesy	1 2 3 4 5

Comments:

A copy of this form is provided as Figure B-60 in Appendix B.

---

before the training effort began, specifies the goal, learning objectives, and key performance measures.

Let's take a look at the results that were called for in the contract for the refreshment stand example from Chapter 2.

Reviewing the Goal

When the training contract was created, Dave Martin, the refreshment stand manager of a large theater, had just received a call from the theater manager. Because the theater had been receiving complaints about one out of every four refreshment stand employees, the theater manager, Gianna Grecco, had an important message for Dave; "Your staff needs training! Now!"

When Dave requested help from the training manager, he had a definite goal in mind; "I want every one of our counter people to be efficient and more courteous to customers." When the trainer asked Dave how he would be able to tell that the training was successful, Dave made it simple; "I'll stop getting complaints, or at least they'll decrease significantly." Dave's entire staff has received training. Now it's time to answer the bottom-line question: Did it work?

Measuring Progress Toward the Goal

Your role as a trainer is to guide Dave through the measurement and reporting process of the training. In some cases, the Training Department may agree to be responsible for capturing the measurement and tracking process, but in this case Dave wants to be directly involved.

How can you begin to measure business results for the refreshment stand? Figure 9-8 provides you with a sample business results form. The top of the form repeats the overall goal: Increase customer satisfaction levels, and decrease customer complaints. It also tells you what to measure to track progress toward this goal and how to do it. The bottom portion of the form does the same for the three learning objectives related to the training goal.

Now that you have reviewed this form with Dave, how do you begin to capture the results for the refreshment stand? Column three of Figure 9-8 is your guide for capturing the data required to measure progress:

- Dave will give you the number of customer complaints for the months of December and January.
- You will work with Dave's assistant, Mary, to select standard time frames to measure the number of sales conducted without assistance. (Mary selected Fridays from 2 P.M. to 4 P.M. and Mondays from 8 P.M. to 10 P.M.
- Dave will save all voided transaction slips and capture the weekly number of voids.
- Mary regularly inventories soft drink and popcorn containers and tracks sales against usage.

Tabulating the Results

Dave and Mary captured all the relevant data for both the overall training goal and the three learning objectives for the months of December and January. Dave also figured out the percent of improvement (see Figure 9-9).

Presenting the Results

Dave has asked for your help in getting ready to share the results with the theater manager, Gianna Grecco. As a trainer, you know that pictures are worth a thousand words, so you guide Dave as he transforms the data into a graphic display of the results. Your goal, as you shared with Dave, is to keep the display simple and easy to understand. You also want to be able to support the findings. Figures 9-10 to 9-13 show the bar charts Dave has selected

(text continues on page 207)

Figure 9-8. Sample business results form.

Measuring Business Results

Overall Training Goal: Increase customer satisfaction levels and decrease customer complaints.

Part 1

Overall Training Goal	What to Measure	How to Measure
Customer satisfaction	Number of complaints	Measure the number of customer complaints received for two months

Part 2

Learning Objective	Measurement	How to Measure
1. Ring orders without assistance	Number of sales conducted without assistance	During a 2-hour time frame, measure the number of sales conducted without assistance
2. Ring orders correctly	Number of voided transactions	Every other Monday, measure the number of voided transactions for the day
3. Charge correct amount	Number of inventory variances	Measure the number of inventory (soft drink and popcorn) containers against sales

A form based on this figure is provided as Figure B-61 in Appendix B.

Figure 9-9. Data captured.

Overall Training Goal: Increase customer satisfaction levels and decrease customer complaints.

Part 1

Overall Training Goal	What to Measure	December 1999	January 2000	+/-	% Improvement
Customer satisfaction	Number of complaints	40	19	−21	−52.5%

Part 2

Learning Objective	Measurement	December 1999	January 2000	+/-	% Improvement
1. Ring orders without assistance	Number of sales conducted without assistance (during 2-hour time frame)	31	55	+24	43.6%
2. Ring orders correctly	Number of voided transactions	40	23	−17	−42.5%
3. Charge correct amount	Number of inventory variances	253	178	−75	−29.7%

A form based on this figure is provided as Figure B-62 in Appendix B.

Figure 9-10.   Number of customer complaints.

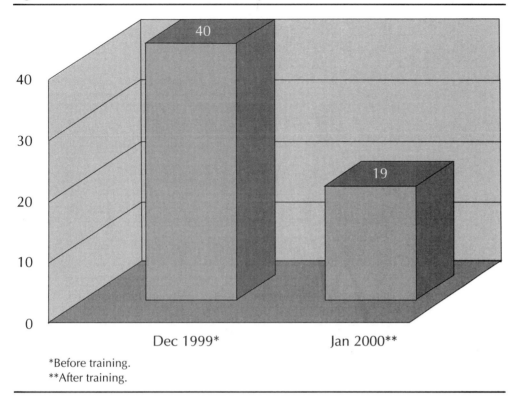

*Before training.
**After training.

Figure 9-11.   Orders rung without assistance.

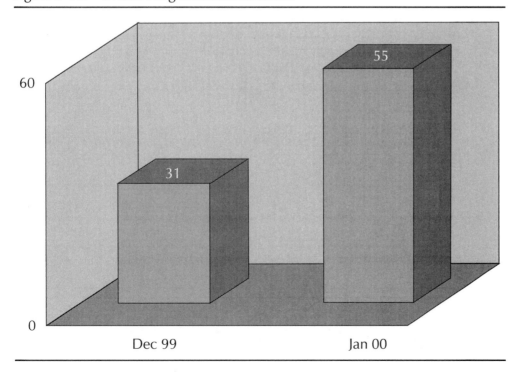

Figure 9-12.   Number of voids (month).

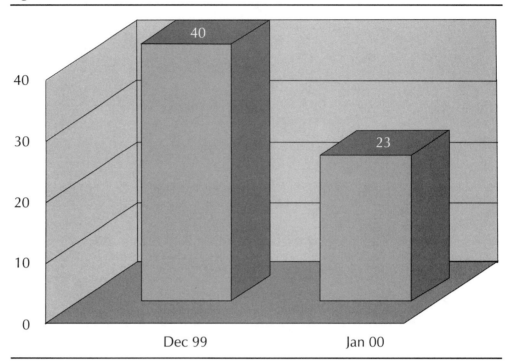

Figure 9-13.   Inventory variances.

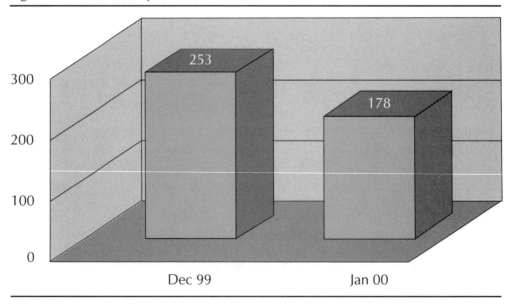

for his presentation to Gianna Grecco. While this process can be extensive, time-consuming, and costly, it can also be simple, efficient, and cost-effective (as depicted in the theater example).

If Gianna Grecco wants to know the details of the training effort and plans to share them with her regional managers, you can provide her with the training summary report discussed and outlined in Chapter 10.

Note

1. Based on the Metamatrix Map developed and presented by August Jaccaci at the 1995 conference of the Creative Leadership Association in Buffalo, New York.

10

Putting It All Together

Review/Training Summary Report

Now that we have reviewed all the components of the LEARN acronym and the training cycle, it's time to put the puzzle back together and look at the entire process of *Turning Training Into Learning* (see Figure 10-1). As we fit the pieces of the puzzle back together, we will take a few minutes to discuss some problems that can inadvertently occur in the training process and offer some don't-let-this-happen-to-you advice.

Common Pitfalls and Safety Net Solutions: Don't Let This Happen to You

As trainers, educators, presenters, or facilitators, there are many embarrassing moments we all wish we could forget. These are the moments that can

Figure 10-1. Guide to Chapter 10.

Learning Stage	Secrets to Success
PUTTING IT ALL TOGETHER 	**Review/Training Summary Report** 1. **Common Pitfalls and Safety Net Solutions: Don't Let This Happen to You** 2. **Tips to Remember** 3. **Putting It All Together** 4. **Training Summary Report** ▪ Overview ▪ Distribution of the training summary report

sidetrack or even derail a training program. The good news is, it's OK to make mistakes as long as you learn from them. To help you avoid some of the mistakes we have made or witnessed others make, we offer the following list of twenty pitfalls, along with solutions for avoiding or correcting them.

Pitfall	*Safety Net Solution*
Annoying Your Participants With Behaviors/Phrases	■ *Recognize annoying behaviors.* Think of some habits that may annoy you—clicking noises, repetitious movements, adjusting clothing, etc. Some people use phrases like "Mm-hmm, mm-hmm," "Right," "That's what I'm saying," or "Do you hear what I'm saying?" to fill silent pauses in a conversation. Annoying habits and phrases can actually keep participants from learning by creating enough distractions to keep messages from transferring to long-term memory. If participants are occupied with the process of counting the number of times the facilitator taps a pencil on the table, jingles pocket change, paces back and forth, or repeats an irritating phrase, they aren't concentrating on the content. ■ *Become aware of your own annoying behaviors.* It may be a good idea to videotape yourself to see if you have any annoying or redundant habits. After viewing the videotape, you may be shocked to see that you possess some of the annoying habits that interfere with participant learning. This will give you an opportunity to work on eliminating them. ■ *Make a conscious effort to change.* Sometimes just being conscious of a habit can help you to stop it, or at least to minimize the occurrence of it. If you commit to trying to stop an annoying behavior, you will be much more aware of it every time you slip up and use it.
Delaying Implementation	■ *Schedule training to coincide with implementation.* When too much time elapses between the completion of a training course and the implementation on the job of the skills learned, participants have a hard time remembering what they have learned. This makes application much less likely. Make sure your training, especially if it is tied to larger organizational initiatives, will be given no more than three weeks before implementation.

Pitfall	Safety Net Solution
Having Difficult Participants Who Distract From Learning	Participants can be difficult for a number of reasons. Often it's just because they enjoy hearing the sound of their own voices. Sometimes it's because they are required to attend training and simply don't want to be there. There are a variety of techniques for dealing with these people.

- *Body language.* If a participant is engaging in side conversation that is disrupting the group, minimize the distance between you and that person. This implies that you are facing the challenge and taking control of the situation without making a verbal statement to the disruptive participant.

- *Humor.* To stop a side conversation, smile as you ask the participant to share his or her conversation with the group.

- *Direct request.* If a participant is talking at length and monopolizing the class, you can ask if these questions can be discussed after class or at the break.

- *Break.* Occasionally participants will try your patience to the point of breaking it. If you feel your patience beginning to evaporate, you may call a break during which you can deal with any participant who is causing a disruption.

- *Exit opportunity.* If this person truly does not want to be in the class, it might be an appropriate time for this person to return to his or her job. Give the difficult or dominant participant the opportunity to walk out with his or her dignity intact.

Cramming In Too Much Content

- *Allow time for practice.* When you plan the course, be sure to allow time for practice, practice, practice. It is much more effective for participants to learn a few concepts and skills well rather than sit through a course that is packed full of content that is simply covered.

- *Watch for overload cues.* As soon as participants become overloaded, they shut down and stop receiving. This is particularly true with difficult material. Always ask yourself, How difficult will this material be for the learner? Present difficult concepts in bite-size pieces. Overload cues include side conversations, blank stares, letter writing, and preoccupation with anything other than the course and topic at hand.

Pitfall	Safety Net Solution
	■ *Stay in pace with your learners.* Check with participants frequently to be sure you are in pace with them and that they are still receiving.
Failing to listen	■ *Communicate.* Learning involves communication, which is a two-way activity. You can't expect participants to listen to and understand you if you don't listen to them and understand what's on their minds.
	■ *Ask for input and listen to it.* As trainers, educators, or facilitators, we do not always listen effectively to the messages our participants are sending us.
	■ *Watch for body language.* Effective listening involves not only the words we say but how our words are said and what body language accompanies our words. Stay alert for nonverbal messages from your participants.
Inflexibility	■ *Know when to change a charted course.* You need to be constantly receptive to your audience's needs and reactions. Know when they're not getting it and be flexible enough to switch to plan B to accommodate your learners.
Not Testing Your Training	■ *Field-test your course.* When you field-test, or pilot, your course prior to a large-scale rollout, you are able to preview the reactions to your materials prior to implementation and to know where you are likely to need to change course and go to plan B.
Lecturing Only	■ *Switch delivery approaches.* Change your delivery approach several times each session to appeal to all your learners, who have different learning styles. Using various multimedia techniques allows you to charge up your delivery and helps your learners to remain engaged. Be creative in your design approach; use videos, exercises, activities, rotating flip charts, small-group discussions, role plays, and creative overheads to drive your messages home.
Using Humor Inappropriately	■ *Collect cartoons and appropriate anecdotes.* Humor can add variety to your training program and help you to demonstrate specific learning points. Humor can put your learners at ease and help them to remember.

Pitfall	Safety Net Solution
	■ *Test your humor with colleagues.* Humor should not be offensive or off-color. Before you use a story, you might want to stage a trial run with a few of your colleagues to gauge their reactions. You need to make sure that your humor adds to the learning effort instead of distracting from it.
Getting off Track	■ *Use the "parking lot" approach.* Keeping your learning group on track may be a challenge at times. If you notice that the group is diverging or going off on tangents, use the "parking lot" approach. Write the words "Parking Lot" at the top of a flip chart. Explain that this "parking lot" is reserved for questions and comments that may not fit into this particular session. When a participant veers from the topic at hand, walk to the flip chart and write a line about the question or topic. Then you can interrupt the participant and indicate that the idea is in the "parking lot." At a break or immediately following the session, address the items in the "parking lot" and suggest where participants can get more information or answers.
Omitting Introductions	■ *Remember to set the tone.* If you are eager to get started, you might forget to introduce yourself and to have your participants introduce themselves. Introductions set the tone for the day, give your participants the opportunity to express their goals for the session, and provide them with an opportunity to meet other participants.
Using Ineffective Visuals	Everyone has their own style when it comes to developing overheads. Even with variable styles, there are some tips to remember:
	■ *Font.* Make sure the font is large enough so the overheads can be read.
	■ *Frames.* Put overheads in frame protectors so they don't slide off the machine (if you are not conducting the presentation electronically).
	■ *Pacing.* Don't race through the overheads; make sure your learners have time to read them.
	■ *Hard-copy handouts.* Provide hard copies of important overheads in the course material.
Using Toxic Markers	■ *Don't pollute the air.* Some flip-chart or whiteboard markers can be toxic—the fumes emit a foul

Pitfall	Safety Net Solution
	odor. Use flavor-scented markers that are nontoxic. These markers give off an appealing smell.
Rushing	■ *Pace your presentation activities.* As you are planning the delivery of the course, estimate the time allocated to each section of the course; make sure you are not rushing through the material. If you rush, chances are that your learners will feel rushed too, and they may mentally check out because they are not effectively grasping the material.
Reinventing the Wheel	■ *Explore creative resources.* Don't reinvent the wheel. There are cost-effective methods for getting sound and viable content pertaining to specific training topics off the Internet. You can get content-specific materials related to personal-style inventories, management style, communication, and other topics.
Overrehearsing Your Course	■ *Maintain spontaneity.* Being prepared is a good thing, and practicing the delivery of material is important. But sounding like a robot is not good. If your delivery sounds canned, it will not be effective because it missed the reality factor. Be sure that you know the material you are presenting well enough to explain it clearly, but try not to memorize the exact words you will say.
Having Poor Personal Hygiene	Have you ever worked for someone who had a personal hygiene problem? When you present in front of a group, you need to ensure that your appearance is neat and clean. Here are some tips to remember: ■ Be diligent with your hygiene. ■ Make sure your clothes are not too tight (so you can avoid embarrassing moments). ■ Be certain your clothes (especially knit fabrics) are clean. ■ Make sure your appearance fits with your organization's culture. ■ Avoid garlic-filled lunches before afternoon classes!
Being a Victim of Trainer's Ego	■ *Check your ego at the door.* You definitely want to be perceived as knowledgeable, not egotistical. A

Pitfall	Safety Net Solution
	rule of thumb is: Check your ego at the door instead of bringing it into the classroom. If you are perceived as approachable, knowledgeable, open, and honest with your participants, you will have a more successful learning environment. ■ *Be honest with your participants.* Don't try to fake it. If you don't have the answer to something that is asked, be honest with your participants. Ask other participants in the class to share their solutions. Offer to find the answer, or tell them where they can find it.
Having a Wrong Course Length	■ *Avoid courses that last an entire day.* If you can possibly avoid them, do not schedule courses that last an entire day. Learners have a tendency to be "filled up" after about three to four hours of training. If you continue beyond that point, you may lessen the effectiveness of the session. Instead, schedule two half-days, either on consecutive days or several days apart.
Using the Wrong Type of Room	As you choose your training environment, remember that logistics are critical. Your training environment supports all the learning you are delivering. Make sure that: ■ The room accommodates your learning needs (size, flexibility of setup). ■ The room is comfortable to be in for the duration of the course. ■ You orient your participants to the nearest rest rooms, phones, water fountains, etc.

Tips to Remember

We have discussed several pitfalls you may encounter during the training process, but we also want to identify some tips to remember so your training efforts will not fail!

Tips to Remember	In order to be prepared:
Be Prepared With Backup Materials/Plans	■ Have a set of overheads in case the LCD projector fails. ■ Have an extra lightbulb for the overhead. ■ Have extra pencils, pens, markers, flip-chart paper, tape, etc.

Tips to Remember	In order to be prepared:
	▪ Test the electrical connections before class.
	▪ Have the phone numbers of catering, audiovisual, maintenance, etc., available at all times.
	▪ Locate the nearest phone.
Have Fun!	▪ *Enjoy the training.* Realize the privilege you have of sharing the learning experience with your participants. Chances are, if you're having fun, your learners are, too.
Manage Course Time Effectively	▪ *Stick to the time limits of the course.* You can set participant expectations and encourage timely return from breaks if you start on time, stay on time, and end on time.
Respect Personal Space	▪ *Arrange the room to show respect for personal space.* Studies show that a distance of three feet is what we all perceive to be personal space. Decreasing this three-foot boundary signifies that you are invading someone's personal space. Be aware of this space limit when you arrange participant chairs and set up your facilitator area. Although you don't want to deny training/learning to participants, it is better to put some of your participants on a waiting list and have two sessions rather than to have one session in which personal space is invaded because there simply is not enough room.
Respect Your Participants' Experience and Knowledge	▪ *We can't emphasize enough how important it is to value the experiences of your adult learners and build on them.* There is nothing worse than making adult learners feel inadequate or disrespected. If someone raises a controversial point, do not immediately dismiss it. Ask why the learner feels that way, and ask your other participants their opinions. Ensure that you honor all opinions, even if you do not agree with some of them.
Tell Stories	▪ *Collect stories.* There is nothing more effective and interesting to all learners than a good story. You can personalize a story or describe a past participant's experience to drive your learning objectives home.
	▪ *Become a good storyteller.* Practice your ability to slow down and take your time telling stories. Be-

Tips to Remember	In order to be prepared:
	cause participants will probably remember your stories long after they have forgotten the content of the course, make sure that you link important learning concepts to each story.
Use Performance Measures	■ *Link your training to performance and evaluation.* Too often training efforts that do not include performance measures are seen as a vacation from work. To avoid this pitfall, ensure that your learning links to agreed-upon goals and performance measures. Make concrete plans to evaluate the application of learning on the job.

Putting It All Together

Chapters 5 through 9 covered the entire LEARN process. We illustrated all the components you need to know in order to successfully turn your training into real learning. Once you have achieved this level of learning with your participants, you will want to communicate the results. The next section presents the training summary report, which you can compile for all interested audiences once you have completed the entire LEARN process.

Training Summary Report

Overview

The purpose of this report is to consolidate training results and share the findings with your learners, your supervisors, the OD steering committee, and the Training Department to measure training impact. Sharing the training summary report allows you to close the learning loop and, subsequently, fulfill the initial training request. Demonstrating increased learning/knowledge levels is a powerful way of helping the manager who requested the training, the participants, the OD committee, and your own manager to understand both the value of the training effort and the results. The report provides both quantitative and qualitative measurements.

The training summary report has seven major sections. The outline shown in Figure 10-2 lists the components of the report. Now that we've reviewed the structure, let's look at each section in more detail.

Background Information. You may begin the background section by stating the title of the training, when it was conducted, and how long it lasted. Then you should continue by describing who was at the training and why they were at the training, as well as any other additional relevant information. The example below uses a hypothetical Problem Solving training course:

Figure 10-2. Training summary report outline.

Component	Description
1. **Background information**	The background section should describe: ■ What training was delivered (learning objectives) ■ When the training was delivered and how long it lasted ■ Who the training was delivered to ■ Why the training was delivered (purpose) ■ Who requested and approved the training
2. **Training results**	Any quantitative and qualitative scores received from pre- and postevaluations as well as from surveys distributed during and after the training
3. **Business results**	Key measurements determined in the training contract
4. **Key findings**	The trainer's overall assessment of the training, based on the results
5. **Recommendations**	The trainer's recommendations for the sponsoring department
6. **Proposed next steps**	Actions the trainer identifies that need to continue and that support learning
7. **Appendixes**	Actual course pre- and posttest results (for example, if you run a department of 120 employees through training but use 6 separate sessions, you might want to include the results from each session to support the overall averages depicted in the summary report)

The *Problem Solving* training course was conducted from February 17, 2000 through February 19, 2000. There was a *total of 45 participants* from the *Human Resources Department* in the training with 15 participants at each session. The training sessions were *three hours in length*. The *sponsor of the training, Lewis Lindell, Vice President of Human Resources*, approved the course methodology plan and signed the training contract.

Training Results. A preassessment and postevaluation were distributed to participants prior to and after the Problem Solving training course to measure proficiency levels of specified learning objectives. Additionally, the participant feedback form was distributed thirty days after the training to measure the application and transferral to the job. Then, forty-five days after the training, we collected data to complete the business results form.

Figure 10-3 presents the quantitative results from the course's participants. Figure 10-4 presents the qualitative feedback from the course's participants.

Additional Feedback

- Participants indicated that they would like the course to be repeated in order to reinforce what they have learned.
- Participants also stated that they want additional job-related case scenarios in order to practice the skills they've developed.

Figure 10-5 presents the quantitative results from the participants' supervisors. Figure 10-6 presents the qualitative feedback from the participants' supervisors. Figure 10-7 presents the quantitative results from the participants' coworkers. Figure 10-8 presents the qualitative feedback from the participants' coworkers. Figure 10-9 presents the quantitative results from the customers who were surveyed. Figure 10-10 presents the qualitative feedback from the customers who were surveyed.

Figure 10-3. Participant summary chart—quantitative results.

Learning Objectives	Percentage of Employees Applying Skills on the Job	Frequency*	Level of Success**
Learning Objective A	80	2.0	3.0
Learning Objective B	72	1.0	2.8
Learning Objective C	88	3.0	4.2

*Frequency scale: 0 (never), 1 (once), 2 (often), 3 (all the time).
**Success scale: Not successful, 1—very successful, 5.

A copy of this figure is provided as Figure B-63 in Appendix B.

Figure 10-4. Participant summary chart—qualitative feedback.

As a result of the training, I have been able to:
- Solve problems more quickly.
- Identify a problem.
- Identify root causes of a problem.
- Involve my colleagues in developing possible solutions.
- Develop new solutions effectively.

Figure 10-5.   Supervisory summary chart—quantitative results.

Learning Objectives	Percentage of Employees I've Witnessed Applying Skills on the Job	Frequency*	Level of Success**
Learning Objective A	75	2.0	3.3
Learning Objective B	78	2.2	2.7
Learning Objective C	90	2.8	4.2

*Frequency scale: 0 (never), 1 (once), 2 (often), 3 (all the time).
**Success scale: Not successful, 1—very successful, 5.

Figure 10-6.   Supervisory summary chart—qualitative feedback.

As a result of the training, my employees:
- Are solving their problems more independently.
- Seem to have more confidence in developing solutions.
- Are working together better than before the training.

Figure 10-7.   Coworker summary chart—quantitative results.

Sample Statements (Related to Learning Objectives)	Percentage of Employees Applying Skills on the Job	Frequency*	Level of Success**
▪ I have noticed that my colleague is using a more structured approach to problem solving.	79	1.5	3.7
▪ My colleague includes me in decisions that I need to be included in.	73	2.4	4.8

*Frequency scale: 0 (never), 1 (once), 2 (often), 3 (all the time).
**Success scale: Not successful, 1—very successful, 5.

Figure 10-8.   Coworker summary chart—qualitative feedback.

I would also add:

- Joe is making a difference in the department—he seems much more excited about his job.
- I didn't get a chance to attend the training because I was on vacation. Will another session be held so I can attend?

Figure 10-9.   Customer satisfaction summary chart—quantitative results.

Sample Statements (Related to Learning Objectives)	Level of Satisfaction
- I would rate my overall satisfaction with the service of 'X' department/employee as . . .	3.7
- My questions were answered thoroughly.	4.0
- My problem was resolved completely.	4.3

*Frequency scale: 0 (never), 1 (once), 2 (often), 3 (all the time).
**Satisfaction scale: Not satisfied, 1—very satisfied, 5.

A copy of this form is provided as Figure B-64 in Appendix B.

Figure 10-10.   Customer satisfaction summary chart—qualitative feedback.

I would also add:

- I think the department should increase its response time to voice-mail messages. Once I get through, I feel the service is excellent, but sometimes getting through to the right person is a real problem.
- Can the department handle legal questions?
- If I refer someone, do I get a discount?

Business Results. The business results, which are also termed return on investment (ROI), refer back to the training contract that was developed for the entire training effort. This contract specifies the goal, learning objectives, and key performance measures. See the Business Results section of Chapter 9 for an example of measuring business results (see Figure 9-8) and examples of graphic presentations of business results (see Figures 9-10 to 9-13).

Key Findings. Overall, the ratings demonstrate a significant improvement in problem solving. The following evaluation summary presents a statistical compilation of the evaluation findings from each training session conducted from February 17, 2000 through February 19, 2000. (For detailed evaluation statistics, refer to the appendixes section of the report.) On a scale of 1 to 5 (1 being not effective and 5 being very effective), participants rated their level of proficiency with regard to problem solving before the training (pretraining), after the training (post-training), and on the job. These findings are summarized in Figure 10-11.

Group 1 and 3:   A significant learning curve was demonstrated within groups 1 and 3. This may be due to the fact that their knowledge of problem solving prior to the training was minimal.

Group 2:   The findings from group 2 indicate that proficiency ratings, both pre- and post-workshop, were significantly higher than those for the other two groups. The assumption is that this group was a higher-level management group with more experience, supported by the participant registration list.

While both sets of scores indicate improvement, there is room to further increase learning and to move the ratings up.

Recommendations. Use this portion of the report to communicate any recommendations you have determined as a result of the training. For example:

- Problem-solving reinforcement support should be performed on the job via case scenario meetings.
- A recognition program should be implemented on the job to support performance improvement related to problem solving.
- The development of a second-level Problem Solving course should be considered.

Proposed Next Steps. This portion of the report lists both immediate steps and long-term activities. This can be viewed as a reinforcement tool to communicate and support any postcourse follow-up you think should be conducted to support the training as well as specific future activities to be conducted. For example:

Figure 10-11.   Overall problem-solving score by group.

Group	Pretraining	Posttraining	On the Job
1	2.7	4.0	4.3
2	3.9	4.4	4.4
3	2.2	4.1	4.5
Combined Average Score	**2.9**	**4.2**	**4.4**

A copy of this form is provided as Figure B-65 in Appendix B.

- Management support will work with the trainer to develop an action plan to support learning on the job.
- The OD steering committee will review the training summary report and determine business objectives.
- The trainer will follow up with participants and management to track posttraining activities.

Appendixes. As part of the training summary report, appendixes are included that contribute to the findings in the report. These can include actual feedback forms, verbatim comments, case scenarios, etc.

Distribution of the Training Summary Report

Once you have completed the training summary report, distribute it to the appropriate audience(s). You may want to consider these four distinct audiences when distributing your training report:

1. Training participants
2. Training/HR departments
3. Sponsor(s) of the training (person(s) who initiated the training request as well as managers or supervisors responsible for reinforcing training on the job)
4. OD steering committee

When you have distributed your report and received feedback, DO NOT simply file it for future reference. Instead, use it as a source of key information that triggers future organizational learning and development needs. In doing so, review the impact the training effort has had on the benefits you were looking for in the original driving forces model (see Figure 1-7).

Once you have completed this initiative, you are ready to begin the LEARN process for the next learning project.

Appendix A

The LEARN Process

Appendix A provides you with a pictorial overview of the complete LEARN process. LEARN will enable you to turn your own training initiatives into learning events. You can use this appendix as a quick, complete reference guide to assess, develop, deliver, and evaluate your own programs that improve performance and get results.

Table of Contents

Appendix Figure	Based on Figure	Title	Page
A-1	I-2	The complete training process puzzle.	226
A-2	I-1	The LEARN Process.	226
A-3	P1-2	The training process puzzle.	226
A-4	P1-1	Stages of the training process.	227
A-5	I-2	The center of the training process puzzle—LEARN.	227
A-6	I-3	Outline of Chapters 5–9— the LEARN process.	227

Figure A-1.   The complete training process puzzle.

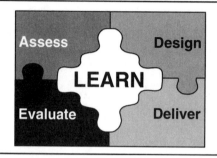

Figure A-2.   The LEARN process.

L   Listen and Understand—If you capture my attention and interest, I'll listen to what you have to offer and try to understand it.

E   Evaluate and Decide—When you help me see what's in it for me, I'll evaluate the competencies you've introduced and decide how I can use them on the job or in my life outside the job.

A   Attempt and Build—If you help me build my skills step-by-step in a safe environment, I'll make a serious attempt to learn.

R   Return and Apply—When I feel comfortable with the skills and abilities I've learned, I'll return to the job and actually use what you've taught me. I'll be able to apply them to my own situation.

N   Natural Transition—Now these skills and abilities are mine. I own them. I may pass them on to other people or take them to the next level and learn more on my own.

Figure A-3.   The training process puzzle.

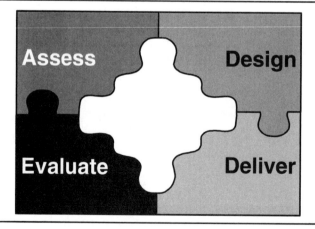

Figure A-4. Stages of the training process.

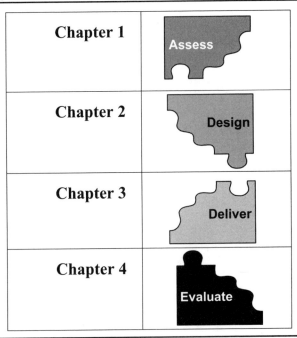

Figure A-5. The center of the training process puzzle—LEARN.

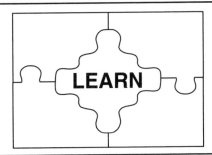

Figure A-6. Outline of Chapters 5–9—the LEARN Process.

Chapter	Acronym Letter	Meaning	Chapter Subtitle (Secret to Success)
5	L	Listen and Understand	Capture my attention and interest
6	E	Evaluate and Decide	Help me see what's in it for me
7	A	Attempt and Build	Help me build my skills step-by-step
8	R	Return and Apply	Send me back to use them on the job
9	N	Natural Transition	Now they're mine

Appendix B

LEARN Tools

How can you begin to implement the LEARN process? Use Appendix B as your tool kit. The sixty-five tools in this section, which are illustrated and described throughout the book, are provided for your convenience. You can use them as they are, or customize them to meet your own particular training needs.

Table of Contents

Appendix Figure	Based on Figure	Title	Page
B-12	2-7	Training request form.	246
B-13	2-13	Supervisor commitment grid.	247
B-14	2-14	Training partner matrix.	248
B-15	2-17	Sample course plan.	249
B-16	2-18	Subject matter expert invitation.	250
B-17	2-19	Subject matter expert biography.	251
B-18	2-20	Logistics requirement checklist.	252
B-19	2-26	Precourse checklist.	253
B-20	3-2	Checklist of adult learning experiences.	254
B-21	3-4	Template for mind mapping.	255
B-22	3-6	Reaching your visual learners.	256
B-23	3-7	Reaching your auditory learners.	257
B-24	3-8	Reaching your kinesthetic learners.	258
B-25	3-11	Checklist for "hardwiring" skills into memory.	259
B-26	4-4	Evaluation Form A.	260
B-27	4-5	Evaluation Form B.	261
B-28	4-6	Evaluation Form C.	262
B-29	4-7	Evaluation Form D.	263
B-30	4-8	Worksheet for calculating quantitative evaluation results.	264
B-31	4-16	Evaluation Form E.	265
B-32	5-2	Checklist for establishing a safe learning environment.	266

Appendix Figure	Based on Figure	Title	Page
B-33	5-6	Questions for participants.	267
B-34	5-8	Symbols for creative introduction.	268
B-35	5-9	Bingo beginnings.	269
B-36	5-11	Scavenger hunt scramble.	270
B-37	5-12	Team résumé.	271
B-38	6-2	Four-step situational questioning process.	272
B-39	6-7	Training features and benefits worksheet.	273
B-40	6-9	Building a bridge from where your participants are to where you want them to be.	274
B-41	7-1	Ancient Chinese proverb.	275
B-42	7-10	Factors to consider in selecting a game.	276
B-43	7-14	Template for ensuring practice, practice, practice.	278
B-44	7-17	Role play A (first communicator).	279
B-45	7-17	Role play A (second communicator).	280
B-46	7-18	Role play B (first communicator).	281
B-47	7-18	Role play B (second communicator).	282
B-48	7-18	Role play B (third communicator).	283
B-49	7-19	Template for evaluating simulations.	284
B-50	8-10	Supervisor feedback form (application and results assessment).	285

Appendix Figure	Based on Figure	Title	Page
B-51	8-12	Case scenario meeting form.	286
B-52	8-13	Checklist of learner recognition strategies.	287
B-53	8-14	Support activities follow-up form.	288
B-54	8-15	Participant action plan.	289
B-55	8-17	Buddy contract.	290
B-56	8-18	Participant contact list.	291
B-57	8-20/ 9-4	Participant feedback form.	292
B-58	9-5	Supervisor feedback form.	293
B-59	9-6	Coworker feedback form.	294
B-60	9-7	Customer feedback form.	295
B-61	9-8	Business results form.	296
B-62	9-9	Data captured form.	297
B-63	10-3	Participant summary chart—quantitative results.	298
B-64	10-9 10-10	Customer satisfaction summary chart—quantitative results.	299
B-65	10-11	Overall score by group.	300

Figure B-1. Training checklist.

Who Needs Training?

1. Describe the intended audience.

   ❐ *Intact work team* who are depended on each other to accomplish daily work and meet goals (e.g., book publishing team made up of acquisitions editor, marketing manager, production manager, art director, and team leader).
   Description:

   ❐ *Staff members who share the same function* and work toward the same goal but are not considered a team (e.g., cashiers from all shifts of a large supermarket).
   Description:

   ❐ *Members of special project teams* whose work flows directly from one department to another (e.g., hospital admitting representatives who capture insurance information, medical records representatives who code patient charts for billing, and billers who seek reimbursement from third-party payers.)
   Description:

   ❐ *Any staff member at a specific level who chooses to attend* (e.g., any manager or supervisor who elects to attend).
   Description:

   ❐ *Any staff member who chooses to attend* (e.g., any staff member who voluntarily elects to attend and obtains permission).
   Description:

2. Will this training be required? ❐ Yes (mandatory)   ❐ No (voluntary)

   If yes, who is requiring the training?

   How will this requirement be communicated?

From *Turning Training Into Learning*
by Sheila W. Furjanic and Laurie A. Trotman (New York: AMACOM, 2000).

Figure B-2.   Background questions.

___

Assessing the Training Request

1. Which employees are the intended training participants?

2. What part does each one play in the work that is done in the department?

3. Which participants are the most skilled at performing their jobs?

4. How well do the participants know each other?

5. Are there natural leaders among the participants? Who are they?

6. How familiar are the participants with the training subject?

7. Are there one or two participants who know the subject well?

8. Are any participants likely to resist training? Why?

9. Do any participants need special attention during the learning process?

10. What other types of training have these employees received?

11. How will employees perceive this particular training effort (positive, negative)?

12. Is there anything that hasn't been asked that will help assess this training request?

___

From *Turning Training Into Learning*
by Sheila W. Furjanic and Laurie A. Trotman (New York: AMACOM, 2000).

Figure B-3.   Telephone interview with intended participants.

Hi. My name is _____ and I've been asked to facilitate a course in
             (your name)

_____ for all _____ at _____.
   (subject area)   (intended group of participants)   (name of organization)

Have you heard about this course? It is scheduled for _____.
                                                   (date, time location of course if available)

I'm trying to talk with each of the people who are scheduled to participate in the course, to gather some basic information that will help me develop a course that addresses your needs. Is this a good time to talk?

1. How long have you been with _____?
                              (name of organization)

2. How long have you been a _____?
                            (position)

3. How many people report directly to you?

4. What has been your biggest challenge in this position?

5. What has been your biggest success?

6. What topics/skills should this course focus on to be of most help to you?

7. Do you have any hints, tips, or suggestions you can share with other participants?

8. What else should I know before I begin planning this course?

From *Turning Training Into Learning*
by Sheila W. Furjanic and Laurie A. Trotman (New York: AMACOM, 2000).

Figure B-4.   Analyzing the training request.

Questions to ask the person requesting the training:

1. What prompted you to request this training?

2. How long has this been a problem?

3. How often does it occur?

4. What is the process that leads up to the problem?

5. Have you already tried training as a solution? What happened?

From *Turning Training Into Learning*
by Sheila W. Furjanic and Laurie A. Trotman (New York: AMACOM, 2000).

Figure B-5.   Fixing a process problem.

_____

Questions to ask the person requesting the training:

Clarify the request.

1. What is the nature of the problem? Describe it to me and give examples.

2. How will the requested training solve the problem?

Determine the root cause.

1. Why is it a problem? What happens as a result of this problem?

2. What do you think is the root cause of this problem?

3. Why do you think so?

Identify options.

1. Are there other options?

2. Is there another way to accomplish this process?

3. What are the alternatives?

Select the best solution.

1. What is the best solution for the organization and the participants?

2. Why is this solution best?

Develop an action plan.

1. If the process is being changed, what is the timeline for this change?

2. Who will develop the new process?

3. How will it be tested?

4. How will it be communicated?

5. How will it be evaluated?

From *Turning Training Into Learning*
by Sheila W. Furjanic and Laurie A. Trotman (New York: AMACOM, 2000).

Figure B-6.   Questions to ask when clarifying support for participants.

1. How important is this training to your department's operations? Explain.

2. How long do you feel this training effort should take?

3. What do you want participants to accomplish in that length of time? Be as specific as possible.

4. If more sessions are required, will your staff be encouraged to participate? What factors will affect this decision?

5. How are you prepared to support the training on the job? Give examples if possible.

6. How will you measure the success of the training? Be specific.

7. Are you or are members of your staff willing to serve as mentors to the participants when they return to the job? Which staff members should we plan to work with?

8. Have you tried training for this before? If yes, why are you doing it again? Describe the original training effort and the results.

9. If follow-up activities or sessions are necessary, will your staff members be encouraged to participate?

From *Turning Training Into Learning*
by Sheila W. Furjanic and Laurie A. Trotman (New York: AMACOM, 2000).

Figure B-7. Decision matrix.

C O N F I D E N T I A L

IS THE PROBLEM WORTH FIXING?

Question	Yes	Maybe	No
1. Does the client (person requesting training) have realistic expectations?			
Explain:			
2. If we do nothing, will the problem go away?			
Explain:			
3. If we do nothing, will the problem get worse?			
Explain:			
4. Will correction of this problem have a positive effect on the goals of the organization?			
Explain:			
5. Will failure to correct the problem have a negative effect on the goals of the organization?			
Explain:			
6. Are higher priority programs competing for training resources earmarked for this effort?			
Explain:			
7. Is this training effort strongly supported by management?			

(continues)

Figure B-7. (Continued)

Question	Yes	Maybe	No
			Explain:
8. Is the value of this training effort being questioned by management?			
			Explain:
9. Will this training effort be supported when the participants return to the job?			
			Explain:
10. Can this training be handled effectively in the department without the help of the training department?			
			Explain:

From *Turning Training Into Learning*
by Sheila W. Furjanic and Laurie A. Trotman (New York: AMACOM, 2000).

Figure B-8. Proposed training matrix.

THE BIG DECISION:
SHOULD THIS TRAINING TAKE PLACE?

This matrix will help you determine whether the requested training should take place. Possible scores range from 7 to 35. The higher the score, the more certain you can be that training is the appropriate response to the request.

Consideration	5	4	3	2	1
1. Is the problem really a process problem?	☐ The process is sound. Training will help staff members learn to use the process.	☐	☐ The process might be able to be improved, but the improvement is impractical at this time.	☐	☐ An improvement in the process could increase productivity and make the requested training to be unnecessary.
2. What are the driving forces behind the training?	☐ Strong driving forces both internally and externally. Solidly backed by senior management.	☐	☐ Some degree of both internal and external driving forces, but not a priority training effort.	☐	☐ No strong driving forces, either internally or externally.
3. Will the learning be supported when the participant returns to the job?	☐ There is a support plan in place. A mentor has been appointed. The participant will be encouraged to apply the learning and return for help if needed.	☐	☐ The participant's supervisor seems mildly enthusiastic about the training, but no support plan is in place.	☐	☐ The supervisor is reluctant to let the participant attend class, and considers this training a waste of valuable time.

(continues)

Figure B-8. (Continued)

		□		□		□
4. Will there be barriers to success in implementation?		The training requested is "do-able," and the time allotted, both for preparation and implementation, are appropriate.		There may be some delay in implementing the training due to equipment or systems problems, but they are being corrected.		There will be no implementation for at least 3 months while system and equipment problems are resolved.
5. Is this a "magic wand" request?		The requester's expectations are right on target.		The requester may be expecting too much.		This is clearly a "magic wand" request. Even Houdini couldn't make this happen.
6. Is the problem worth fixing?		Yes. If it is not fixed, there will be serious consequences. This problem will not go away on its own.		The problem is worth fixing, but there are other higher-priority problems that should be addressed first. There will be no serious consequences if it is not addressed now.		The problem will either go away or cause no serious consequences if it is not addressed.
7. Is the training available from another resource?		No. This has to be a custom-made training effort.		Outside resources are available, but they will have to be customized or supplemented to fit this effort.		Yes. Outside resources are readily available, and will address the needs of the requester.

From *Turning Training Into Learning*
by Sheila W. Furjanic and Laurie A. Trotman (New York: AMACOM, 2000).

Figure B-7.   Decision matrix.

CONFIDENTIAL

IS THE PROBLEM WORTH FIXING?

Question	Yes	Maybe	No
1. Does the client (person requesting training) have realistic expectations?			
Explain:			
2. If we do nothing, will the problem go away?			
Explain:			
3. If we do nothing, will the problem get worse?			
Explain:			
4. Will correction of this problem have a positive effect on the goals of the organization?			
Explain:			
5. Will failure to correct the problem have a negative effect on the goals of the organization?			
Explain:			
6. Are higher priority programs competing for training resources earmarked for this effort?			
Explain:			
7. Is this training effort strongly supported by management?			

(continues)

Figure B-7.   (Continued)

Question	Yes	Maybe	No
Explain:			
8. Is the value of this training effort being questioned by management?			
Explain:			
9. Will this training effort be supported when the participants return to the job?			
Explain:			
10. Can this training be handled effectively in the department without the help of the training department?			
Explain:			

From *Turning Training Into Learning*
by Sheila W. Furjanic and Laurie A. Trotman (New York: AMACOM, 2000).

Figure B-9. Training contract.

Training Contract	
Requesting Department: _____ **Sponsoring Manager:** _____ **Date:** _____	**Telephone Number:** _____ **FAX Number:** _____ **E-Mail Address:** _____

Background Information
- Identify why training is needed

- Identify relevant events that prompted the training request

Training Goal
- Identify the overall goal for the training program

Training Learning Objectives
- Identify the learning objectives to be achieved during the training

Key Performance Measures
- Answer the question, How will you know training has been successful? What changes are required?

Target Audience(s)
- Identify the participants/audiences you are targeting for the training

Requirements
- List any requirements the requester would be responsible for performing prior to and during training

Budget/Cost *(only applicable for internal chargebacks)*
- Identify any cost/budget requirements

Manager Follow-Up Activities
- Identify follow-up activities the requesting sponsor (management) needs to perform

Approval	
I agree with the terms of this contract. _____ Requester Approval	I agree with the terms of this contract. _____ Training Department Approval

Dates of Actual Training:
Participants:
Comments:

From *Turning Training Into Learning*
by Sheila W. Furjanic and Laurie A. Trotman (New York: AMACOM, 2000).

Figure B-10.   Skill gap question template.

What Should Employees Be Able to Do?	*How Well Should They Do It?*	*How Can You Tell It's Being Done This Way?*
1.		
2.		
3.		
4.		
5.		
6.		
7.		
8.		

From *Turning Training Into Learning*
by Sheila W. Furjanic and Laurie A. Trotman (New York: AMACOM, 2000).

Figure B-11.   Skill gap assessment guide template.

Training Skill Required	Assessment of Trainee Skill	Skill Gap
Skill: How Well?		
Skill: How Well?		
Skill: How Well?		
Skill: How Well?		
Skill: How Well?		
Skill: How Well?		
Skill: How Well?		
Skill: How Well?		

Figure B-12.   Training request form.

Name _____	Date Requested _____
Department _____	Date to Be Conducted _____

| **Department Head** _____

Department Head Approval Required?
Yes ☐   No ☐ | **Telephone** _____

E-Mail _____

Fax _____ |

Project Description:

Training Requested:

Learning Needs	Related Competencies	Key Performance Measures
(What are the learning needs?)	*(What skills are related to the learning needs?)*	*(How will effectiveness of the training be measured?)*

From *Turning Training Into Learning*
by Sheila W. Furjanic and Laurie A. Trotman (New York: AMACOM, 2000).

Figure B-13.   Supervisor commitment grid.

Training Planned _____

Participant _____

Supervisor/Manager _____

Department Head _____

Level of Commitment

Use the grid below to gauge the level of commitment that the supervisor, who will support your participant on the job, has with regard to the training.

	Level	Commitment Description
❏	1	**Not Committed:** Is not in favor of training. Reluctantly has agreed to let staff members attend. Has not had time to discuss needs or implementation plans.
❏	2	**Passive Participant:** Seldom has time to discuss training needs. Supports training but believes that the responsibility for implementation belongs to the staff member and the trainer. Has not had time to discuss implementation.
❏	3	**May Be Moldable:** Has consulted with you about training needs and supports training but indicates that he or she has no time to devote to implementation.
❏	4	**Active Supporter:** Has actively participated in discussing and contributing to learning needs, supports training, and is willing to serve as mentor to staff members when they return to the job.
❏	5	**Cheerleader:** Enthusiastically supports training. Has helped you create relevant content. May even participate in the pilot session. Is a model mentor, allowing staff members to become comfortable using their new skills on the job.

*Note: If commitment level is not above 3, review training requirements with your trainee's supervisor/manager and discuss the importance of his or her level of commitment to achieve buy-in. Reiterate the message that most training efforts fail to be transferred to the job because there are no follow-up support mechanisms in place once participants return to work.

From *Turning Training Into Learning*
by Sheila W. Furjanic and Laurie A. Trotman (New York: AMACOM, 2000).

Figure B-14.   Training partner matrix.

Use the matrix below to:

- List participants.
- Identify supervisor/manager who supports each participant.
- Identify training needs.
- Indicate whether supervisor/manager has been actively involved in communicating the training needs to the participant. Insert date of last discussion.
- Determine the commitment level (see Figure 2-13).

Participant	*Supervisor/ Manager*	*Training Need*	*Actively Involved (Yes or no and date)*	*Commitment Level (1 not committed– 5 very committed)*

This form is primarily useful in supporting the training contract and serves as a background reference document to the contract.

From *Turning Training Into Learning*
by Sheila W. Furjanic and Laurie A. Trotman (New York: AMACOM, 2000).

Figure B-15. Sample course plan.

Course/Session Title:

Date:

Objective	Content (topics)	Time Frame	Presenter	Teaching Method

From *Turning Training Into Learning*
by Sheila W. Furjanic and Laurie A. Trotman (New York: AMACOM, 2000).

Figure B-16.   Subject matter expert invitation.

MEMORANDUM

To:

From:

Date:

Re:

Thank you for agreeing to be the subject-matter expert for the _____
                                                                                                          (course name)

_____ to be held on _____, in room _____.
                                                          (date)   (room at time)

To assist with the ongoing training and education efforts, the _____
                                                                                                                  (course name)

course will be offered to _____. The objective of this
                                                          (intended participants)

course is to _____.
                              (object of course)

As a subject-matter expert, we would like you to complete the attached training plan. This plan enables the training department to identify, at a glance, your expectations for participants in this course. Also attached is a biography for you to complete so we can advertise the course, identifying your background.

If you are unable to attend the course, it is critical that you find a replacement with a relevant background to teach the course or notify us at least two weeks in advance so we can reschedule the course.

Please complete the training plan and the bio and return them to our office no later

than _____. Feel free to either e-mail them to _____ or fax
              (return due date)   (e-mail address)

them to _____.
              (fax number)

We look forward to working with you at the _____.
                                                                          (course name and date)

From *Turning Training Into Learning*
by Sheila W. Furjanic and Laurie A. Trotman (New York: AMACOM, 2000).

Figure B-17. Subject matter expert biography.

SUBJECT MATTER EXPERT BIOGRAPHY

Name:	**Telephone number:**
Fax number:	**E-Mail address:**
Mailing address:	**Secretary/administrative assistant (name and number):**

Please describe your last three positions (and length of time in each position), as well as the organization and your job responsibilities below.

1. Current position, organization, length of time in position, and description:

_____

_____

_____

2. Previous position, organization, length of time in position, and description:

_____

_____

_____

3. Previous position, organization, length of time in position, and description:

_____

_____

_____

Use the space below to describe additional relevant experiences

_____

_____

_____

_____

Education

Degree	*School*	*Major/Minor*
_____	_____	_____
_____	_____	_____
_____	_____	_____

Certifications/Licenses

_____

_____

From *Turning Training Into Learning*
by Sheila W. Furjanic and Laurie A. Trotman (New York: AMACOM, 2000).

Figure B-18.   Logistics requirement checklist.

Course Name _____

Instructor _____   **Date** _____

Use the following checklist to determine logistics requirements for training. This may be used with or without your client.

Equipment

❏ Overhead   ❏ Flip charts *(quantity)*   ❏ Electronic LCD panel
                                                       projection
❏ Microphone   ❏ TV/VCR
                                                   ❏ Slide projector
❏ PC   ❏ Podium
                                                   ❏ Facilitator tables *(quantity)*

                                                   ❏ Other _____

⊗ Contact the Audiovisual Department with request.

Room Schematic (Layout) *(see diagrams in Figures 2-20 to 2-24)*

Location (room number and floor) _____
❏ Individual   ❏ Large group   ❏ Classroom style
❏ Small group   ❏ Boardroom style   ❏ Other

Breakout session space/rooms required?
❏ Yes   ❏ No

⊗ Contact the Building Services Department with request.

Training Materials
❏ Overhead transparencies of course materials
❏ Prepared flip charts
❏ Icebreaker props/exercises
❏ Group exercise materials
❏ Name tents/cards
❏ Masking tape/pushpins
❏ Handouts (list)   _____

                            _____

                            _____

                            _____

Refreshments
❏ Breakfast   ❏ Lunch   ❏ Dinner   ❏ A.M. Break   ❏ P.M. Break

⊗ Contact the Catering Department with request.

From *Turning Training Into Learning*
by Sheila W. Furjanic and Laurie A. Trotman (New York: AMACOM, 2000).

Figure B-19.   Precourse checklist.

1. Visit room and check:

- ❐ Lighting
- ❐ Electrical outlets (actually working)
- ❐ Room setup (select schematic)
- ❐ Window shades (appropriate for effective illumination of AV equipment)

2. Contact all enabling departments to ensure delivery of their services.

Catering:

- ❐ Menu
- ❐ Beverages
- ❐ Timing
- ❐ Cleanup
- ❐ Contact name and number (in case of problem)

Audiovisual:

- ❐ Equipment
- ❐ Delivery time
- ❐ Pickup time
- ❐ Contact name and number (in case of problem)

Environmental Services:

- ❐ Room setup
- ❐ Moving of equipment/furniture
- ❐ Delivery time
- ❐ Pickup time
- ❐ Contact name and number (in case of problem)

Security:

- ❐ Confirm room unlocked/locked at appropriate times
- ❐ Number and contact name (in case of an emergency)

From *Turning Training Into Learning*
by Sheila W. Furjanic and Laurie A. Trotman (New York: AMACOM, 2000).

Figure B-20.   Checklist of adult learning experiences.

**Are Your Sessions Geared to the
Needs of Adult Learners?**

Your answers to these questions will help you determine if your sessions are suited to adult learners.	*Seldom*	*Sometimes*	*Usually*
1. I build options into my lessons for the participants to choose from.	❏	❏	❏
2. I value the experience my adult participants have had and try to base learning on their real-life examples.	❏	❏	❏
3. I build practical, hands-on experiences into each session.	❏	❏	❏
4. I try to avoid teaching theory that participants won't find practical and useful.	❏	❏	❏
5. I relate learning to real life and help participants see how it can help them become better problem solvers.	❏	❏	❏

From *Turning Training Into Learning*
by Sheila W. Furjanic and Laurie A. Trotman (New York: AMACOM, 2000).

Figure B-21. Template for mind mapping.

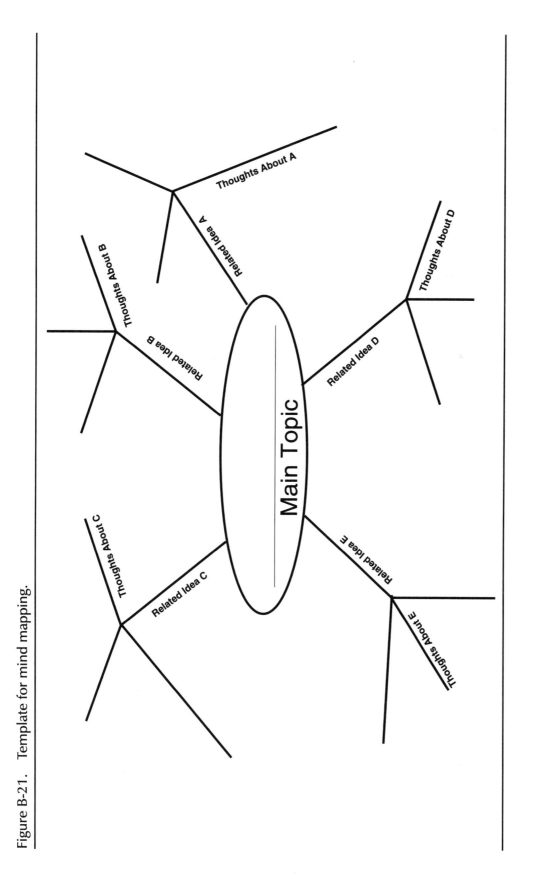

From *Turning Training Into Learning*
by Sheila W. Furjanic and Laurie A. Trotman (New York: AMACOM, 2000).

Figure B-22.   Reaching your visual learners.

You can reach your visual learners by using methods from this checklist.

❐ **Pictures**—The old saying that a picture is worth a thousand words is true for these learners. Select pictures to represent each of the important points you are presenting.

❐ **Graphic illustrations**—Try to diagram what you are saying. Representative figures will stick in the visual learner's mind long after your words have evaporated.

❐ **Tables/charts**—Organize your material into table or chart form. When you do this, you will enable the visual learner to get a picture of all the key concepts as they should be arranged to reach him or her. The visual learner will have the table or chart to memorize information and to use as a self-test.

❐ **Video clips**—Show a brief section from a popular movie to appeal to the visual learner, who will be able to associate the pictures on-screen with the concepts being learned and long after the video clip has ended.

❐ **Mind maps**—Have your participants help you create a mind map that illustrates the relationship among the main concepts and their questions.

❐ **Flash cards**—Encourage your visual learners to make their own flash cards. The exercise of recalling the learning and dividing it into logical words and phrases for the cards will provide a learning opportunity in itself. When the flash cards have been made, they are portable and ready for review whenever the learner wants them.

❐ **Color coding and highlighting**—Add meaningful color codes and highlights to the materials participants are trying to learn. Both you and the learners can effectively reinforce learning.

From *Turning Training Into Learning*
by Sheila W. Furjanic and Laurie A. Trotman (New York: AMACOM, 2000).

Figure B-23.   Reaching your auditory learners.

You can reach your auditory learners by using methods from this checklist.

❒ **Storytelling**—Almost all learners, not just children, enjoy learning through story-telling, and auditory learners lead the group of people who will respond to case situations, examples, and personal stories that illustrate the points you are trying to make.

❒ **Small-group discussions**—Auditory learners will benefit from listening to other members of a small group as much as from contributing to it. However, auditory learners are often good speakers, so they will make substantial contributions to discussion groups.

❒ **Debates**—As keen listeners and good speakers, auditory learners are natural de-baters. They can remember key points without notes and expend little effort hearing, understanding, and preparing rebuttal for opposing arguments.

❒ **Audiotapes**—If you encourage your auditory learners to prepare their own au-diotapes, they will benefit from organizing the information to record it and from having the tapes available to listen to repeatedly.

❒ **Mnemonics**—If you can, create mnemonics that will help auditory learners bet-ter remember what is being taught; it will be a great help to them. If you are unable to do this, you can encourage your participants to come up with their own mnemonics based on examples you might provide.

From *Turning Training Into Learning*
by Sheila W. Furjanic and Laurie A. Trotman (New York: AMACOM, 2000).

Figure B-24.   Reaching your kinesthetic learners.

You can reach your kinesthetic learners by using methods from this checklist.

❒ **Role playing**—Your kinesthetic learners will be eager for you to stop talking so they can get into the role-playing exercise. They need to be up moving around and will be your most animated role players.

❒ **Practice**—Any opportunity for hands-on practice will appeal to these learners. Let's say you are learning about print advertising. Your kinesthetic learners won't be comfortable with the learning process until they have pens, scissors, and glue in hand and can create an ad that exemplifies the concept you are presenting.

❒ **Site visits**—Kinesthetic learners will be eager participants in any learning that allows them to leave the traditional classroom setting. They will learn rapidly if they have a chance to participate in hands-on demonstrations during site visits.

❒ **Lab work**—Kinesthetic learners will gravitate to the computer lab to try the technical concepts you have been teaching them. While participants from all three learning styles need time in the lab to make sure learning sticks, these learners can't wait to get their hands on the keyboard.

❒ **Games**—Any learning game that makes sense and reinforces the content presented in class will be a welcome activity for your kinesthetic learners, who may be your most eager participants.

From *Turning Training Into Learning*
by Sheila W. Furjanic and Laurie A. Trotman (New York: AMACOM, 2000).

Figure B-25.   Checklist for "hardwiring" skills into memory.

❐ Describe to the learners the skill you are going to present. Make sure they know why you are presenting it and why it is important for them to learn it.

❐ Acknowledge learners who have some ability in this area.

❐ Demonstrate the entire skill set slowly and carefully.

❐ Divide it into logical learning modules if the skill is a complex one. For example, the process of registering hospital patients is a complex one that can be taught in five logical modules.

❐ Arrange an opportunity for participants to practice *each* of the five modules until they have reached a level of proficiency. Provide appropriate feedback on each of the modules to ensure mastery of the skills associated with it. For example, if a participant has difficulty entering the patient's name and address on the hospital computer system, let that person practice the skill until he or she is comfortable.

❐ Arrange an opportunity for participants to practice the *entire* process from beginning to end.

❐ Schedule practice sessions with appropriate feedback that enable the participant to demonstrate the entire skill *five more times*. The insurance broker will demonstrate the ability to process six separate claim forms.

From *Turning Training Into Learning*
by Sheila W. Furjanic and Laurie A. Trotman (New York: AMACOM, 2000).

Figure B-26.   Evaluation Form A.

OPINION-BASED EVALUATION

Course: _____   Date: _____

Please take a moment to evaluate this training session by placing a mark on each of the lines below to indicate your opinion of the training. Position your mark at the appropriate spot between the two statements.

    I believe this workshop was . . .

                                       5   3   1

A. Time well spent   L------------I------------J A total waste of time

B. Relevant to me   L------------I------------J Not relevant and I could care less

C. Useful   L------------I------------J Not useful at all

D. Interesting   L------------I------------J Boring me to death

E. Stimulating   L------------I------------J Putting me to sleep

F. Able to involve me L------------I------------J Impersonal—the instructor didn't know I was here!

G. Clear   L------------I------------J Unclear—what was it about?

H. Flexible   L------------I------------J Rigid—the instructor wouldn't budge an inch

I. Comments:

From *Turning Training Into Learning*
by Sheila W. Furjanic and Laurie A. Trotman (New York: AMACOM, 2000).

Figure B-27.   Evaluation Form B.

QUALITATIVE EVALUATION

Course: _____   **Date:** _____

1. The three most useful parts of the course were:

   A.

   B.

   C.

2. The three least useful parts of the course were:

   A.

   B.

   C.

3. The course helped me understand how to _____.

   _____

   _____

4. The course could have helped me understand _____.

   _____

   _____

5. I would improve future courses by _____.

   _____

   _____

6. What I liked most about the course was _____.

   _____

   _____

7. What I liked least about the course was _____.

   _____

   _____

From *Turning Training Into Learning*
by Sheila W. Furjanic and Laurie A. Trotman (New York: AMACOM, 2000).

Figure B-28.   Evaluation Form C.

POST-COURSE EVALUATION

Course: _____   Date: _____

Please take a few moments to evaluate the content and learning process in this course.

Concerning the content . . .

	Not at All		**To a Great Extent**	
1. I understand how to _____	1	2	3	4
2. I understand how to _____	1	2	3	4

3. As a result of this course, I will be able to use the following skills in my job:

_____

Concerning the process . . .

	Not Effective		**Very Effective**	
4. How effective were the materials for the program? I would suggest _____	1	2	3	4
5. How effective was the length of the program? I would suggest _____	1	2	3	4
6. How effective was (were) the instructor(s)? I would suggest _____	1	2	3	4

7. What interested me most in the session was: _____

_____

8. What interested me least in the session was: _____

_____

9. To improve future training sessions, I would suggest: _____

_____

10. I would also be interested in learning about the following training
    (check all appropriate boxes):
    ❑ Written communication   ❑ Oral communication   ❑ Effective listening
    ❑ Project management   ❑ Leadership   ❑ Presentation skills
    ❑ Software applications   ❑ Other suggestions: _____
                                                       _____

11. What training length do you think is most appropriate?
    ❑ 1 full day   ❑ ½ day   ❑ 2 one-hour segments   ❑ 2 full days   ❑ 1 week

---

From *Turning Training Into Learning*
by Sheila W. Furjanic and Laurie A. Trotman (New York: AMACOM, 2000).

Figure B-29.   Evaluation Form D.

DESCRIPTIVE EVALUATION

Course: _____   Date: _____

Please circle the descriptive answers that most closely match your evaluation of this course.

1. Did the course content meet your expectations?				
(5) It exceeded my expectations. It was just what I needed. I'm glad I attended.	(4) It was what I expected and needed. I'm glad I attended.	(3) Some of it met my needs; I did not need other parts of the course. I have mixed feelings about whether I should have attended or not.	(2) Although a portion of it met my needs, it was not the course I expected. If I had known this ahead of time, I probably would not have attended.	(1) It was not what I expected, and it did not meet any of my needs in this area. Frankly, it was a waste of 3 hours.
Comments:				

2. As a result of the session, do you feel that you can _____				
(5) I'm confident that I can _____ _____ _____	(4) I'm pretty sure I'll be able to _____ _____ _____	(3) I'm going to try, but I'm not sure.	(2) I doubt it. I'm not sure I understood some of the concepts.	(1) Absolutely not! I didn't understand a word the instructor was talking about.
Comments:				

3. Will you be able to apply the _____ you learned in your current position?				
(5) Absolutely! I'm going to start today.	(4) I think so. If I'm able to apply them, it will be helpful, so I'll try.	(3) I'm going to try, but I'm not sure.	(2) I doubt it, but I'll see if there is any way I can use them.	(1) Absolutely not! There is no way I'll be able to use this stuff.
Comments:				

4. Did the instructor present the materials in a way that helped you understand them?				
(5) Absolutely! I think the instructor really knew her stuff.	(4) Yes, I got all of it.	(3) I'm not really sure. Sometimes I thought she knew what she was talking about, and other times I wasn't not sure she knew.	(2) Not really, I didn't understand.	(1) Absolutely not! She didn't have a clue.
Comments:				

5. Did the instructor capture and hold your attention throughout the session?				
(5) Always! What an instructor! I never felt bored.	(4) Yes, she did a good job of keeping me engaged.	(3) Sometimes, but I did daydream on occasion.	(2) Not really. I was thinking more about the work I would have to go back to.	(1) Absolutely not! My brain left a while ago.
Comments:				

From *Turning Training Into Learning*
by Sheila W. Furjanic and Laurie A. Trotman (New York: AMACOM, 2000).

Figure B-30.   Worksheet for calculating quantitative evaluation results.

Evaluation Question	1	2	3	4	Total
1					
2					
3					
4					
5					
6					
Denominator formula: 20 evaluations × 4-point rating scale = 80					

From *Turning Training Into Learning*
by Sheila W. Furjanic and Laurie A. Trotman (New York: AMACOM, 2000).

Figure B-31. Evaluation Form E.

COMFORT-LEVEL EVALUATION

Course: _____ Date: _____

Please take a minute to indicate how comfortable you are with the skills you learned in today's session.

Technique or Skill	*Piece of Cake* I didn't have any trouble with this and will be able to use it easily.	*Let Me Practice* I'm catching on, but I need more practice time.	*Show Me Again* I'm having trouble with this and need more instruction.
1.			
2.			
3.			
4.			
5.			

From *Turning Training Into Learning*
by Sheila W. Furjanic and Laurie A. Trotman (New York: AMACOM, 2000).

Figure B-32.   Checklist for establishing a safe learning environment.

❒ Arrive early and make sure you have all your materials and equipment.

❒ Check the room temperature.

❒ Check the refreshments. Unwrap the plates/trays from catering.

❒ Check the laptop connections, backup overhead, and other audiovisual equipment.

❒ Set up the flip charts. Make sure there are markers and that they work.

❒ Ensure that physical barriers have been removed so all participants have access to the room, especially those who have special needs.

❒ Have a sign-in sheet (if you're using one) ready for participants to sign as they enter, or have it ready to circulate after participants are all seated.

❒ Place your agendas and handouts on the table in front of each seat, or place them at the door for participants to take when they enter the room.

❒ Fold paper into table tents and place one on the table in front of each seat. (See Figure 5-3 for table tent directions.)

❒ Place enough markers on the table to provide easy access to them by all participants.

❒ Verify that the clock in the room is working properly, or place a small clock at the front of the room for your use. (This will ensure that you don't have to keep looking at your watch to keep the session on target.)

❒ Locate the nearest rest rooms, telephones, water fountains, and emergency exits if you are unfamiliar with the room. Be prepared to give participants the lay of the land at the beginning of the session. Make sure you know how to get help in case of an emergency.

From *Turning Training Into Learning*
by Sheila W. Furjanic and Laurie A. Trotman (New York: AMACOM, 2000).

Figure B-33. Questions for participants.

Participant Introduction

Name:

Department:

I have been with the company ____ years.

In this course, I hope to learn _____
_____
_____.

From *Turning Training Into Learning*
by Sheila W. Furjanic and Laurie A. Trotman (New York: AMACOM, 2000).

Figure B-34. Symbols for creative introduction.

Select a symbol that best represents you and explain why.

From *Turning Training Into Learning*
by Sheila W. Furjanic and Laurie A. Trotman (New York: AMACOM, 2000).

Figure B-35.   Bingo beginnings.

Has been at the company less than one year	Rides a bicycle	Plays golf	Has two children	Walks to work
Has four children	Enjoys scuba diving	Drives a Buick	Takes the train to work	Has a cat
Has a dog	Plays tennis	FREE	Speaks Spanish	Has tropical fish
Drives a Ford	Has been at the company more than five years	Speaks French	Reads *Time* magazine	Drives to work
Likes football	Hates football	Likes to dance	Enjoys swimming	Hates broccoli

From *Turning Training Into Learning*
by Sheila W. Furjanic and Laurie A. Trotman (New York: AMACOM, 2000).

Figure B-36. Scavenger hunt scramble.

Scavenger Hunt Fact	First Name
1. Speaks Spanish	_____
2. Plays chess	_____
3. Likes skiing	_____
4. Has two sisters	_____
5. Plays racquetball	_____
6. Likes crossword puzzles	_____
7. Goes to the movies often	_____
8. Reads mysteries	_____
9. Has three children	_____
10. Has a dog	_____
11. Has a cat	_____
12. Traveled to Europe last year	_____
13. Likes ballroom dancing	_____
14. Plays the piano	_____

From *Turning Training Into Learning*
by Sheila W. Furjanic and Laurie A. Trotman (New York: AMACOM, 2000).

Figure B-37.   Team résumé.

Team Résumé Worksheet

1. Our team has held the following jobs:

2. Our team has experience in:

3. Our team likes to do the following extracurricular activities:

4. Our team . . .

From *Turning Training Into Learning*
by Sheila W. Furjanic and Laurie A. Trotman (New York: AMACOM, 2000).

Figure B-38.   Four-step situational questioning process.

Step 1.   **Identify a concept or skill that participants will be learning in the session.**

Concept:

Step 2.   **Recall a realistic situation in which the concept applies.**

Situation:

Step 3.   **Determine the link between your example and the concept.**

Link:

Step 4.   **Write a question asking participants if they have ever been in a similar situation.**

Question:

From *Turning Training Into Learning*
by Sheila W. Furjanic and Laurie A. Trotman (New York: AMACOM, 2000).

Figure B-39. Training features and benefits worksheet.

Transforming Features Into Benefits

Course	Feature (Content)	Benefits

From *Turning Training Into Learning*
by Sheila W. Furjanic and Laurie A. Trotman (New York: AMACOM, 2000).

Figure B-40.   Building a bridge from where your participants are to where you want them to be.

Subject of Course: _____

Description of Participants: _____

_____

_____

STEPS	PLAN
1. Get into the minds of your learners and try to understand what they are thinking about the subject at hand.	
2. Begin by addressing their thoughts and feelings.	
3. Explain where you want them to be.	
4. Involve them in designing the plan for getting there.	
5. Move in logical steps from what they know to what you want them to know.	
6. Keep them involved.	
7. Give them lots of feedback.	

From *Turning Training Into Learning*
by Sheila W. Furjanic and Laurie A. Trotman (New York: AMACOM, 2000).

Figure B-41.   Ancient Chinese proverb.

Tell me and I'll forget.
Show me and I may remember.
Involve me and I'll understand.

From *Turning Training Into Learning*
by Sheila W. Furjanic and Laurie A. Trotman (New York: AMACOM, 2000).

Figure B-42.   Factors to consider in selecting a game.

Question	Yes	No
1. Does the game relate to the objectives of the course? The game should help participants master concepts that relate to the ultimate objectives of the course. The lowest level of game that should be used is one that tests vocabulary terms against the meaning of those terms. A game that should **NOT** be used is a word finder that asks participants to simply circle words without indicating that they have an understanding of what those words mean.	❏	❏
2. Has the game been tested for consistency in directions/rules/ scoring? The game may sound good on paper, but you can't anticipate difficulties participants might have in understanding the directions, rules, and scoring if you don't test the game before you use it. An easy way to test a new game is to round up coworkers and offer them a pizza lunch for participating in your trial run. Directions that seem perfectly clear are often identified as confusing during this trial run and can be rewritten before the game is used in class.	❏	❏
3. Can the game rules be taught in order to facilitate playing? Sometimes game rules are, of necessity, somewhat complex. It's a good idea to practice teaching them to prospective players during your trial run. Often the way that rules are explained and demonstrated can get a game off and running correctly with no false starts.	❏	❏
4. Does the strategy for winning correspond with the learning objectives of the session? Make sure that the participants who show the best command of the course content are the ones who have the best chance of winning. This means that you will have to test several game scenarios to make sure that lucky participants who show little or no understanding of the content can't win.	❏	❏
5. If the game calls for physical movement by the participants, does this movement work within the physical limitations of your room? Here again, the trial run is important. If participants have to move around and are hampered by chairs that can trip them or tables that force them to squeeze by sideways, the game is not an appropriate one for the room. You should either change rooms or use another game. When designing these games, you should also consider the needs of disabled participants.	❏	❏

6. **If the game calls for using bells, buzzers, or other signaling devices, will these devices be accepted (or tolerated) by occupants of surrounding classrooms and offices?** If the room you are using for your class is in close proximity to other classrooms or offices, you can be a very unpopular person if your game interferes with the work of others. Bright-colored signs that are raised by the participants can be used as substitutes for noisy signaling devices if noise is a problem. You may also want to alert your "neighbors" that the class may become a little loud even if you are using noiseless signaling devices, because enthusiastic game contestants can easily forget that they are in class. ☐ ☐

7. **Are all players allowed to actively participate?** Games that call for one representative from each team to compete while the rest watch should be modified to allow everyone a chance to participate on a rotating basis. The disadvantage of using a rotation is that participants who know they will not be participating for several turns can lose interest. An alternative technique is to put the names of the participants from each team in a hat and draw them at random for each round. Then all participants have to stay alert because they never know when they will be called on. ☐ ☐

8. **Will the time invested in the game yield a worthwhile amount of learning, or can the concepts be better taught in another way?** Concepts can almost always be taught in another way, but games provide an opportunity to help participants master knowledge that might be harder to master through simple discussion and study. Because games take more time than discussion, it's important to make sure the concepts that are taught and tested through games are the ones that are the most important as participants master the goals of the course. ☐ ☐

From *Turning Training Into Learning*
by Sheila W. Furjanic and Laurie A. Trotman (New York: AMACOM, 2000).

Figure B-43.   Template for ensuring practice, practice, practice.

Step	*Plan*
1. **Explain the skill in words**	
2. **Demonstrate the whole skill**	
3. **Divide the skill into steps**	
4. **Demonstrate step 1**	
5. **Drill step 1 to mastery**	
6. **Demonstrate step 2**	
7. **Drill step 2 to mastery**	
8. **Demonstrate step 3**	
9. **Drill step 3 to mastery**	
10. **Continue demonstrating and mastering each step until the entire skill is learned**	
11. **Practice the entire skill**	
12. **Repeat practice with feedback**	
13. **Follow up**	

From *Turning Training Into Learning*
by Sheila W. Furjanic and Laurie A. Trotman (New York: AMACOM, 2000).

Figure B-44. Role play A (first communicator).

ROLE ASSIGNMENT

First Communicator (Pat)

It's 7:30 Tuesday morning, and Randy Johnson's dog has done it again! You put the garbage cans out half an hour ago. Now, when you're ready to leave for work, you find Sparkie spreading the contents of the cans all over the lawn. You've been on good terms with the Johnson family since you moved into the neighborhood 5 years ago, and you've been comfortable with the fact that Sparkie has been allowed to run freely like all the other neighborhood dogs. This didn't seem to be a problem before this week, but now that Sparkie is about 6 months old, he is growing quickly. Unfortunately, he has just learned how to charge your garbage cans hard enough to knock them over. When it happened last week, you picked up the trash and made a mental note to talk with your neighbor, but you never got around to it. Now you're really angry. This has to stop! You've just called Randy and asked for a minute of his time. Take the next 5 minutes to plan your discussion with Randy. Then have the actual conversation.

From *Turning Training Into Learning*
by Sheila W. Furjanic and Laurie A. Trotman (New York: AMACOM, 2000).

Figure B-45. Role play A (second communicator).

ROLE ASSIGNMENT

Second Communicator (Randy)

You and your two children have lived on Windsor Terrace for 7 years. Your neighbor Pat Dyce has lived down the block for 5 years. Pat has just called and asked to see you for a minute. Last year Pat collected for the National Cancer Society, and you suspect that he is collecting again. You locate your checkbook and wait for Pat to ring the doorbell.

From *Turning Training Into Learning*
by Sheila W. Furjanic and Laurie A. Trotman (New York: AMACOM, 2000).

Figure B-46.   Role play B (first communicator).

ROLE ASSIGNMENT

First Communicator (Mark)

It's 3:30 Thursday afternoon, and you're overloaded with work. You report to two directors, Ashley and Jennifer. They are equal in level and title. Yesterday they both gave you high-priority projects that are due tomorrow afternoon. You realize now that you will have to stay late tonight just to finish one of them by the deadline. You might be able to get some help from your coworker, Angela, but one of the directors will have to rearrange Angela's work load. If she does help you, there's about a 50 percent chance that you will be able to meet both deadlines. If you can only get one project done by tomorrow afternoon, you don't know which one it should be.

Because both directors have asked for a status report, you've decided to talk with both of them at the same time. Take the next 5 minutes to prepare what you will say. Then meet with them.

From *Turning Training Into Learning*
by Sheila W. Furjanic and Laurie A. Trotman (New York: AMACOM, 2000).

Figure B-47. Role play B (second communicator).

ROLE ASSIGNMENT

Second Communicator (Ashley)

Mark is one of the brightest and best workers in your office. You have given him an important report to prepare before the end of the day Friday. Because this report contains politically sensitive information, you want it on Friday so you can make any necessary changes before you present it at a meeting next Wednesday. When you ask Mark how the report is coming, he says he wants to talk with you for a moment in the conference room. Go there now and talk with him.

From *Turning Training Into Learning*
by Sheila W. Furjanic and Laurie A. Trotman (New York: AMACOM, 2000).

Figure B-48.   Role play B (third communicator)

ROLE ASSIGNMENT

Third Communicator (Jennifer)

Mark is one of the brightest and best workers in your office. You have given him a complex project that absolutely *must* be ready tomorrow at 5:00. You are leaving for Washington at 9:30 Friday evening and are scheduled to make a presentation, using the information in the report, on Saturday morning. When you ask Mark how the report is coming, he says he wants to talk with you for a moment in the conference room. Go there now and talk with him.

From *Turning Training Into Learning*
by Sheila W. Furjanic and Laurie A. Trotman (New York: AMACOM, 2000).

Figure B-49.   Template for evaluating simulations.

Question	Yes	No
1. Are the educational objectives for each role or position clearly defined?	☐	☐
2. Do the objectives relate directly to the course objectives?	☐	☐
3. Do the objectives relate to the real world?	☐	☐
4. Are participants asked to make decisions that approximate real-life decisions?	☐	☐
5. Are participants given feedback on the results of their decisions?	☐	☐
6. Do the required activities correspond with the educational objectives of the simulation?	☐	☐
7. Do the required activities within the simulation correspond with the activities of the real world?	☐	☐
8. Are the directions easy to understand?	☐	☐
9. Is the amount of necessary preparation time realistic for your situation?	☐	☐
10. Will the time invested in the simulation yield more worthwhile learning than if the concepts involved were taught in another way?	☐	☐

From *Turning Training Into Learning*
by Sheila W. Furjanic and Laurie A. Trotman (New York: AMACOM, 2000).

Figure B-50.   Supervisor feedback form (application and results assessment).

SUPERVISOR FEEDBACK FORM

How is your employee doing? Please take a minute to rate your employee's ability to apply the objectives learned during the training on the job, using the scale below.

Learning Objectives	Applied on the Job	Frequency*	Level of Success**
Learning objective A	☐ Yes ☐ No	0 1 2 3	1 2 3 4 5
Learning objective B	☐ Yes ☐ No	0 1 2 3	1 2 3 4 5
Learning objective C	☐ Yes ☐ No	0 1 2 3	1 2 3 4 5

 *Frequency scale: 0 (never), 1 (once), 2 (often), 3 (all the time).
**Success scale: Not successful, 1—very successful, 5.

As a result of the training, my employee has been able to . . .

What can the training department do to assist you in supporting your employee in applying the skills on the job?

    ☐ Call me; I need help supporting my employee's application.
    ☐ I'm doing just fine.
    ☐ The support tools are not working because _____

_____

_____

    ☐ Give me more information on _____

    ☐ I would suggest *(please describe)* _____

Overall, I believe my employee's performance has improved:

Not at all				Significantly
1	2	3	4	5

From *Turning Training Into Learning*
by Sheila W. Furjanic and Laurie A. Trotman (New York: AMACOM, 2000).

Figure B-51.   Case scenario meeting form.

CASE SCENARIO MEETING			
Volunteer:			
Course:			
Scenario:			
Group Discussion Notes:			
Outcome	*What Went Well (Pros)*	*What Did Not Go Well (Cons)*	*Lessons Learned*
Action Steps:			

From *Turning Training Into Learning*
by Sheila W. Furjanic and Laurie A. Trotman (New York: AMACOM, 2000).

Figure B-52.   Checklist of learner recognition strategies.

Recognition Strategy	Component	Action
1. Informal recognition	▪ Verbally recognize improved performance to the individuals and their colleagues.	❏
	▪ Host a surprise luncheon.	❏
	▪ Invite employees to participate on a new team.	❏
	▪ Ask employees what special assignment/ project they want to work on.	❏
	▪ Provide comp time off.	❏
2. Formal recognition	▪ Identify the performance achievement in the company newsletter.	❏
	▪ Post the achievement on a Web site.	❏
	▪ Conduct small-group and large-group performance-based recognition meetings.	❏
	▪ Invite senior management to deliver the recognition messages (note, phone call, e-mail, or in person).	❏
3. Awards	▪ Distribute formal plaques, certificates, or trophies.	❏
	▪ Provide gift certificates.	❏
	▪ Provide prizes, trips, theater tickets, sporting event tickets, etc.	❏
4. Celebrations	▪ Let your employees decide how they want to celebrate performance achievements and give them a budget to do so.	❏

From *Turning Training Into Learning*
by Sheila W. Furjanic and Laurie A. Trotman (New York: AMACOM, 2000).

Figure B-53.   Support activities follow-up form.

Manager/supervisor Support Activities
Follow-Up Plan

Question	Yes	No
1. Have you conducted weekly case scenario meetings?	☐	☐
2. If yes, how effective were the meetings?		
3. If you answered yes to question 1, did you use the weekly case scenario planning form?	☐	☐
4. Have you conducted any recognition programs?	☐	☐
5. If yes, how effective do you believe these programs were in reinforcing performance?		
6. Have you conducted any support activities other than the weekly case scenario meetings or recognition programs?	☐	☐
7. If yes, describe the activity you conducted.		

8. On a scale of 1 to 5, how would you rate the overall effectiveness of weekly case scenario meetings? (please circle)

Not Effective   *Very Effective*

1   2   3   4   5

9. On a scale of 1 to 5, how would you rate the overall effectiveness of recognition programs? (please circle)

Not Effective   *Very Effective*

1   2   3   4   5

10. What would you suggest to improve performance support programs?

From *Turning Training Into Learning*
by Sheila W. Furjanic and Laurie A. Trotman (New York: AMACOM, 2000).

Figure B-54.   Participant action plan.

ACTION PLAN

Training course: _____	**Date delivered:** _____
Department request: _____	**Participants:** _____ _____ _____ _____ _____
Activity:	**Date Due:**
1.	**Frequency (daily, weekly, etc.):** ___ **Start date:** _____
2.	**Frequency (daily, weekly, etc.):** ___ **Start date:** _____
3.	**Frequency (daily, weekly, etc.):** ___ **Start date:** _____

From *Turning Training Into Learning*
by Sheila W. Furjanic and Laurie A. Trotman (New York: AMACOM, 2000).

Figure B-55.   Buddy contract.

Training course: _____   **Training course date:** _____

Participant A's name: _____   **Participant B's name:** _____

Telephone #: _____   **Telephone #:** _____

E-mail address: _____   **E-mail address:** _____

Fax #: _____   **Fax #:** _____

Guiding Principles

- We will share our experiences and lessons learned.
- We will offer to help each other whenever necessary.
  Others . . .

Next Steps

Over the next month, we will:
- Meet at least 2 times to discuss our progress to date.
- Brainstorm alternative solutions to the problems we have encountered.
- Implement alternative solutions identified.

Signature   Signature

_____   _____

Participant A: **Participant B:**

From *Turning Training Into Learning*
by Sheila W. Furjanic and Laurie A. Trotman (New York: AMACOM, 2000).

Figure B-56.   Participant contact list.

PARTICIPANT LIST

Course Name: ＿＿＿＿＿＿＿＿＿＿＿   **Facilitator:** ＿＿＿＿＿＿＿＿＿＿＿＿

Date Attended: ＿＿＿＿＿＿＿＿＿＿＿

Participant Name	Department	Telephone/ Fax	E-Mail Address
1.			
2.			
3.			
4.			
5.			
6.			
7.			
8.			
9.			
10.			

From *Turning Training Into Learning*
by Sheila W. Furjanic and Laurie A. Trotman (New York: AMACOM, 2000).

Figure B-57.   Participant feedback form.

PARTICIPANT FEEDBACK FORM

How are you doing? Please take a minute to tell us whether you have been able to use the skills you learned in _____ on the job. If you prepared an action plan, let us know how you did on each of the activities in your plan.

Action Plan Activities	Applied on the Job	Frequency*	Level of Success**
1.	❑ Yes ❑ No	0 1 2 3	1 2 3 4 5
2.	❑ Yes ❑ No	0 1 2 3	1 2 3 4 5
3.	❑ Yes ❑ No	0 1 2 3	1 2 3 4 5

 *Frequency scale: 0 (never), 1 (once), 2 (often), 3 (all the time).
**Success scale: Not successful, 1—very successful, 5.

4. As a result of the training, I have been able to . . .

5. What can the training department do to assist you in supporting your skill application on the job?

   ❑ I'm doing just fine.
   ❑ Call me; I need help applying the skills on the job.
   ❑ The skills I learned are not working because _____
   ❑ Call my manager; I think he/she needs help in supporting me.
   ❑ Give me more information on _____
   ❑ I would suggest *(please describe)* _____

6. Overall, I would say that this course helped my performance on the job improve:

Not at all				Greatly
1	2	3	4	5

From *Turning Training Into Learning*
by Sheila W. Furjanic and Laurie A. Trotman (New York: AMACOM, 2000).

Figure B-58.   Supervisor feedback form.

SUPERVISOR FEEDBACK FORM

How is your employee doing? Please take a minute to rate your employee's ability to apply the objectives learned during the training on the job, using the scale below.

Learning Objectives	Applied on the Job	Frequency*	Level of Success**
1.	☐ Yes ☐ No	0 1 2 3	1 2 3 4 5
2.	☐ Yes ☐ No	0 1 2 3	1 2 3 4 5
3.	☐ Yes ☐ No	0 1 2 3	1 2 3 4 5

*Frequency scale: 0 (never), 1 (once), 2 (often), 3 (all the time).
**Success scale: Not successful, 1—very successful, 5.

4. As a result of the training, my employee has been able to . . .

5. What can the training department do to assist you in supporting your employee in applying the skills on the job?

    ☐ Call me; I need help supporting my employee's application.
    ☐ I'm doing just fine.
    ☐ The support tools are not working because _____

    ☐ Give me more information on _____
    ☐ I would suggest *(please describe)* _____

6. Overall, I believe my employee's performance has improved:

Not at all				Significantly
1	2	3	4	5

7. Since the training, I would rate employee impact on the job as:

No impact				Significant impact
1	2	3	4	5

8. Since the training, I believe my employee's performance has had an impact on the department by . . .

From *Turning Training Into Learning*
by Sheila W. Furjanic and Laurie A. Trotman (New York: AMACOM, 2000).

Figure B-59.   Coworker feedback form.

COWORKER FEEDBACK FORM

Dear _____ :

As you may know, I recently attended a course on _____
and have been trying to improve my _____ .

As a follow-up requirement from that course, I am asking several coworkers for their feedback. Please take a minute to complete this form and send it to _____
_____ .

_____

[participant's signature]

Learning Objectives	Applied on the Job	Frequency*	Level of Success**
1.	☐ Yes ☐ No	0 1 2 3	1 2 3 4 5
2.	☐ Yes ☐ No	0 1 2 3	1 2 3 4 5
3.	☐ Yes ☐ No	0 1 2 3	1 2 3 4 5

*Frequency scale: 0 (never), 1 (once), 2 (often), 3 (all the time).
**Success scale: Not successful, 1—very successful, 5.

4. Since this training I notice that you:

From *Turning Training Into Learning*
by Sheila W. Furjanic and Laurie A. Trotman (New York: AMACOM, 2000).

Figure B-60. Customer feedback form.

CUSTOMER FEEDBACK FORM	
Dear _____: _____ Department is committed to providing the best service for our customers. Please take a moment to fill out this survey and tell us how we're doing. _____ [department manager's signature]	

	Performance *(Not satisfied = 1 to very satisfied = 5)*
1. On-time service	1 2 3 4 5
Comments:	
2. Problem solving	1 2 3 4 5
Comments:	
3. Courtesy	1 2 3 4 5
Comments:	

From *Turning Training Into Learning*
by Sheila W. Furjanic and Laurie A. Trotman (New York: AMACOM, 2000).

Figure B-61.   Business results form.

Measuring Business Results

Overall Training Goal:

Part 1

Overall Training Goal	What to Measure	How to Measure

Part 2

Learning Objective	Measurement	How to Measure
1.		
2.		
3.		

From *Turning Training Into Learning*
by Sheila W. Furjanic and Laurie A. Trotman (New York: AMACOM, 2000).

Figure B-62. Data captured form.

Overall Training Goal:

Part 1

Overall Training Goal	What to Measure	Date 1	Date 2	Score +/−	% Improvement

Part 2

Learning Objective	Measurement	Date 1	Date 2	Score +/−	% Improvement
1.					
2.					
3.					

From *Turning Training Into Learning*
by Sheila W. Furjanic and Laurie A. Trotman (New York: AMACOM, 2000).

Figure B-63.   Participant summary chart—quantitative results.

PARTICIPANT SUMMARY CHART

Learning Objectives	Percentage of Employees Applying Skills on the Job	Frequency*	Level of Success**
A.			
B.			
C.			

  *Frequency scale: 0 (never), 1 (once), 2 (often), 3 (all the time).
**Success scale: Not successful, 1—very successful, 5.

From *Turning Training Into Learning*
by Sheila W. Furjanic and Laurie A. Trotman (New York: AMACOM, 2000).

Figure B-64. Customer satisfaction summary chart—quantitative results.

CUSTOMER SATISFACTION SUMMARY CHART

Level of
Satisfaction

Department: _____

Date(s) of Service: _____

- I would rate my overall satisfaction with the level of service provided by the department as . . .

- I would rate my overall satisfaction with the level of service provided by the employee(s) as . . .

- My questions were answered thoroughly.

- My problem was resolved completely.

- To improve the service in this department, I would suggest:

---

*Frequency scale: 0 (never), 1 (once), 2 (often), 3 (all the time).
**Satisfaction scale: not satisfied, 1—very satisfied, 5.

From *Turning Training Into Learning*
by Sheila W. Furjanic and Laurie A. Trotman (New York: AMACOM, 2000).

Figure B-65.   Overall score by group.

TRAINING RESULTS SUMMARY

Session	Pretraining Score	Posttraining Score	On the Job
1			
2			
3			

Combined Average Score

Analysis

Session

1. Date/audience/number of participants:

   Description:

2. Date/audience/number of participants:

   Description:

3. Date/audience/number of participants:

   Description:

From *Turning Training Into Learning*
by Sheila W. Furjanic and Laurie A. Trotman (New York: AMACOM, 2000).

Index